D1517458

Doctors and Therapists Praise Gemstone Energy Medicine

"It is my belief that gemstone energy medicine will, in the near future, develop into an art and science that can stand equal with homeopathy and acupuncture as a major contribution to the field of energy medicine." *Gary N. Klepper, D.C., N.D.*

"From the Chinese medicine perspective, it is not surprising that therapeutic gemstones have such powerful effects. For me, holistic medicine is vibrational medicine—meaning that any therapeutic substance is effective primarily because of its vibration. I have seen the gemstones produce a very strong vibrational response."

Heiner Fruehauf, Ph.D., L.Ac.
Chair, Chinese Medicine Department
National College of Naturopathic Medicine

"I have seen remarkable results with therapeutic gemstones, including performance enhancement with professional and Olympic athletes. In order to advance in science, we often try new things to achieve greater results than previously proven. In the future, I have no doubt that further research will confirm the demonstrated clinical efficacy of therapeutic gemstones."

Ada Gonzalez, N.D.
International Speaker and Educator

"Gemstone energy medicine has transformed my ability to use natural medicine in profound ways. As more practitioners in many healing disciplines experience the depth and breadth of these therapies, medicine itself will be transformed."

Sara Hazel, N.D.
Founder, Barefoot Sage Spa

"I have been working with therapeutic gemstone spheres both personally and professionally for over eight years, and the benefits are spectacular. I feel therapeutic gemstones are the most valuable energy healing tool available. There is no other intervention that is so simple and precise in how it works with the mind-body energy system. I am grateful every day that this resource is available to me, my family, and my clients."

Carol Tuttle, MRET
Author of Remembering Wholeness

"In my healthcare practice I have found that the effects of gemstones are truly powerful. Clinical treatment with gemstones often results in profound and lasting improvements in my clients' physical and inner health, changes that clearly manifest in their everyday lives. My experience has borne out the value of these tools over and over again."

Alan Coffman, L.Ac.

"This is indeed the therapy of the future. Therapeutic gemstone spheres have the most powerful therapeutic effect I have ever experienced in my life."

Lourdes Rabago, C.M.T., RPh

"I continually receive feedback from clients and friends on the beneficial effects of therapeutic gemstones. Their beauty and healing energy register a profound and lasting impression on those who experience them."

Linda A. Lile, Ph.D., RCST

"I use therapeutic gemstones in my work as an acupuncturist, because they address a complete spectrum of issues safely and effectively. There is simply no substitute for the work done by therapeutic gemstones."

Blaise Desesa, Ph.D., L.Ac.

"I think the most significant difference I have felt since wearing therapeutic gemstones has been related to my relationship with my wife. We have both noticed that since she has been wearing her Pink Tourmaline and I have been wearing my Green Tourmaline, I am much more attentive and affectionate towards her. The changes are very obvious and include not only a sexual enhancement aspect but the overwhelming desire to simply be in close proximity to my wife. This is a pronounced difference, evident even to some outsiders.

"Many of the other observations reported regarding athletic performance and endurance as a result of the Tourmaline necklace have not been observed by me. However, having been on Trans-D Tropin™ (a GHRH analog) for over five years, my athletic performance, endurance, and recovery are already well beyond what could be expected. Nevertheless, based on my own personal experience, I can see how Green Tourmaline may help to enhance athletic performance.

"I use Green Tourmaline and other gems on a regular basis. The bottom line is that the gemstones do make a difference—although sometimes I have a difficult time believing it myself!"

Rashid A. Buttar, D.O., FAAPM, FACAM, FAAIM
Medical Director, Center for Advanced Medicine™

Gemstone
Energy Medicine

Healing Body, Mind and Spirit

Michael Katz

Natural Healing Press

ISBN 0-924700-24-6

Library of Congress Catalog Card Number 2004111794

Gemstone Energy Medicine: Healing Body, Mind and Spirit
SECOND PRINTING

Editing: Katherine Hall

Book Design: Nada Katz

Cover Design: Nada Katz

Typography: Bill Brunson

Illustrations: Nicole Rodgers
Brian Kerr

Photography: David Gorsek

THE INFORMATION CONTAINED IN THIS BOOK IS FOR EDUCATIONAL PURPOSES ONLY.

IT SHOULD NOT BE CONSIDERED AS A SUBSTITUTE FOR CONSULTATION WITH A LICENSED HEALTHCARE

PROFESSIONAL OR AS A REPLACEMENT FOR ANY MEDICAL TREATMENT.

THE GEMSTONES REFERRED TO IN THIS BOOK ARE OF THERAPEUTIC QUALITY, WHICH MEANS THEY

MEET SPECIFIC STANDARDS OF COLOR, CLARITY, AND CONSISTENCY. THERAPEUTIC-QUALITY

GEMSTONES ARE OF THE FINEST QUALITY AND SHOULD NOT BE CONFUSED WITH

MORE COMMONLY AVAILABLE GEMSTONES.

My Deepest Gratitude

To Katherine Hall, my editor, dear friend, and partner in the creation and writing of this book. I thank her from the depths of my heart and soul. Her clarity, kindness, dedication, and brilliance have made this book what it is; without her, it would not have been born. To my beloved wife Nada, for her devotion, kind heart, creative vision, and tireless support for me and this work. Her inspired design has instilled grace and style into the cover and every page of this book. To Dr. Ada Gonzalez, whose wise and generous nature, insights into gemstone energy medicine, and unique abilities to share those insights with others have been an invaluable boon to me and to this new healing modality.

To Dr. Rashid Buttar, premier physician who is helping to change the world and bring medicine to its highest level, my thanks for having the courage of his convictions. I appreciate his willingness to experience gemstone energy medicine and to use this exciting modality to help his many patients. A big thanks to Dr. Sara Hazel for her commitment to share her expertise in gemstone energy medicine with others, and to Dr. Heiner Fruehauf, Alan Coffman, Linda Lile, and the many other doctors, therapists, and practitioners who continue to support this important and innovative field.

To Sarah Sanderson, whose unwavering integrity, support, and dedication I count on every day. To Bill Hall, whose steadfast friendship, confidence, and expertise I treasure dearly. To Francesco Patricolo, whose compassion and caring have been an invaluable support in my work. For their efforts to help bring gemstone energy medicine to the world, I thank Sam Sanderson, Carol Jarka, Sandeep Amar, Katie Downing, Michelle Emery, Rachael Vollmer, Denelle Eknes, Tracy Nyari, and John Areh. To Nicole Rodgers, whose illustrations grace these pages and whose unconditional love and support for this work is a great gift. To Alexandra Carol, on whose selfless support and keen eye I've come to depend. To my dear friends and partners, Shiao Ming and

Mei Chi, my most sincere thanks. And to my other friends and co-workers, seen and unseen (you know who you are), I offer you all my deepest gratitude.

To Bob Silverstein, whose insights and encouragement helped clarify the form and purpose of this book. To Heidi Rickabaugh, whose friendship and mastery of design shine out in the look of these pages. To Nancy Trent, Walter Sperr, and their associates, who have helped brilliantly to bring gemstone energy medicine into an ever-brighter light.

To my dad, who has always given me his loving encouragement, and to my mother, who would appreciate knowing that this book is beautifully completed. To my dear children, Emily, Eleena, and Eranel, who have my eternal gratitude for choosing me to be their dad. I love you all.

Contents

Foreword

I am often asked by other physicians when I am lecturing what I think the future of medicine will be. In my personal opinion, energy medicine will certainly be a major constituent of the medicine of the future, although this sentiment is not original. Historically, as far back as 5,000 years ago, healers have used various forms of energy in treating the ailments of society. Whether one refers to the use of energy in medicine as in five-dimensional scalar waves or the Far Eastern forms of energy healing using *chi*, the essense is the same. If one considers using the mathematical formulas Einstein developed, which show that time and space are relative, and we accept the theory of relativity, which essentially states that as we travel at the speed of light, time slows down, then it is no longer a leap to extrapolate the resulting increase in longevity and health if one can generate the appropriate types of energy fields.

The subject of using various forms of energy in healing and possibly in prolonging life fascinated me from the start. I first read *Vibrational Medicine*, by Richard Gerber, M.D., while I was still in medical school and then read *The Body Electric*, by Robert O. Becker, M.D., as I started my residency in general surgery. The book you now hold, *Gemstone Energy Medicine: Healing Body, Mind and Spirit*, by Michael Katz, is fascinating and intriguing because it brings within the reach of each individual a method by which he or she can not only learn how to harness but actually generate the appropriate type of energy fields needed or desired by the person or healthcare provider. It allows the means by which to attain this previously difficult and intangible goal and brings it within the reach of the individual.

Research indicates that specific fields of energy enhance the immune system, evidenced by increased DNA synthesis in lymphocytes. Already, the evidence exists that trans-membrane potential is substantially increased by using "field technology" instead of direct electrical induction. Recently, a mobius strip, blind loop induced scalar wave generated by a band worn on the wrist has generated scientific research into the biological effects of this new type of non-Hertzian electromagnetic energy. These findings lend support to the theory of the life-enhancing properties provided by various methods of potentiating energy.[1]

The neutralization of many of the harmful electromagnetic frequencies generated in our modern society alone is enough to warrant further research into any device that indicates the ability or potential to protect the biological system. Patients have reported many benefits during and after their experiences of using various forms of energy healing, including having an increased sense of well-being, more energy, better sleep, and improved pain control. Acupuncture, in fact, is nothing more than enhancing and opening up energy channels that have been blocked or, in other cases, blocking certain energy channels along specific meridians to achieve a desired effect. Plants exposed to specific types of energy fields have also been noted to grow faster than they do in other parts of the building that lack the field exposure.

Although numerous studies indicate the biological significance of linear, transverse, electromagnetic, and acoustic waves, relatively little is known about the role of nonlinear, non-Hertzian, naturally occuring resonance energy (or what I have coined "NOR energy") waves in biological systems. The conclusion has been that certain types of energy are more biologically active than traditional electromagnetic fields. The function of non-Hertzian energy is more than likely to be significant, since quantum mechanical analysis of biological processes has revealed that biological systems are of a nonlinear nature. With the additional possibility of energy being programmable as a result of intention, or conscious thought, theoretically this type of NOR energy effect can be potentiated.

Energy can be oriented to create a natural, life-enhancing amorphogenic resonance energy field that produces a positive biologic effect. I believe the effects reported by individuals wearing therapeutic gemstones, including the Olympic athletes who have reported improvement in athletic performance, may actually be indicative of this amorphogenic

---

1 *See* Biological Interactions with Scalar Energy Cellular Mechanisms of Action and Effect of Non-Hertzian Scalar Waves on the Immune System, *by Dr. Glen Rein, Stanford University Medical Center.*

NOR energy, which in its rawest form can be seen in scalar waves or mental thoughts. When used in conjunction with intention, or conscious effort, the possibilities increase exponentially and become endless. The overall effect of this NOR energy is to excite the electromagnetic field of any substance, organic or non-organic, and thus allow the substance to morph (as in metamorphosis) into a state that is more like its original, natural, electrical matrix form.

As an example of the potential of NOR energy, let's consider Kirlian photography. Kirlian photography is a well-known method of measuring electromagnetic energy fields of objects. Dead tissue has a low or dim pattern, whereas a live biological system has a very bright pattern. It is the energy field of an object that determines the brightness of the pattern disclosed on the Kirlian photograph, with disease producing a lower energy image. Kirlian photographic analysis of inanimate but organic objects exposed to some of these forms of energy has been recorded and noted to show a consistent increase in energy patterns on the images of the substances exposed to these fields of energy.

Most people have heard of the phantom pain experienced by patients who have had an extremity amputated. Doctors explain that this phantom pain "exists in your head" and will often treat it with analgesics and antidepressants. However, when Kirlian photographs are taken of these recently amputated limbs, the amputated extremity is still amazingly visible on the Kirlian photograph. Although the amputated part shows up with a dim pattern and the intact portion of the limb appears brighter, the Kirlian photograph does pick up the resonance frequency generated by the remaining intact cells, resulting in the dim pattern on the photograph of a part of the body that is no longer physically present.

I believe that it is the innate NOR energy that is being picked up and recorded by the Kirlian photograph. It is this NOR energy that is characteristic and common to every cell in a particular individual's body— as unique as the DNA that defines the individual's genetic uniqueness. Therefore, this NOR energy must be a function of the DNA, because the DNA is the only substance that is identical in every cell and unique to each individual. Remember that the DNA from one cell contains the entire blueprint for each individual, with all information necessary to create an identical copy of that individual.

It is important to recall from basic, elementary science that the smallest building blocks for all substances, whether organic or non-organic, are made up of atoms. And an atom is a flux of energy defined as a proton and a neutron in the center, with electrons flying around the proton and neutron. If an atom is the smallest building block and is defined as a flux of energy, then everything by definition is a flux of energy, since everything is comprised of atoms. Thus, the DNA also is a flux of energy and has its own NOR frequency, unique to the individual and identical in all the individual's cells. This NOR energy is characteristic of all substances that have their own unique resonance signature, or NOR energy signature.

We now understand that the DNA is resonating at the same inherent NOR frequency as all the rest of the cells in the body. And we also recognize that the identical DNA structure existing in each cell continues resonating at its NOR energy regardless of what happens to any other cells or parts of the body, thus allowing for the energy pattern of the collective whole to continue resonating at the specific frequency as when the limb was intact. The amputation of the extremity does *not* change the NOR energy of the DNA in the rest of the cells in the intact portions of body. In other words, the intact cells resonate and create the energy pattern of the entire body, even though a portion of the body is now gone. But the resonance from the intact cells is sufficient to create the image of the missing extremity viewable on the Kirlian photograph, although it appears lighter or fainter than the rest of the intact body, since the NOR energy of that particular portion of the body no longer exists.

Dr. Victor Marcial-Vega, an oncologist and close friend from Florida, has done high resolution blood imaging and dark field microscopy blood tests on patients before and after being exposed to scalar waves generating a form of NOR energy, and he has compared these specimens with previous blood samples from the same patients. According to Dr. Vega, changes, such as a high level of chylomicrons and triglicerides considered abnormal have been cleared by 80 percent or more. Severe fibrin patterns observed by Dr. Vega characteristically in cancer patients, especially those with end-stage metastatic disease, have significantly improved and often are resolved. The blood drawn afterwards showed more debris and waste material than the blood specimens drawn before exposure to these induced NOR energy fields, possibly explaining the detoxification symptoms (headaches, sore throat, achiness, etc.) that most people initially experience.

Based on the latest developments in Fractal Mathematics, Chaos Theory and Acausal Physics, these thoughts I have expressed become more and more likely to one day soon leap from the esoteric arena into the field of conservative medicine. Already, there is a peer-reviewed journal, *Subtle Energies and Energy Medicine Journal*, designed to provide guidelines, scientific background, and scientific credibility for subtle-energy applications, while providing a venue for technical papers involving theory and application of energy in the field of medicine. But due to the resistance of conventional and traditional medicine and the constraints of politics, much of the necessary research to quantify these subtle but essential and accumulative effects of energy medicine will probably not take place for years to come.

In the interim, I believe that therapeutic gemstones provide the easiest and most convienient method of increasing and poteniating the naturally occuring resonance energies that are an intricate but virtually ignored part not only of our own bodies, but of every living substance on this planet. This book will provide the reader with the fundamental knowledge and opportunity to learn more about this intriguing field and its application in healing. The information is well written, easy to understand, and organized in a manner that is user friendly. As I have always done with my patients, I encourage and challenge readers to open themselves to the immense possibilities, seek the truth, and evaluate the outcomes for themselves. This book will help you take the first step.

Rashid A. Buttar, DO, FAAPM, FACAM, FAAIM
Medical Director, Center for Advanced Medicine™
Director of Clinical Research, V-SAB Medical Labs, Inc.

Gem Therapy Comes of Age

In the years since I first began to work with therapeutic gems and uncover their hidden potential for healing, the field of energy medicine has undergone a transformation. In 1988, when I began my exploration of these powerful healing tools, energy medicine in its various forms was practiced in the West by a few pioneering physicians and enjoyed by a relatively small number of people looking for alternatives to conventional medicine. While the ancient science of acupuncture was taking root in Western medical offices, practices such as homeopathy and Reiki were at the crest of a wave that would soon sweep the West.

Since then, a minor revolution has taken place. The paradigm on which energy medicine practices are based has become more widely accepted. This paradigm sees the human being as an integral part of a universe in which, on a fundamental level, matter is a form of energy. In this paradigm, each person is a unique system of interconnected fields of energy and information. Treatments used in energy medicine address this most fundamental level of the human form, affecting the very stuff of which we are made. These treatments target the underlying causes of illness and discontent, rather than merely the symptoms. By using this approach, energy medicine aims not only to improve our health but to transform it. Today this new, energetic model of the human being and human health is not only embraced by large numbers of people, it has excited the interest of many physicians and medical researchers.

Doctors and patients are experiencing that energy medicine works—often where conventional medicine does not. Chronic debilitating illnesses, common ailments, aches, pains, and everything in between have responded to energy medicine practices. Energy medicine is shedding light on the true nature of health and disease and offering solutions to seemingly intractable health problems—often leaving those who practice it healthier and more vital than they thought possible.

One of the most powerful forms of energy medicine is gem therapy. Here, too, a change has taken place. Once relegated to the fringes of the healing arts, the therapeutic uses of gems were not widely adopted by either doctors or the public. Offering neither a coherent model of the human being's energetic nature nor precise therapy protocols and tools, gem therapy practices were inconsistent at best and ineffective at worst. Today, all that has changed. Pioneering information and effective new practices are allowing gem therapy to take its rightful place as a cornerstone of energy medicine.

In 1988, I began a serious exploration of the application of therapeutic gems for healing. Through a series of illuminating intuitive experiences, I was introduced to extraordinary new information about the uses of gems for enhancing health on all levels. Since then, this information has been confirmed and expanded through further exploration, research, and testing. From these experiences emerged a deeper understanding of our energetic physiology, with profound implications for human health. From them also emerged new ways to evaluate, refine, and shape the gems themselves into reliable and potent therapeutic tools. Equally important, I learned techniques for using gems that are precise, systematic, and effective—techniques that lift gem therapy out of the realm of intuition, hunches, and folklore to a new form of energy medicine—*gemstone energy medicine*. This book presents an introduction to these discoveries and to the practical ways anyone can use therapeutic gems to enhance health and improve the experience of life.

Since I first published my early explorations, thousands of people around the world—physicians, homemakers, Olympic athletes, business people, celebrities, and many others—have come to experience remarkable healing by applying therapeutic gems with these new methods. Confirmed during over a decade of clinical experience, these discoveries have yielded gem therapies that work—both as primary treatments and as complements to other healing modalities. Emotional maladies, mental complaints, and acute and chronic illnesses of all kinds have responded to these gem therapies in unprecedented and exciting ways.

How can therapeutic gems accomplish all this? Physicists tell us that all matter is energy in physical form. Gemstones are certainly no exception. Formed over eons, often at high pressure, the Earth's gemstones embody intense concentrations of energy. The energetic and physical properties of gemstones are already employed in many aspects of technology. The ability of crystals to conduct and transform energy is no longer a new idea to us. For example, every television, quartz clock, portable phone, and personal computer runs smoothly thanks to Quartz crystals. Today the energetic properties of gems are also being used to improve people's health at a fundamental level.

Efforts to use gems for healing have a long history. In many lands and in many ways, people have sought to uncover the abilities that lay hidden within the intensely compressed crystalline structures of gemstones—particularly the ability to heal. Over the centuries, our attempts have met with varying degrees of success and failure. Yet, when using gems for health, something was always missing—for, until recently, we have been unable to discover a systematic way to unlock the full therapeutic powers of gems and to achieve consistent, long-lasting results.

To discover why success with gems for healing was elusive for so long, one place to look is to the gems themselves. Essential to the success of any form of medicine is the nature of its therapeutic tools. To be most effective and reliable, medicine must be pure and high in quality. The purity and quality requirements of the gems we use for healing parallel those of any other form of medicine. Meeting these strict requirements can make or break a gem's therapeutic worth. For gemstone energy medicine to be effective and consistent, the use of only therapeutic-quality gemstones is required.

The past sixteen years have also shown that a gem's shape profoundly affects the way it can express its energy—and thus its ability to deliver its healing properties. The ideal shape for a therapeutic gem is the sphere. The spherical shape unleashes a gem's potential to reach and heal the deepest energetic aspects of our being, where the root causes of disease and distress lie. Therapeutic gemstone spheres radiate an incomparable energy that can affect all our dimensions, physical and subtle, and hence heal and transform our entire being.

Together, these two concepts—the selection of only the highest quality gems and the use of gems cut into the proper shape—represent a simple, yet seismic, shift in the understanding of how gems can work therapeutically. Proper selection, shaping, and use of gemstones transform them into therapeutic power tools. The potent healing energy of therapeutic gems can deeply heal and nourish every aspect of the human form.

Fortunately, enjoying the health benefits of gemstone spheres is exceptionally easy and straightforward. Based on this new information, over 100 therapy protocols using gem spheres have been developed. However, powerful benefits can be obtained simply by wearing therapeutic gems around the neck. Wearing a therapeutic gemstone necklace allows the gems' healing energy to penetrate the deepest levels of the wearer's physical and energetic dimensions. There, the gems' energy goes to work dissolving energetic blockages and producing beneficial changes in body, mind, and emotions.

The experiences of thousands of people have shown that the information presented in these pages represents a quiet but growing revolution in the healing arts. These remarkable, documented experiences of healing provide our first glimpses of what becomes possible when we put this new form of energy medicine into practice. More empirical research and testing are on their way. In the meantime, preliminary clinical trials and the testimony of pioneering gemstone users indicate that this new form of energy medicine has much to offer. Therapeutic gemstones work. With them, we have entered a new era of healing—one that harnesses the therapeutic powers of gems and fulfills their once-elusive promise as tools for our personal healing and transformation.

The Multidimensional Human Form

Many people wonder how something as simple and earthbound as a gemstone can accomplish a feat as extraordinary as healing the mind, body, and emotions. Many wonder how something so solid and—well, *stone*-like can produce such dynamic effects. To unlock this apparent mystery requires two paradigm shifts.

The first and most fundamental of these shifts is the concept that the human form is a multidimensional system of subtle energies that create and sustain the physical body. In many alternative medical fields, these systems continue to be mapped, studied, and utilized for healing. Oriental medicine, for instance, has been studying the relationship of physical matter and subtle energies for thousands of years. Every application of an acupuncture needle attempts to access these energies to affect the body and mind.

The second paradigm shift involves the tools of gemstone energy medicine. In one sense, it may seem paradoxical to use a stone—the embodiment of earthly material—to affect subtle, nonphysical energies. Yet a closer look reveals what may not be immediately apparent—that the crystalline nature of certain gemstones and their ability to process energy have much in common with the liquid crystalline forms in our own cells. Once the mechanisms of human energy systems are more thoroughly understood and compared with those of gemstone energy medicine, the elegance and power of gems as therapeutic tools can be more readily understood.

In short, to understand how therapeutic gemstones can nourish, heal, and illuminate all aspects of our lives, we must first understand our own nature and the true nature of health and illness.

Most of us are aware that we are far more than our physical anatomy. Indeed, each of us is a complex being comprised of many aspects, seen and unseen. In addition to a physical body, each of us has a multi-faceted inner life, comprised of emotions, thoughts, memories, dreams, and intuitions. And deep within each of us, underlying and pervading every waking and dreaming moment, lies our awareness, or consciousness. This spiritual element exists beyond the body, emotions, and mind.

Within our being are still other aspects that have long been familiar to Eastern physicians and that, more recently, Western doctors have begun to explore. These are the "energetic" aspects. Some of these have been identified as the *acupuncture points* and *meridians*, the *chakras*, and the *aura*. Whether or not we are fully conscious of it, life energy flows constantly through these nonphysical channels and structures to nourish all facets of our being.

Yet, as the ever-growing field of energy medicine reveals, these are only a few of the highly complex structures that make up our energetic "physiology." All of our nonphysical structures and components are as vital to our existence as our heart and lungs. These components, together with the physical body and our spiritual essence, comprise the multidimensional human form.

The Subtle Bodies

Although our inner dimensions are integral to our experience of life, scientists are still striving to define the nature of these nonphysical elements. For example, how and where exactly do emotions originate? Our common experience is that emotions come from somewhere "inside." Our thoughts, memories, and intuitive nudges also seem to arise from some internal source. What is that source? Where do our emotions, thoughts, and intuitions come from?

Answering these questions holds an essential key to understanding how gemstones can affect us so profoundly. To answer them, we must expand the current model of human physiology and turn to one that includes the physiology of our *inner* lives.

If we could somehow see beyond our physical body and into our inner dimensions, we would see that the energetic components in which our emotional responses originate essentially form another body. For the purposes of this discussion, we can call this body the *emotional body*, though it is also sometimes referred to as the *astral body*. The emotional body is a *subtle body*, because its substance is more subtle, or less material, than that of the physical body. Although we cannot see it with our physical eyes, the emotional body is just as real and just as integral a part of us as the physical body.

If we could peer even more deeply into our own being, we would see another, even more subtle body. This is the energetic aspect of our being in which our past experiences and patterns of stimulus and response are stored. We can call this storehouse of memories and patterns, the *causal body*.

Even deeper within us is another body, which we can call the *mental body*. This body is the source of the river of thoughts that flows continually through the mind. Deeper still is the *intuitive body*, or the aspect of our being from which our intuitions arise. Most subtle is the aspect, which cannot, in truth, be called a body. In essence, it is pure spirit, also known as soul, or the highest self. Beyond the highest self lies the infinite source of all life. It is the origin of the life force itself and the source of all our bodies, physical and subtle.

As life force flows from its infinite source into the physical world, it forms, animates, and fuels all of our bodies with its vital essence. Within and between all of these bodies lie many channels that allow this life energy to flow through the bodies to enliven and nourish them. In addition, these subtle-body channels connect all the bodies and allow them to communicate with each other.

The *chakras*, or energy centers, are key components of this channel system. The seven major chakras, which are located on the front of the physical body, also have counterparts or reflections in the subtle bodies. Among many other vital functions, the chakras act as major corridors through which life energy flows into and out of each subtle body. The chakras also act as major pathways for life energy from the subtle bodies to enter the physical body. This energy is then distributed throughout the physical body via the system of *meridians* identified many centuries ago.

The subtle bodies have many other components, as well. These components are similar to the physical body's cells, organs and systems, thus making our subtle-body anatomy just as complex as that of the physical body.

Another essential aspect of our energetic physiology is the *aura*. The aura is the energetic field that surrounds the physical body and can be seen through Kirlian photography and by some highly sensitive individuals. Each of our bodies—physical and subtle—generates its own aura, or energetic reflection of itself. Together, these various auras form the energetic field that is often called simply, "the aura." The intimate relationship of the subtle bodies to their auras is key to understanding how therapeutic gemstones work and will be explored further in upcoming chapters.

The Nature of Health and Illness

This understanding of how we human beings are constructed can offer us insight into the nature of health and help explain how we go astray from it. In an optimally healthy person, the physical and subtle bodies are well aligned with each other, and the channels through which energy flows are connected and clear. The life force can flow freely from the innermost core of our being, through our subtle bodies, to the physical body. Nothing impedes this vital flow, and all the bodies receive the energy they need to perform at a peak level. This free flow of life force blesses the individual with radiant vitality, mental acuity, and a joyful inner peace.

Unfortunately, for most of us, this state of vibrant health remains a goal to which we only aspire. Various impediments and blockages within our bodies and energy channels diminish the flow of life force within each body and from one body to another. This causes them to stray from a state of optimal health.

In this sense, illness is multidimensional. When blockages arise in any of the subtle bodies or their connections, these blockages reduce the amount of life force flowing to the physical body. Thus, illness can originate in one subtle body, or dimension of being, and also manifest in another. We experience this, for example, when emotional strain or mental stress triggers exhaustion, the onset of a cold, or perhaps another more serious physical ailment. Thus, emotional and mental disharmonies lead not only to inner distress but often manifest as physical problems, too.

Where do the impediments and blockages within our bodies originate? Over the course of one's life, we all experience times of less-than-ideal nutrition, emotional ups and downs, exposure to environmental toxins, and other stresses of living. Although we don't always feel it at the time, these experiences leave their marks on us at various levels of our being. Such marks, which can be both physical and energetic, can be deposited anywhere within our physical and subtle bodies.

Of course, overwhelming and painful traumas also leave their marks. These marks, however, are far deeper and have a profoundly negative impact on our subtle physiology. The effects of a major trauma are similar to those of a large rock falling into a mountain stream. It slows the current and can even divert its course. The effects of our more minor, daily stresses are like those of sticks and leaves slowly piling up around the rock. As these foreign objects collect in the stream, the flow of water is increasingly obstructed, and areas downstream experience a diminished flow.

This is similar to what happens within each of us as we go about our lives. As energetic marks and deposits accumulate within us, they act as blockages and disruptions in the flow of life force through our subtle bodies to the physical body. Optimal health requires that the flow of life force throughout our being remain strong and unimpeded. Energetic deposits in one subtle body not only disrupt the flow of energy within that body; they can also block the flow to other bodies. As the flow of life force is choked off, areas "downstream" become stagnant. Just as obstructions in the mountain stream can degrade the environment downstream, so can disruptions in the flow of life force give rise to disharmony, pain, and disease. Indeed, it is these disruptions that are the fundamental causes of illness.

Consequently, to effect a complete healing of any condition, be it physical, emotional, mental or spiritual, we must eliminate its underlying causes—namely, the energetic deposits and disruptions blocking the flow of energy within us. Therapeutic gemstones are ideal tools for the job. When used properly, they can neutralize these energetic blockages and bring vital energetic nourishment to the parts of us that have become stagnant. Thus, therapeutic gemstones can help restore us to the vital and radiant expressions of life force we were born to be.

Therapeutic Gemstones Address the Causes of Ill Health

How can gemstones fill such a tall order? Modern physics reveals that all matter is energy in material form. The Earth's gemstones exemplify this natural law. Gemstones embody intense concentrations of energy. Indeed, the energy concentrated in gemstones is the same energy that sustains, nourishes, and enlivens all living things, including human beings. Gemstones are concentrated packets of this energy.

Every element of life, including the entire mineral kingdom, is comprised of molecules in motion, vibrating at rates unique to the substance they comprise. A gemstone's chemical substance—the elements that make it up—not only give the gem its distinctive color; it also generates a unique and characteristic vibration, or energy.

When certain gemstones are used properly, the energy within them resonates and interacts with the life energy in people. The gemstone's energy radiates into the user's aura and bodies, where it locates and dissolves energetic blockages. The gem's energy transforms these disharmonious energies into powerful, harmonious vibrations and returns them to our bodies. Thus, gemstones bring vital nourishment to areas that have been suffering from the deficiencies of energy caused by these blockages. In this way, therapeutic gemstones eliminate the blockages that bring about discomfort and disease. They powerfully uplift our entire being. Like sunshine breaking through clouds, the vibrant energy radiated by gemstones neutralizes the obstructions to our own inner radiance and illuminates the areas that have been in shadow.

The implications of this therapeutic action are profound. Despite enjoying the benefits of our remarkable advances in modern medicine, many people continue to suffer with ailments of all kinds. Why should this be so? A primary reason is that our physicians can only observe and measure the manifestation of illness from a physical viewpoint. Even the emotional and psychological components of disease are assessed and treated from a limited point of view.

Missing from most therapeutic systems is an understanding of the vast portions of our being where the true causes of disease lie. These regions encompass the cells, organs, channels, structures, and systems that function in the inner, unseen dimensions of our being. With no way to perceive, diagnose, and treat these dimensions, most physicians lack the means to offer true and lasting solutions to our ill health and distress.

Therapeutic gemstones provide a unique and powerful way to fill this need. They are physical tools that can not only benefit the physical body and help eliminate its manifestations of disease, but can also directly affect every aspect of our multidimensional selves. Thus, the potent energy in therapeutic gemstones makes them uniquely able to address the very causes of disease—and to restore the multifaceted human organism to its natural state of vitality and joy.

Transforming Gemstones into Therapeutic Tools

People have always been powerfully drawn to gemstones. Indeed, gemstones are among the most beloved treasures on the planet. Gems are beautiful. Yet it is more than just their beauty that attracts people so profoundly. Deep within, people know that there is more to gemstones than meets the eye.

The promise of something "more" has drawn people to gemstones for countless ages. Gemstones and human beings seem to share a profound resonance—one felt by our distant ancestors and our modern selves. Gems have called to us in every age and culture. Certainly, all great civilizations have valued gems and used them for purposes that transcend their appearance. History recounts attempts to use gems in hopes of curing ailments, attracting wealth, ensuring protection, and even experiencing higher states of consciousness. For example, the ancient Egyptians prized the powers of Lapis Lazuli; the Minoans honored Carnelian and used it widely; in China, the near-ubiquitous use of Jade continues today in a tradition thousands of years old; and in India, the time-honored system of Ayurvedic medicine employs a variety of gems in its practices.

In more recent times, as alternative medical practices have gained in public awareness, interest in gems for healing has intensified. Pioneering healers have turned to gems for assistance and helped to reawaken Western culture to the healing and transforming powers of the Earth's minerals. Many popular authors have promoted gemstones for their healing and spiritual properties. Dedicated researchers, such as the late Dr. Marcel Vogel, in the United States, and Michael Gienger, in Germany, have applied innovative scientific methods to uncover some of the energetic effects of gems on the human form.

Yet, unlike some alternative medical modalities—such as acupuncture, homeopathy, and medicinal herbs—the use of gemstones for healing is only beginning to reach beyond the inner circles of energy medicine.

Despite renewed interest in gems for healing and our longstanding attraction to them, until now gems and crystals have been only superficially embraced as therapeutic tools. To be sure, many people have reported wonderful experiences with the energies of crystals and gems. Yet missing from these reports are consistent, dramatic, and long-term results. The question is: Why? Why have we been unable to take full advantage of the healing energy available in gemstones? Why have we not yet fully enjoyed the personal transformation that crystals and gems seem to promise?

To uncover an important answer to these questions, we must look to the gemstones themselves. Vital to the success or failure of any form of medicine is the nature of its therapeutic tools. By looking to the gems, we can discover two important reasons that our experiments with gemstones for healing have, in the past, not yielded consistent and long-lasting results: (1) the forms of gemstones we have commonly used and (2) the physical purity and quality of gems we have generally used. These two elements—form and quality—are essential keys to unlocking the healing energies of gemstones—and to transforming them into reliable, powerful, and truly therapeutic tools.

Key #1: Shape Matters

The Earth is a cornucopia of gifts. Its air, water, soil, and fruitful products sustain the life of all its inhabitants. From our earliest beginnings, we human beings have harvested these gifts and prospered by molding them to our uses. We sow the Earth's raw fruits, then process and transform them into other products we can digest or use. We cut seeds and grind them into flour for our nourishment, we harvest plant fibers to spin and weave into clothing, and so on.

Like many of the Earth's gifts, crystals and other gems also become most useful to people when they are harvested in their raw form and then "processed" in some way. For example, we use cut and polished gemstones in many aspects of technology, from lasers to computers, lenses, watches, and other precision instruments. Indeed, gemstones stand at the cutting edge of modern technology: Quartz crystals in computers and telecommunications devices help to propel information around the globe, and Rubies and Sapphires make delicate laser surgery possible.

However, in an attempt to tap a gemstone's *healing* force, historically people have primarily used the raw, crystalline form of gems. Yet, by its very nature, this form limits the flow of gemstone energy and therefore can offer only limited benefits for healing. Using a gemstone in its raw, unprocessed form is like using penicillin, or many other medicines, in their raw form—ineffective and risky. Like any other medicine or therapy tools, gemstones must be carefully selected and properly processed to be reliable and effective. With gemstones, an essential part of this processing is cutting a gemstone into a specific *shape* that allows it to affect all dimensions of our being.

How Energy Flows Through Crystals

Within the Earth, crystals are spectacularly varied: they occur naturally in clumps and clusters and in many other unique manifestations. Common to most crystals, however, is a basic form that includes two ends: one pointed and the other non-pointed. It is the nature of a gemstone crystal to continuously draw into itself energies from its immediate environment. These can include the various energies generated by a person or any other random energies present in the crystal's immediate surroundings. Because of a raw crystal's shape, this energy is compelled to flow through it in one direction: into the non-pointed end and out of the pointed end.

As energy moves into and through the gemstone's crystalline matrix, an important change takes place: the energy drawn into the crystal takes on certain properties of that gemstone. Thus, each type of gemstone essentially converts the energy from its environment into an energetic frequency characteristic of that type of gem. In other words, Blue Sapphire transforms ambient energy into Blue Sapphire energy, Amethyst transforms ambient energy into Amethyst energy, and

Rhodochrosite transforms ambient energy into Rhodochrosite energy. What this means is that the gemstone's unique chemical makeup is reflected in the energy it produces. Its chemical composition gives this energy a vibratory signature, or pattern, unique to that type of gemstone. Many forms of energy medicine therapy, such as homeopathy, produce effects by introducing specific vibratory patterns to the body. This is also true of gemstone energy medicine.

The flow of energy through a crystal—and its transformation into a specific type of gemstone energy—is constant. As energy exits through the crystal's point, some of this energy flows out into the environment in a focused beam. However, much of the gemstone's energy is immediately drawn back into the crystal through the crystal's non-pointed end, or base (see Fig. 2-1). Sometimes, when people hold or wear a crystal, they feel the concentrated energy inherent in the crystal itself and the flow of uplifting energy through and around the crystal.

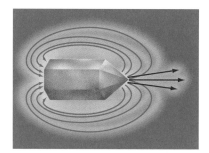

Fig. 2-1 Energy flow in a raw crystal

The Limitations of Crystals

This energy can feel good to the person wearing it, holding it, or carrying a crystal in a pocket. Yet it is the nature of this flow that is the primary reason that crystals are limited as therapy tools. First, because a significant portion of its energy is immediately pulled back into the crystal through its base, the volume of gemstone energy that can reach into a person's aura, or energetic field, is limited. And, second, the portion of energy that does stream out of the crystal's point touches only a very small part of the person's aura and cannot penetrate the aura deeply.

We know that to produce a deep and lasting healing of any condition, we must resolve its inner causes. We must reach into the fabric of our physical and subtle bodies and eliminate the underlying energetic blockages wherever they occur. Because a crystal's energy stays in a layer of the aura close to the physical body, its ability to address and resolve a condition on all levels is profoundly limited. While the energy that flows through a crystal is life-giving, this energy does not reach deeply into our nonphysical dimensions, nor can it affect them significantly. This is a principal limitation of crystal therapy.

Using either end of a crystal for therapy also poses serious drawbacks. One drawback arises when a crystal's point is applied to a person's body or aura: the highly focused beam of energy radiating from the crystal can potentially "burn" the person's energetic fabric. The resulting disruption in the subtle fabric usually isn't obvious immediately and may take weeks, months, or even years to manifest in an unwanted condition.

The second drawback arises when the base of a crystal is placed on a human body—for example, on an ailing chakra or a distressed organ. Because of the way energy flows through a crystal, the crystal naturally draws energy out of the body and into itself. Although this process may sound beneficial, currently there is no way of knowing whether the crystal is pulling disharmonious energy or positive life force out of the body.

Gifted clairvoyants and highly sensitive practitioners can sometimes employ a crystal's focus to obtain some therapeutic benefits. Yet, for most people, placing pointed crystals on the body in any orientation is unpredictable and potentially hazardous. Despite the limitations of crystals, these kinds of applications are among the most common ways that people have used gems to promote healing. The limitations of these applications and of the raw crystalline shape are among the primary reasons that gemstones have not yet taken their rightful, central place in energy medicine.

The Good News About Crystals

Although the therapeutic uses of the raw, crystalline form of gemstones are limited, we can benefit from the unique way that energy flows through and around crystals. The energy of a raw crystal primarily affects the physical aspect of its environment. For this reason, a crystal placed anywhere in one's home environment can radiate life, good feeling, and harmony into the area in which it is placed. For example, an Aquamarine or Amethyst crystal set out in the home can uplift and brighten the home environment.

Introducing the Gemstone Sphere

How, then, can the healing energies of gemstones be safely and effectively used by people? One important part of the answer is simply to shape them into *spheres*. When harnessing the healing energies of gemstones, shape matters. A gemstone's shape profoundly affects the way a gem receives and expresses its energy—and thus our ability to benefit from its healing properties. Cutting a gemstone crystal into a sphere fundamentally changes the way that energy flows through the gemstone.

A sphere both *draws in* and *radiates out* energy from its entire surface. Among many other benefits, this eliminates the drawbacks that arise from having a pointed and non-pointed end.

Most important, cutting a gemstone into a sphere fulfills its potential to work with all of our dimensions, physical and subtle—and thus to heal and transform our entire being. A sphere represents wholeness and infinite potential. The spherical shape unleashes a gemstone's full healing capacity—the capacity we have long sensed but had been unable to use to full advantage. Indeed, using gemstone spheres for healing represents a breakthrough that is helping to raise gem therapy to a viable, effective form of energy medicine.

How Energy Flows through Spheres

Just as a crystal continually draws in energy through its base, a gemstone sphere continually draws in energy from its entire surface. This provides a much greater proportion of surface area from which to draw in and radiate energy. The spherical shape also allows a unique phenomenon to take place within the gem—a spectacular transformation that allows the energy of a gemstone sphere to affect all dimensions of our being.

This process of transformation can best be explained with a little help from physics. We understand from physics that as energy moves toward the center of a sphere, it becomes more concentrated. This is what happens inside a gemstone that has been cut into a spherical shape. As energy in the sphere's environment is drawn from the surface toward the sphere's center, the energy becomes highly compressed and concentrated. This intense compression triggers the transformation of ambient energy into the type of energy characteristic of the gemstone. At the same time, the compression sparks a virtual explosion of this energy out from the center of the sphere and back into the environment (see Fig. 2-2).

What happens in the center of a gemstone sphere is analogous to what takes place in the center of the sun: intense compression generates

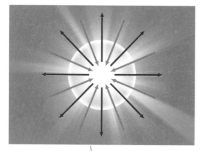

Fig. 2-2 Energy flow in a gemstone sphere

a continual transformation that results in energy being radiated out to the sun's surface and beyond. Similarly, the "explosion" of energy within a gemstone sphere causes the sphere to unleash its energy with great power in all directions.

The transformation process in a gemstone sphere begins when energy in the sphere's environment touches the surface of the sphere. The electrons on the sphere's surface pick up this energy. Then, because of the sphere's shape and the gem's crystalline nature, the surface electrons are compelled to transfer this energy to other electrons that lie closer to the center of the sphere. Like an electronic bucket brigade, molecule by molecule, the gem's electrons continually transfer energy toward the sphere's center. There, the energy becomes more and more compressed and concentrated. The resulting explosion of energy charges the electrons around the sphere's center and sparks a unique reaction: ambient energy is transformed into the type of energy characteristic of that particular gemstone.

At the same time, some of the gem's energy takes a leap into other, more subtle, nonphysical dimensions. This leap of some of the gemstone energy into more subtle dimensions is crucial. It allows the energy emanated by gemstone spheres to resonate with and penetrate all the subtle dimensions of our own being. Herein lies one of the essential reasons for the extraordinary therapeutic potency of gemstone spheres.

The explosion in the sphere's center rapidly pushes all of the newly generated gemstone energy back to the sphere's surface and beyond, into the sphere's environment. Again, because each type of gemstone has a unique chemical composition and molecular structure, the character of the transformed energy is unique to that type of gemstone. Thus, Aventurine spheres radiate Aventurine energy, Malachite spheres radiate Malachite energy, and so on. This process of energy entering the sphere, becoming transformed, and then radiating back out from the surface is constant and unceasing.

Key #2: The Importance of Therapeutic Quality

When it comes to using any therapeutic tool, we always seek—and need—the very best. We demand purity and quality, and rightly so. Most of us would not knowingly use inferior-quality medicine or medicine containing impurities. Not only does a poor-grade medicine fail to provide the consistent results we are looking for; it might provide some unwanted results as well. The same is true for therapeutic gemstones.

This principle holds another key to understanding why, throughout history and until now, the results of using crystals and other gems have been spotty and often disappointing. Cutting gems into the proper shape is the first key to unleashing their potential as healing tools. Yet if the quality of the gem itself is insufficient—if it is filled with impurities and flaws—its energy will be distorted and weakened. The gemstones we use for therapy must be high enough in quality to deliver the healing and transformation we seek from them. Anything less than the highest quality gemstones will most likely disappoint the user and at worst bring unwanted consequences. Then, even cutting the gem into a proper shape will not be enough. Both proper shape and proper quality must be present in the gems we use for therapy. Only then do they yield the consistency and reliability required to take their appropriate place as therapeutic tools.

What Constitutes Therapeutic Quality?

Within the mineral kingdom is a wide range of naturally occurring grades of purity. Indeed, an infinite number of gradations exist between gemstones whose physical nature is so pure that they can express their energies freely, and gemstones that are so riddled with contaminants, inferior coloration, and poor clarity that their therapeutic energies are inhibited, trapped, corrupted, or virtually nonexistent.

To be therapeutic, a gemstone's physical matrix must be virtually free of foreign matter. It must also exhibit all its own unique parameters for therapeutic quality, and these parameters must be present in proper proportion. Anything less may distort the character of the gemstone's energy and make that gemstone unsuitable for medicinal purposes.

Gemstones that don't meet certain stringent requirements of purity, color, clarity, shape, and cut are not capable of transmitting therapeutic-quality energy. Such gems may even look beautiful to the casual observer. However, gems that don't meet these requirements will not only have significantly less, if any, therapeutic effect; they can even have detrimental effects on their users. The cracks, irregularities, or foreign matter commonly found in most gems can seriously inhibit the flow of healing energy through a gemstone sphere. Instead of radiating into a user's aura like the sun, the sphere's energy bounces around the molecular structure of the contaminants and flaws. The energy that manages to escape is often distorted (see Fig. 2-3).

As one might expect, therapeutic-quality gemstones are rare. The vast majority of rounded gems available today simply don't meet the therapeutic-quality requirements for purity, cut, color or shape. Furthermore, a large number of gemstones are dyed and some are even irradiated to improve their appearance. Although these gems might look beautiful in a piece of jewelry, dye smothers a gemstone's energy and renders it therapeutically useless. Irradiation does even more damage: it destroys the energy of a gemstone and replaces it with a disharmonious one. This energy can actually be harmful if projected into the gemstone user's body and aura.

Energy flow in a therapeutic-quality sphere

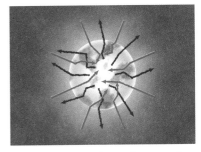

Energy flow in a sphere with flaws

Fig. 2-3

Each Gemstone Type Has Unique Requirements

For every type of gemstone there is a different set of criteria that makes that gem therapeutic. In fact, the characteristics that make one type of gemstone therapeutic do not necessarily apply to other gemstones. For example, certain characteristics of therapeutic Quartz spheres don't apply to Lavender, Aquamarine, or Leopardskin Jasper; some characteristics that make Dark Green Aventurine spheres therapeutic differ from those that apply even to Light Green Aventurine, and so on.

For example, a degree of cloudiness is desirable in therapeutic Lavender but unacceptable in clear Quartz. Another example is Leopardskin Jasper: the more various the colors in a Leopardskin Jasper necklace, the more potent the necklace is, whereas a single, uniform color is a must in a therapeutic Aquamarine necklace.

The Seven C's of Therapeutic Quality

A gemstone is judged for therapeutic quality by criteria that are unique to each type of gem. These criteria fall into seven categories: character, color, clarity, consistency, cut, cleanliness, and *candescence*. Each individual bead must meet the requirements for its type in all seven categories. For example, an Amethyst bead must meet the requirements for therapeutic-grade Amethyst in all seven categories.

Character

Unique to each gem, character describes the nature of the gemstone itself and is determined by its unique ratio of mineral components. For example:

- Therapeutic Aventurine is composed of silicon dioxide colored green by tiny platelets of green chromium mica, called fuchsite. Its appearance is characterized by dark-green capsules floating in a translucent light-green base. Among other requirements, the flecks must appear as solid, discrete capsules and not as loose clouds or streaks.
- Therapeutic Lapis Lazuli is a combination of lazurite and other minerals, including Sodalight, calcite, and pyrite. Its appearance is characterized by a specific proportion of golden pyrite flecks in a base of royal blue color.

Color

To be therapeutic, a gem must accurately represent the optimal color for its type. As a gem strays from its optimal color, its therapeutic effectiveness decreases. Off colors, inappropriate shades, or muddiness add undesirable energies. For example, Amethyst that is too light or too dark purple is not therapeutic; nor is grass-green Dark Green Aventurine, which should be closer to a deep forest-green.

Clarity

Clarity requirements are unique to each gemstone type and can vary widely. For example, some gems are adversely affected by certain internal flaws or cloudiness, while others are not. For example:

- Therapeutic Quartz and Citrine must be optical or near-optical in quality.
- Ideal Lavender displays a mixture of cloudy and transparent areas.

Consistency

Consistency is a quality that is desirable both within a sphere and within a therapeutic necklace as a whole. In general, the quality of all spheres in a necklace should be similar to each other, without a high degree of variability. Consistency is more important for some gemstones than it is with others. For example:

- In a Blue Sapphire necklace, consistency is critical. Lack of consistency, even in bead size, can render an otherwise therapeutic Sapphire necklace non-therapeutic.
- Within an Opalight necklace, a wide variation of characteristic colors can contribute to the necklace's effectiveness.

Cut

Because of the central role of shape in a gem's therapeutic effectiveness, precision in cutting and drilling therapeutic gems is essential. Spheres and other rounded forms should contain a minimum of chips, nicks, and uncharacteristic irregularities. Spheres should have no flat spots, and other rounded forms should be well formed and proportioned. Drill holes should be clean and consistent in size.

Cleanliness

To be therapeutic, most gems must be free of adulteration, such as dye, irradiation, or kerosene. These treatments can seriously disrupt a gem's therapeutic energies and even render them harmful to the user. For example:

- Roselle (Rose Quartz) is often dyed to deepen its pink color, yet dye renders it non-therapeutic.
- The machines used to cut Leopardskin Jasper spheres are usually lubricated with kerosene, yet the kerosene clogs the surface of the finished spheres and disrupts the natural expression of the gems' healing energies.
- Aquamarine is sometimes irradiated to enhance the color of a poor-quality gem. However, this treatment destroys the energy of the gem and replaces it with a severely disharmonious energy.

Candescence

Gem *candescence* is an optical quality that makes a gem look like a brilliant drop of liquid color. This liquid appearance reflects an energetic quality that, when present in certain gems, indicates exceptional therapeutic potency. It is an extremely rare quality that is most often seen in colored crystalline gems, such as Sapphire, Emerald, Amethyst, Citrine, and others.

Other Rounded Forms

Because of the way a small number of gems radiate their specific energies, an exact spherical shape is not required to produce the greatest degree of therapeutic benefits in those gemstones. Other rounded shapes can also support the work of these gems and, in some cases, help them express their energies more effectively. Three of these rounded forms are rounded chips, rondels, and cylinders.

Rounded Chips

When cut properly, the flow of gemstone energy through the rounded yet irregular form known as a *rounded chip* is similar to that of a sphere. The primary difference between gemstone chips and spheres is that energy radiates from a sphere in a perfectly regular fashion, and energy radiates from a rounded chip in an irregular one. Consequently, a rounded chip tends to have more cutting, penetrating action than a sphere. For a small number of gemstones, such as Citrine and Aquamarine, this action actually enhances their effects (see Fig. 2-4).

Fig. 2-4 Rounded chip

Rondels

A *rondel* is a sphere that is somewhat flattened on two opposite sides. Several precious gemstones, including Emerald, Ruby, and Blue Sapphire, are often cut into rondels (see Fig. 2-5).

Cylinders

Like a gemstone sphere, a gemstone *cylinder* can project its energy deep into the aura. However, because of its flat ends, a cylinder does not radiate its energy equally in all directions. Instead, it radiates laterally, accentuating the movement of energy around the entire physical body. (See page 259 for a photograph of Purple Rainbow Fluorite cylinders in a necklace.)

Fig. 2-5 Rondel

The Role of Faceted Gems

Faceted gems, such as those commonly used in rings and pendants, are used in a number of therapeutic systems, including Ayurvedic medicine. A faceted gem is typically cut to form a flat top, or *table*, and a pointed base, or *culet*. A faceted gem pulls energy in through its culet and radiates it out through its table and some surrounding facets. Like a crystal, a faceted gem radiates nearly all of its energy in one direction. Thus, a faceted gem's energy can touch only limited parts of the aura.

Furthermore, to wear a faceted gemstone, it is usually mounted in metal. Any kind of metal mounting severely restricts a gemstone's energy flow. Even if both the table and culet of the gem are exposed, the majority of the gem's energy stays contained within the gem.

Consequently, while it does no harm to wear and enjoy a gemstone ring or pendant, the metal setting will significantly diminish the gem's therapeutic potential.

Nevertheless, faceted gemstones have a powerful role to play in advanced gemstone energy medicine. When certain faceted gems are applied in highly specific protocols and not mounted in metal, they can serve as potent tools for stirring and awakening certain aspects of consciousness.

Tools for Holistic Advancement

When we shape pure, high-quality gemstones into spheres and use them properly, the full benefits of gemstone energy medicine become available to us. This is the gift of gemstone energy medicine—to fulfill the age-old promise of the Earth's minerals as effective tools for healing. The chapters that follow explore the ways we can use these potent tools for our own holistic advancement and the remarkable transformation of our health.

The Power of Gemstone Necklaces

Perhaps it is hard for some people to imagine that the therapeutic gemstone necklace represents one of the most powerful tools in energy medicine today—but indeed it is true. Although a therapeutic necklace can look like a simple piece of jewelry, such appearances can be misleading—for a necklace of therapeutic gemstone spheres is much more than that. It is capable of healing and transforming the physical and subtle physiology of the human organism.

Various healing traditions have called for gemstones to be carried in a pocket or pouch like talismans; to be worn in pendants; or, as in some Ayurvedic prescriptions, to be mounted in rings. Yet it is the unassuming necklace of gemstone spheres that is actually the most reliable, consistent, and powerful gemstone tool for treating and transforming one's entire being. The gemstone-sphere necklace is the crowning jewel of gemstone energy medicine—one that has helped raise it to the status of a truly holistic form of energy medicine.

Gemstone Sphere Necklaces: Versatile and Powerful Tools

Gemstone energy medicine offers a wide range of therapeutic tools based on the gemstone sphere. It also offers many techniques for using rounded gems therapeutically. These techniques marry an energetic model of the human organism with knowledge of the therapeutic actions of gemstones to create diverse, reliable, and effective therapies. These therapies go to the roots of many forms of human distress and offer real means to resolve them.

Yet the primary—and often most powerful—way to experience the healing properties of gems is to string them together in the form of a necklace. A necklace of therapeutic gemstone spheres is a powerful and versatile tool for healing and transformation. It can be worn around the neck for profound overall benefits or placed on different parts of the body for specific effects.

When one wears a necklace of gemstone spheres around the neck, the gems essentially surround the core of one's being. The location of the gems and their rounded shape enable the gems' energy to radiate in all directions—deep into the physical body and the *aura*, or energetic field, surrounding the body. There, the gemstones work on neutralizing the energetic blockages that limit positive growth and lead to ill health. At the same time, the gemstones' energy uplifts and nourishes all aspects of our being to energize and inspire us, to help us restore our health, and to make our healing changes permanent.

The advantages of this form of gemstone energy medicine are many. A gemstone-sphere necklace worn around the neck silently works for us as we go about our daily activity and even when we are sleeping at night. With virtually no effort on our part, the gemstones work continually and ever more deeply on that which holds us back from the health, happiness and well-being we desire. A necklace can also be used in many other ways to focus the gems' energies in highly specific therapies.

The Human Aura: Doorway and Information Storehouse

Gemstone sphere therapy is a form of energy medicine. In essence, this means that gemstone energy interacts with our energetic field to produce certain therapeutic effects. In fact, it is the ability of a gemstone-sphere necklace to fill a person's aura with its energy that makes a gemstone necklace so effective and capable of healing and transformation on many different levels.

The aura is an energetic reflection of the physical and subtle bodies. Indeed, each of our bodies—physical and subtle—generates its own aura, or energetic reflection of itself. To those who can perceive auras, the aura generated by the physical body, also known as the *supra-physical aura*, appears as a very thin layer of energy immediately surrounding the physical body. The emotional body also generates an aura, which appears as a somewhat wider layer of energy surrounding the supra-physical aura. The causal body's aura appears as a layer of energy surrounding the emotional aura, and the mental body's aura appears as a layer surrounding the causal aura. The relatively thin sheath of energy surrounding the mental aura is the intuitive aura, generated by the intuitive body. Taken together, the various "layers" of aura generated by the physical and subtle bodies comprise what is often called simply, "the aura." In reality, the aura is quite complex and a treasure trove of information (see Fig. 3-1).

As an energetic manifestation of a particular body, each layer of the aura serves as a living storehouse of information about that body's condition. This information is in the form of energy. Each layer of the aura holds information about the body it reflects, including which areas are healthy and which are not. Thus, for example, one's thoughts and mental condition are reflected in the mental layer of the aura; one's emotional responses and emotional condition are reflected in the emotional layer; and one's physical condition is reflected in the supra-physical layer of the aura. Because the aura reflects the condition of the physical, emotional, mental, karmic, and intuitive bodies, it contains information about every aspect of one's being and one's experiences, past and present.

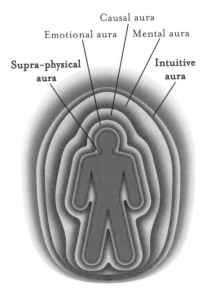

Fig. 3-1 The layers of the aura

How Therapeutic Necklaces Resolve the Inner Causes of Illness

When one wears a gemstone-sphere necklace around the neck, the gemstones' energy radiates in all directions and into the various layers of the aura. As the gemstone energy fills each layer of the aura, this energy gains direct access to the physical and subtle bodies themselves.

It's as if each layer serves as a doorway to the body it reflects. For example, when a gemstone's energy fills the supra-physical layer of the aura, this energy is able to move directly into the physical body; when a gemstone's energy enters the emotional layer of the aura, it moves into the emotional body; and so on.

Fig. 3-2 Action of a gemstone necklace's energy in the aura

When the gemstones' energy has filled a layer of the aura and its corresponding body to a certain degree, the gems' energy starts to neutralize the energetic blockages it finds there. These blockages are deposits of disharmonious energies that accumulate in the physical and subtle bodies in the natural course of living. Such blockages inhibit the flow of life force through the subtle bodies to the physical body, causing distress and disease of all kinds. By obstructing the light of the life force, these blockages effectively create areas of darkness within one's being. As the gemstones' energy shines into the aura and fills the physical and subtle bodies, dark areas are infused with the light of the gemstones' energy. Thus, the gemstone energy transforms and neutralizes the blockages that have obstructed the flow of life force. At the same time, the gemstones' energy acts as vital nourishment for the body, mind, and emotions.

Each type of gemstone has a particular focus to its work. For example, some gemstones focus primarily on physical healing, some focus primarily on emotional renewal, some focus primarily on mental development, and so on. To accomplish this, each type of gemstone targets a particular kind of blockage and tends to concentrate in certain layers of the aura more than it does in others. For example, the primary function of Ruby is emotional transformation, and so it focuses more of its healing energy in the emotional layer than in any other layer of the aura. Other gems focus primarily on the physical layer, the causal layer, or the mental layer, or on a combination of several layers of the aura.

As a gemstone-sphere necklace dissolves energetic impurities and blockages in the physical and subtle bodies, two other important things happen. First, the bodies begin to release into the aura the energetic debris that results from the breakup of blockages. Second, some of this energetic debris is pulled toward and into the necklace's gemstone spheres. It is the nature of a gemstone's crystalline matrix to continually draw energy into itself. When the bodies release their energetic impurities, these discarded energies ride on the continual flow of energy from the aura into the spheres. As the discarded energies are drawn into the gemstones, some of them cling to the surface of the spheres. However, most of the discarded energies are pulled into the centers of the spheres.[1] There, these disharmonious energies undergo the same transformation that life energy undergoes in the center of a gemstone sphere. The discarded energies are transformed into the healing energy characteristic of the gemstone—and thus permanently neutralized (see Fig. 3-2).

More Advantages of Wearing Gemstone Necklaces

By neutralizing energetic impurities and blockages in our aura and bodies, therapeutic gemstone spheres eliminate the very causes of disease. Furthermore, this process—of gemstone energy filling the aura and neutralizing blockages—continues as long as a therapeutic necklace is worn.

In this way, gemstone-sphere necklaces work at ever-deeper levels to dissipate the energetic clouds and other blockages that obscure our natural radiance. At the same time, the gems bring energetic nourishment to the physical and subtle bodies. It is this ability that makes gemstone spheres such unique and extraordinary therapeutic tools. No other form of gemstones—and virtually no other form of energy medicine—can bring such nourishment and transformation to all levels of our being.

When properly cared for, many therapeutic gemstone necklaces can remain useful for an entire lifetime—or longer. Again, gemstone spheres also provide their users with a steady supply of healing energies for as long as they remain in the user's aura. This stands in striking contrast to many other types of medicine, whose supply must be constantly renewed and whose potency expires. Also, unlike many medicines that simply mask symptoms, therapeutic gemstones work in such a holistic manner that they can help eliminate a disharmonious condition permanently and move one to a new level of health and vitality.

---

1 These discarded energies can easily be cleansed from the surface of the gemstones. Indeed, to keep the gemstones performing at their peak capacity, these energies should be regularly removed. See Appendix A: "Care and Cleansing of Therapeutic Gems," on page 397, for instructions.

What Else Gemstone Necklaces Can Do—Focused Therapies

While wearing therapeutic gemstone necklaces around the neck is a powerful and convenient way to enjoy their benefits, it is just one way to experience them. The same necklace worn around the neck can be used in other ways to focus the gemstones' action for various purposes.

Let's take therapeutic Carnelian as an example. Among its many other actions, this deep-orange gemstone vitalizes and detoxifies the body's cells. When a Carnelian necklace is worn around the neck, the gems' energies are diffused throughout the body and aura. Areas in need of Carnelian's support spontaneously take advantage of the gems' energies. The direction of the therapy is essentially dictated by one's entire multidimensional organism.

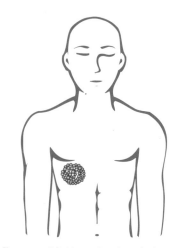

Fig. 3-3 Necklace placed on the liver

One can also place the Carnelian necklace on a specific area of the body to focus its healing energies there. For example, one can curl up a Carnelian necklace and place it on the liver (see Fig. 3-3). This will focus the Carnelian's cleansing and revitalizing energies specifically on the liver. The Carnelian will also work in the areas corresponding to the liver in the subtle bodies. When Carnelian is applied this way, very little of the gemstones' energies will be distributed to other parts of the physical body. Instead, the liver will receive the full focus and benefit of the Carnelian energy—thus accelerating and enhancing the liver's healing. This is one very simple example of how gemstone spheres can be applied in ways that focus the gemstones' effects.

Certain necklaces can also be placed around the head or on the chakras, palms, or soles of the feet to produce specific results. Still other ways to use necklaces include contemplative and diagnostic techniques— ways to reveal the causes of a condition and thus take the first steps toward healing it. Therapeutic gemstone necklaces can be applied in dozens of ways in a myriad of focused therapies. In Chapter 5, the benefits of wearing each of thirty gemstones as a therapeutic necklace are detailed. A sample of one focused therapy is also given for most gemstones.

Multidimensional Healing

Today, not only is conventional medicine expanding to embrace the tools and practices of energy medicine, but a broader concept of health itself is evolving. Even as stately a body as the World Health Organization now defines health as "a state of complete well-being"—one that involves the integration of body, mind, and spirit. Therapeutic gems, with their ability to affect and uplift every dimension of our being, are uniquely suited to help us achieve this more complete vision of true health.

Gemstone Spheres Work Holistically and with Focus

The living system of physical and subtle bodies that comprise each human being is an intricate and interdependent network. To enliven, nourish, and repair every part of us, life energy and information flow from body to body. All our parts are dependent on each other for their well-being. Thus, when one aspect of our being is diminished in some way or is ailing or distressed, other parts are bound to be involved. Disharmonious energies that have accumulated in one body not only stress the body in which they've collected; they also block or distort the flow of energy to other bodies, causing distress there. This is why, for example, mental or emotional upset can lead to physical weakness or even illness.

Consequently, in order to fully resolve any unwanted condition—be it physical, emotional, or mental—all of the condition's underlying causes must be resolved. For a true and lasting resolution of an unwanted condition, all the blockages and disharmonious energies contributing to the condition must be neutralized.

Therapeutic gemstone spheres can address all the underlying causes of a condition because they work holistically—on several dimensions, or bodies, at once. At the same time, most gems also have an affinity with one particular body—physical, emotional, causal, mental, or intuitive—

and tend to focus much of their work there. This unique focus helps define a gemstone's individual purpose. For example, Emerald's primary focus is the physical body, where it helps resolve conditions by neutralizing disharmonious energies. The pink gemstone Rhodonite fosters emotional stability, and thus its primary focus is the emotional body. Blue Sapphire's primary focus is on the mind, and so it brings nourishment, order, and clarity to the mental body.

How, then, do gemstone spheres work holistically? To support its primary focus, each type of gemstone often affects one or more other bodies, as well. Thus, to support its work in the physical body, Emerald also neutralizes any discordant energies in the emotional and mental bodies that are feeding the physical condition. To give Rhodonite's user a secure footing on which to make positive emotional changes, Rhodonite also forges a healthier link between the emotional and physical bodies. To support its primary focus on the mind, Blue Sapphire also clears negative energies from the physical head and brain, which are intimately connected with the mind's functioning.

Although each gemstone has a certain focus to its healing work, all the gemstones described in this book work holistically and, when used properly, bring uplifting benefits.

The Dimensions of Being and the Gemstones that Address Them

Below are descriptions of the dimensions addressed by therapeutic gemstone spheres and the names of gems that focus on each dimension.

Physical Healing and Purification

The primary focus of certain therapeutic gemstones is physical healing. Working with these gems can deeply purify and heal the physical body, help release toxins and negative energies stored in the organs, and support the immune system. Except for Quartz, these gemstones are predominantly green.

These therapeutic gems can help an individual:

- Resolve a chronic or acute illness
- Experience more energy and vitality
- Relieve chronic pain
- Strengthen a weakened organ
- Boost the immune system
- Soothe the body after trauma or surgery

The therapeutic gems that focus on physical healing and purification include:

Quartz	Dark Green Aventurine	Malachite
Emerald	Light Green Aventurine	Bloodstone

Emotional Healing and Upliftment

The primary focus of some therapeutic gemstones is emotional healing. Working with these gems can foster a sense of peace and happiness, improve emotional stability and balance, and help release and heal painful and suppressed emotions. Except for Mother of Pearl, these gemstones are predominantly red or pink.

These therapeutic gems can help an individual:

- Become more emotionally stable
- Soothe a wounded heart
- Release and resolve suppressed feelings
- Heal recent or longstanding grief
- Become more aware of deep feelings
- Experience and express divine love

The therapeutic gems that focus on emotional healing and upliftment include:

Ruby	Rhodonite
Roselle	Mother of Pearl

Karmic Healing and Resolution

The primary focus of some therapeutic gemstones is to help an individual resolve limiting karmic patterns. Working with these gems can help transform negative behavior patterns, break bad habits, and eliminate destructive relationship dynamics. They can also help resolve the negative patterns from the past that perpetuate physical or mental conditions. The results are a greater inner freedom and improved vitality and health. Except for Opalight, these gemstones are predominantly orange.

These therapeutic gems can help an individual:

- Change self-destructive habits
- Climb out of a rut
- Develop new, healthier ways of relating to others
- Eliminate the behavior patterns underlying an unwanted physical condition
- Break free of a pattern of destructive relationships
- Align one's dreams with one's life path

The therapeutic gems that focus on karmic healing and resolution include:

RHODOCHROSITE	CARNELIAN	OPALIGHT

Mental Clarity and Expansion

Mental healing is the primary focus of some therapeutic gemstones. Working with these gems can expand mental potential, clear the mind, increase one's ability to focus, and help heal certain mental imbalances. These gemstones are predominantly blue.

These therapeutic gems can help an individual:

- Experience greater mental clarity
- Focus more easily
- Clear out mental "garbage"
- Improve memory
- Expand the mind to its full potential

The therapeutic gems that focus on mental clarity and expansion include:

Blue Sapphire	Lapis Lazuli	Sodalight

Higher Consciousness and Spiritual Awakening

The primary focus of some therapeutic gemstones is the development and awakening of higher consciousness. Working with these gemstones can help heighten spiritual awareness, abolish impediments to higher states of consciousness, and strengthen intuition. Except for Aquamarine and Citrine, these gemstones are predominantly indigo and purple.

These therapeutic gems can help an individual:

- Let go of certain attachments
- Develop "inner" hearing
- Open to higher states of consciousness
- Strengthen and clarify intuition
- Open to one's inner source of wisdom

The therapeutic gems that focus on higher consciousness and spiritual awakening include:

Lavender	Amethyst	Aquamarine
Indigo	Citrine	Purple Rainbow Fluorite

Masculine and Feminine Healing and Empowerment

The primary focus of these two gemstones is empowering either one's feminine or masculine aspect and fostering balance between these two aspects. These gemstones can restore self-confidence and physical vigor, help resolve relationship issues, and repair endocrine imbalances.

These therapeutic gems can help an individual with the following:

For women

- Empower the feminine aspect
- Improve fertility
- Resolve a gynecological condition
- Relieve menstrual cramps

For men

- Empower the masculine aspect
- Experience more courage, vigor, and endurance
- Resolve an endocrine imbalance
- Enhance sexual prowess

For both men and women

- Strengthen and tone the reproductive system
- Restore or create harmony with a mate
- Protect oneself from other people's negative thoughts and feelings

The therapeutic gems that focus on masculine and feminine healing and empowerment include:

For Men:	Green Tourmaline
For Women:	Pink Tourmaline

Healing and Nourishing with Earth Energies

This special class of therapeutic gemstones includes opaque gemstones whose primary focus is healing, energizing, and nourishing the physical body. In general, the colors of these gemstones are muted, earthy, and variegated.

These therapeutic gems can help an individual:

- Attract whatever the physical body needs for healing
- Feel more grounded and stable
- Accelerate or integrate the positive effects of other therapies
- Develop healthier personal boundaries
- Become more energized and productive

The therapeutic gems that focus on healing and nourishing with Earth energies include:

Agate	Riverstone	Poppy Jasper
Onyx	Quartzite	Leopardskin Jasper

Multidimensional Healing with Five Well-Rounded Gems

Most therapeutic gems focus their work primarily on one dimension, and their work on other dimensions mostly supports their primary purpose. However, there are some gems whose work is particularly diverse and which have profound effects on more than one dimension. For this reason, these gems are especially versatile tools. For example, Citrine can be equally effective at releasing physical tension as it is at awakening a spiritual perspective; Quartz can help bring balance to the mind, body, and emotions. Lavender may be the most versatile of all—it actually focuses its work equally on all the bodies.

This group of particularly "well-rounded" gemstones is listed below. More detailed descriptions of their multiple gifts of healing and transformation can be found in the next chapter.

Quartz	Carnelian	Citrine
Lavender	Aquamarine	

Color Ray Healing with Seven Special Gemstones

The Earth's gems play a surprisingly central role in how color functions, not only in the mineral kingdom but in life itself. This role has far-reaching implications for the healing arts. Indeed, the subject of color healing is such a significant part of gemstone energy medicine that it deserves several books of its own. Thus, what follows is simply a brief introduction to this vast topic.

Color rays are the most fundamental building blocks of all living things. Just as visible light is comprised of the seven colors of the rainbow, so is the life force—the force that enlivens, sustains, and nourishes everything that lives. We human beings are manifestations of this vital force. Thus, at the deepest level we too are made up of spectrums of these seven color rays.

Each color ray has a specific purpose, and all seven color rays are essential for life. Being continually supplied with and nourished by a proper balance of color rays is essential to every aspect of health. In an optimally healthy person, all seven colors are present in balance. Any deviation from that balance moves a person away from ideal health and an optimal expression of life—and will ultimately lead to disease and disharmony.

Seven Color Ray Gemstones

All therapeutic gems embody intense concentrations of energy. They help remove obstructions to the flow of life force in our bodies and being. Seven of these gemstones also serve another, very special function: each of them carries one of the seven color rays of the life force. Embodied in the crystalline matrix of each of these seven gems is the pure and highly concentrated vibration of a certain color ray.

Because the color rays themselves are not physically tangible, it is difficult to work with them directly in their pure form. The gemstones that carry the seven color rays solve this problem. They are the Earth's most powerful tools available for drawing the color rays from their origin through one's inner dimensions, or subtle bodies, to the physical body. Indeed, these seven gemstones are the Earth's premier color healing tools.

The seven color ray gemstones and the color rays they carry are: Ruby (red ray), Carnelian (orange ray), Citrine (yellow ray), Emerald (green ray), Blue Sapphire (blue ray), Indigo (indigo ray), and Amethyst (purple/violet ray).

Each of these gemstones not only contains the concentrated energy of a certain color ray; each also acts as a magnet to continuously draw a current of that color to the physical plane from its unlimited source, the pure life force that lies at the basis of all life. When you wear a necklace of a color ray gemstone, you effectively step into the current of color that the gemstone draws to itself.

As this current moves through your subtle bodies to your physical body, any blockages in your being associated with that color ray are washed away in the current. For example, when you wear a therapeutic Emerald necklace, your entire being is flooded with the green color ray. The green ray helps neutralize the disharmonies that cause physical disease, particularly those centered in the organs. As blockages to the green ray dissolve, any excess of green ray in the body and aura is relieved, and any deficiency of green is filled by the abundant influx of green ray. Through this mechanism, wearing a color-ray gemstone necklace can have profound implications for your life and health at the deepest levels.

Healing the Physical Body with Color

Each of the seven color rays is particularly healing and nourishing to a certain system in the physical body. For this reason, one can greatly benefit a particular system by wearing its corresponding color ray necklace. For example, the red ray nourishes and supports the muscles, tendons, and fascia. Consequently, wearing Ruby can help strengthen these parts of the body and resolve certain conditions related to them.

The following chart lists the color rays and the physical systems that are nourished and supported by each color.

Color Ray Healing and Physical Systems

COLOR RAY	GEMSTONE	PHYSICAL SYSTEM
RED	RUBY	MUSCULAR SYSTEM (muscles, tendons, and fascia)
ORANGE	CARNELIAN	LYMPHATIC SYSTEM SOFT CONNECTIVE TISSUE ENDOCRINE SYSTEM (glands) ADIPOSE TISSUE
YELLOW	CITRINE	ORGANS OF ELIMINATION (skin, bladder, urinary tract, kidneys, intestines, and eliminative aspects of the liver)
GREEN	EMERALD	ORGANS IN THE TORSO BRAIN*
BLUE	BLUE SAPPHIRE	VASCULAR SYSTEM NERVE SHEATHS CEREBROSPINAL FLUID SENSE ORGANS BLOOD BRAIN*
INDIGO	INDIGO	SKELETAL SYSTEM (bones, ligaments, joints, and cartilage)
PURPLE/ VIOLET	AMETHYST	NERVE CELLS BRAIN*

Note that the brain, which serves many functions, is associated with several color rays.

Therapeutic gemstones are jewels of healing and transformation—gifts from the Earth waiting to be opened. To enjoy these gifts, we need only know how to unwrap and use them; yet doing so can be a very simple matter. Simply by shaping therapeutic-quality gemstones into spheres and stringing them into necklaces, we can begin to tap their vast healing potential and reap their far-reaching and multidimensional benefits.

CHAPTER 5

The Healing Benefits of 30 Gemstones

With their ability to touch the many dimensions of our being, therapeutic gemstone necklaces offer unprecedented depth and breadth of healing power. This chapter details the therapeutic actions and benefits of thirty gemstone necklaces when each is worn around the neck. For most of these necklaces, it also provides step-by-step instructions on how to perform a therapy that focuses the gemstones' action on a specific condition or issue. Each of these potent therapeutic tools offers its own unique gift of healing for the multidimensional human form.

30 Therapeutic Gemstone Necklaces

For each therapeutic gemstone necklace, this chapter provides:

- A brief overview of the gemstone's effects
- Indications for using the gemstone
- Benefits of wearing the gemstone as a necklace
- Special considerations for using the gemstone
- The unique requirements for therapeutic quality in the gemstone
- Instructions for performing a therapy that directs the gemstone's benefits to a particular area or issue

Physical Healing and Purification

Quartz

Emerald

Dark Green Aventurine

Light Green Aventurine

Malachite

Bloodstone

Although the following gems are categorized
elsewhere, they also offer significant healing
benefits for the physical body.
Therefore, see also:

Agate • Aquamarine • Carnelian
Citrine • Green Tourmaline
Lavender • Leopardskin Jasper
Pink Tourmaline • Poppy Jasper
Sodalight

Quartz

Attracting Life Force

Quartz attracts life force from the unlimited source of life at the core of your being and brings it into the physical world. As this life force flows through you, it nourishes and balances your mind, emotions, and physical body and corrects color-ray imbalances within them. Because this stream of vital energy touches every facet of your being, all aspects of your life improve. The life energy Quartz draws through your body and into the atmosphere also provides vital spiritual nourishment for the Earth.

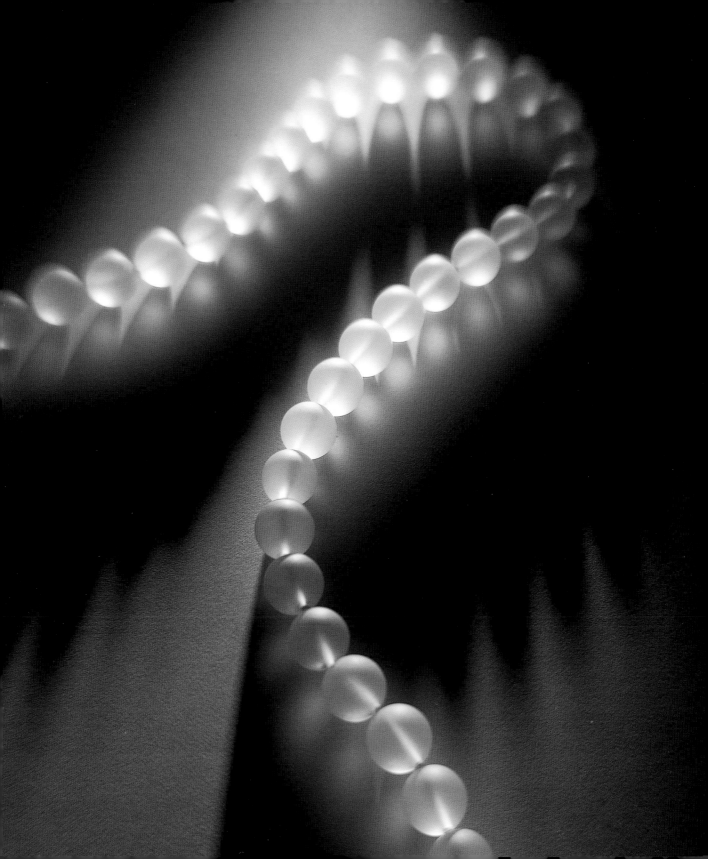

Indications *for Wearing a Therapeutic* Quartz Necklace

YOU ARE EXPERIENCING—

Low or sluggish energy

Feeling out of balance physically, emotionally, or mentally

Feeling overwhelmed

Illness

Injury or pain

YOU WANT TO—

Increase your energy

Bring more balance, grace, and harmony to your life

Enhance the effects of a color ray gemstone

Promote balance in the relationship among your body, mind, and emotions

Foster balance within and among your body's physical processes

Balance your mind's creative and analytical aspects

Regain your balance after a life-changing or traumatic experience

More easily learn from past experiences so you can make better choices

Benefits *of Wearing a Therapeutic* Quartz Necklace

Quartz fosters balance in all aspects of your life. When you are more balanced, more life force can flow through you to touch every aspect of your being. This increased flow fosters even greater balance, which in turn attracts even more life force. Because Quartz's nature is to promote balance, it brings your entire being into balance in a balanced way— slowly and steadily.

When worn around the neck, Quartz balances your whole being; when placed on specific areas of the body, it balances those areas. For example, if you place Quartz spheres on a disharmonious stomach, the Quartz will attract life force to the stomach, promoting greater balance there and helping the stomach become healthier.

When you wear a necklace of Quartz spheres, the Quartz brings balance to your body's physical processes, including those involved in the functioning of your endocrine, organ, nervous, circulatory, digestive, and other systems. Quartz balances these processes one at a time, beginning its work with whatever requires its attention most. As Quartz draws more life force to your physical body, a healing may start to occur. Such healing is not the direct effect of Quartz but of the increased life force that Quartz brings to your body. As you continue to wear Quartz, your health will naturally improve.

When you wear a Quartz necklace, additional life force also permeates your inner aspects—your mind, memory, and emotions. This additional life energy nourishes, balances, and aligns your emotional, karmic, and mental bodies. This is important, because disease is usually more than just physical; it most often originates on the emotional and mental levels.

Quartz fosters a greater awareness of your emotional being. It helps balance emotional energies and incorporate the effects of new experiences into your consciousness. With more emotional balance, you can handle all situations in a more dignified and balanced way. Because of this, Quartz may seem to protect you from the negative emotions of others. However, you will simply become more able to place negative emotions in perspective and to maintain your own balance. Positive emotions will appear enhanced, but only because you will appreciate and enjoy them more.

Those who are familiar with the concept of karma—the law of cause and effect, or the law of action and reaction—know that an individual is ultimately accountable for his actions. Quartz can help you become aware of incidents from the past; it can also help you see that your actions cause reactions. With this awareness, the effects of your actions can become learning experiences rather than simply slaps out of the blue. This awareness will also help you better handle your current life situations that are associated with past experiences.

Quartz also helps you achieve greater mental balance. To accomplish this, it improves either analytical or creative thinking, depending on your needs. Which function is stimulated, which is suppressed, and the degree to which these actions occur will be different for everyone. Once Quartz completes this adjustment, both creative and analytical thinking will be strengthened, enlivened, and improved.

Quartz not only helps balance your physical and subtle bodies, it also helps bring into balance everything that comes into your life. If Quartz is worn continually, it will even work to deflect those forces that upset your balance, and it will attract what is needed to maintain your balance.

Quartz spheres can take the energy that is in your aura, metabolize it, and return it to you in a more usable form. Quartz calls to itself the life force that exists all around you and in your subtle bodies. It can bring this energy into your physical body in a form that the body can "digest" and use for its development. Ultimately, the mission of Quartz is spiritual: when the bodies' energies are balanced, a more stable foundation will be laid from which spiritual growth can flourish.

"Many of my patients are children with cerebral palsy. I have found that when I place a Quartz necklace on a cerebral palsy child after a chiropractic adjustment, it brings deep relaxation, peace, and balance to their bodies, and they hold their adjustments longer. Recently, I placed a Quartz sphere on a little girl who had been unable to move. When I returned to the room, she had picked it up and placed it on her head! I find that Quartz helps today's children find balance."

Dr. Bobby Doscher
Oklahaven Children's Chiropractic Center
Oklahoma City, Oklahoma

Color Ray Healing

Quartz gently attracts a balance of all seven color rays[1] to your body, emotions, and mind. In the process, it corrects any color-ray imbalances in your physical and subtle bodies. When you become more balanced on this fundamental level, all aspects of life improve.

Quartz's ability to attract all seven color rays makes it an ideal partner to wear with a color-ray gemstone necklace. The color ray gemstones include Ruby, Carnelian, Citrine, Emerald, Blue Sapphire, Indigo and Amethyst.[2] Not only does Quartz enhance the flow of life force through all levels of your being, it amplifies the effects of the color ray gemstones and balances the ratios of color rays within you.

Metal and Quartz

A solid Quartz necklace should never contain any kind of metal, such as a metal clasp, chain, or beads. The Quartz would amplify the metal's energetic effects, which in most cases conflict with the action of Quartz.

Frosted Quartz

When therapeutic-quality Quartz is first fashioned into spheres, it is transparent. To prepare Quartz for use in a therapeutic necklace, the surface of the spheres must be roughened through a polishing process that makes the spheres appear white, or "frosted." Only Quartz spheres with this frosted finish should be worn in necklaces. When unfrosted Quartz spheres are drilled for stringing, the drill holes disrupt the energies at both ends of the spectrum of Quartz emanations, making such spheres disharmonious to the wearer. Frosting the spheres re-establishes and maintains a pure, balanced flow of their energies. This property is unique to colorless Quartz.

"When I wear a Quartz necklace, I feel deep inner contentment. I feel very connected to myself, to other people, and to the world around me, and that brings me a great sense of peace and happiness."

Dr. Padeen Quinn
Naturopathic Physician
Portland, Oregon

---

1 *See page 40 for more information on the vital role of color rays in restoring and maintaining health.*

2 *See page 41 for more information on the color ray gemstones.*

Mineral Composition
SiO₂

Found most everywhere in the world, Quartz is the most common single mineral in the Earth's crust. Clear Quartz is pure silicon dioxide, or silicon and oxygen, our planet's most abundant elements. It is usually formed on the outer edges of volcanic flow, where temperatures and pressures are relatively low. Some of the many places Quartz is found include Brazil, Switzerland, Hungary, Japan, India, Madagascar, Arkansas, and New York.

Therapeutic-Quality Quartz

To receive the maximum therapeutic benefits from Quartz, only optical or near-optical quality spheres should be used. Optical-quality Quartz is colorless, clear, and free from flaws to the naked eye. Such flaws include cracks and inclusions, or foreign matter. Near-optical Quartz has very slight flaws in a small portion of the sphere but is otherwise identical to optical quality. If a Quartz sphere has anything more than very slight flaws, its ability to balance your physical, emotional, and mental bodies will be significantly inhibited.

Therapeutic Quartz also has no hint of yellow, gray, brown, or smoky coloration. Color contamination and internal flaws greatly limit the spheres' inflow and outflow of energy.

People who wear lower-quality Quartz may still feel some effects, since any gemstone will influence an individual's energetic field. However, only the highest quality Quartz necklace—one with deeply frosted, optical or near-optical quality spheres and precisely cut drill-holes— will spark the true changes and transformations one seeks from this gemstone. Optical-quality Quartz is extremely rare. Yet it is well worth seeking out, since a necklace made of such Quartz radiates an incomparable energy.

Quartz Therapy
Life Force Infusion

Quartz energy is infused into a painful, injured, or otherwise disharmonious area to bring more life energy and balance to the area. This Quartz infusion can be used as a primary therapy or as a pre-treatment to help prepare any area of the body for another life-giving therapy.

Therapy Tool

One therapeutic necklace of frosted Quartz spheres (8 mm, 10 mm, or 12 mm)

Indications

- When a localized area of your body, such as an organ or muscle, is injured, painful, or tight
- When you are experiencing joint, back, or neck pain
- When you wish to bring additional life force and improved balance to any part of your body
- When you wish to prepare a localized area of your body for another life-supporting therapy, such as a chiropractic adjustment or another gemstone treatment

Effects

When you place Quartz spheres on a disharmonious area of your body, the area and its surrounding aura are infused with Quartz energy. The Quartz attracts additional life force to the area and gently fosters balance there. As the troubled area moves toward a state of greater balance, it naturally releases the disharmonious energies that have contributed to its distress. As a result, the area is soothed and its healing is accelerated.

Often a disharmonious area is so blocked or tight that it does not allow a certain color ray to enter it, even if that color is needed for

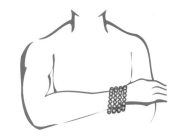

Fig. QTZ-1

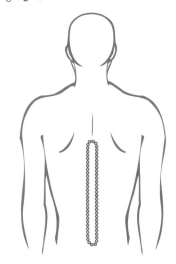

Fig. QTZ-2

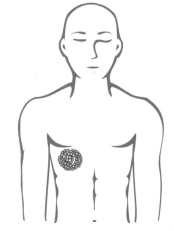

Fig. QTZ-3

optimal balance and health. By drawing life energy to the treatment area, the Quartz attracts all seven color rays of the life force.[3] Because the Quartz introduces these color rays so gently, the area is less likely to resist the colors' healing influence. Instead, the body recognizes the color rays as healing, soothing, and necessary.

Procedure

1. Ideally, position yourself so that the area you wish to treat is exposed to direct sunlight, even if it is just the sunlight coming through an open window on a sunny or cloudy day.

2. Place the Quartz necklace directly on your skin over the area you wish to treat:
   - If you are treating an extremity, such as your wrist, wrap the necklace around it (see Fig. QTZ-1).
   - If you are treating your spine, place the necklace along the length of your spine, centering the necklace on the most troubled spot (see Fig. QTZ-2).
   - If you are treating any other part of your body, arrange the necklace in a neat pile or flat spiral on the ailing area (see Fig. QTZ-3).

3. If you wish, you may secure the Quartz to the area between treatments to maintain a gentle flow of healing energies there. Place the gemstones on your skin and then place a light cotton cloth over the gems. To secure the gems to your body, tape the cloth to your skin with non-plastic first aid tape. Avoid letting the glue from the tape touch the gems.

Caution: Artificial Light and Quartz

The use of sunlight in Quartz therapies can enhance their effects. Artificial light, on the other hand, should never be shined directly on Quartz when it is being used therapeutically. The Quartz can amplify the artificial light spectrums, producing harmful effects. Furthermore,

---

3 *See page 40 for more information on the vital role of color rays in restoring and maintaining health.*

whenever artificial light is directed at Quartz, the Quartz's energy becomes disrupted. However, no harmful effects will result from performing this therapy in ambient artificial light, such as in a room where a lamp is turned on.

Time Guidelines

When performing this treatment in sunlight, keep the Quartz on the treatment area for 30 to 60 minutes once or twice a day. If you secure it to the area between treatments, you can keep it there indefinitely. When performing this therapy as a pre-treatment, apply the Quartz for 15 to 30 minutes immediately before receiving the other therapy.

Post-Treatment Cleansing of Gems

Immediately after completing a treatment, it is important to cleanse the gems of any disharmonious energies released by the body in the course of treatment. See Appendix A: "Care and Cleansing of Therapeutic Gems," on page 397, for cleansing instructions.

Arthritis and Lavender

Although this Quartz therapy can be helpful for arthritis, Lavender is much more effective for treating arthritis pain. See "Lavender Pain Relief and Realignment Technique," on page 236.

Emerald

Healing the Physical Body

Emerald brings life, nourishment, and healing to the physical body. It floods the physical body with the green ray's life-giving energy and gradually neutralizes the disharmonies that cause disease. If enough Emerald is worn, it also works on healing the mental and emotional causes of physical illness. By strengthening your physical body's weakest link, Emerald uplifts, strengthens, and vitalizes your body as a whole, making it easier for you to open to higher states of consciousness.

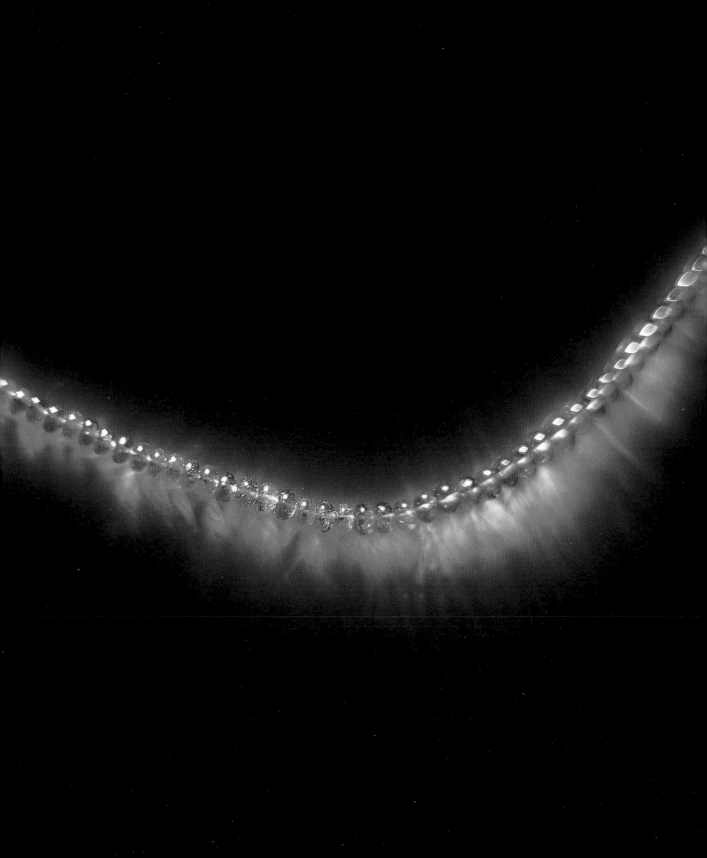

Indications *for Wearing a Therapeutic*
Emerald Necklace

YOU ARE EXPERIENCING—

Any unwanted physical condition—from a serious chronic disease to an acute illness

Chronic fatigue or low energy

Any form of cancer*

Tumors, benign or malignant*

Any physical disease or distress involving one or more organs

YOU WANT TO—

Bring life, nourishment, and healing to your physical body

Release and neutralize disharmonious energy in your body

Maintain a high level of physical functioning

Resolve the emotional and mental causes of physical distress

Take preventive measures to support your health because of a family history of cancer or organ disease*

* To be used as an adjunct to other therapies

Benefits *of Wearing a Therapeutic*
Emerald Necklace

Emerald brings life, nourishment, and healing to your physical body. It helps resolve many types of physical disharmony with the life-giving green ray it carries.[4] Emerald is the gemstone bearer of the green ray, an essential element for the life of all plants, animals, and human beings. The green ray in Emerald raises the vibrations of the physical body and provides it with healing vitality. Emerald's healing effects come from a combination of the green ray it carries and the energy of beryl, the family of crystals to which Emerald belongs. For simplicity's sake, we shall refer to this combination as "Emerald energy."

Emerald focuses its healing effects on the area of greatest disharmony in your body, which is often the source of disease or pain. When you first wear Emerald, its energy floods your aura and locates areas of physical disharmony. Then, like the eagle that has spotted its prey, it swoops down on these areas. Emerald energy enters your body through your skin in a process similar to osmosis. There, it neutralizes and disintegrates the disharmony that manifests as disease and discomfort. Finally, it helps your body release this disharmony.

The origins of physical illness are almost always more than physical. Conflicts and discord in the emotions and mind often lead to physical problems. Inner disharmonies block the flow of life force to the physical body and feed it with disharmonious energy. Emerald not only addresses the physical manifestation of illness; it also helps resolve these inner causes of physical distress.

Emerald increases the flow of life energy throughout your entire being. It does this by energetically lubricating certain components in your subtle bodies. These components, which resemble needle-like

---

4 *See page 40 for more information on the vital role of color rays in restoring and maintaining health.*

fibers, direct life energy through your subtle bodies to your physical body. They perform various other functions, as well: in your emotional body, they direct the emotional energies that eventually manifest as emotions; in your causal body, they manifest as pattern lines; and in your mental body, they represent mechanisms that your mind uses to make its decisions and perform other functions.

As Emerald energy fills your subtle bodies, it provides these important fibers with something like a tune-up: it loosens, cleanses, and lubricates them. As a result, the fibers are freed from obstructions and become more flexible and efficient in their functioning. This allows more life energy to move through these fibers to all aspects of your being.

Although Emerald's effects on the emotional and mental bodies are secondary to its effects on the physical body, when you wear Emerald, you can take comfort in knowing you are using a powerful tool—not only to heal your physical body but to resolve the very causes of your physical condition. Emerald also prepares your emotions and mind for the new state of consciousness that will arise when your physical condition has been resolved.

Emerald and Organs

Each of the seven color rays of the life force is particularly healing and nourishing to certain aspects of the physical body. The green ray nourishes and supports the brain and the organs in the torso. Consequently, wearing Emerald can help strengthen these parts of the body and resolve certain conditions associated with them.

Emerald's Order of Work

Emerald works in stages. When the energy of an Emerald necklace has saturated your aura and resolved a certain degree of disharmony in your physical body, it begins to neutralize the negative emotional energies that are feeding your physical condition. Then, when it has resolved a certain degree of disharmony in your physical and emotional bodies, the Emerald energy penetrates your mental body and begins to work on the mental issues contributing to your condition.

Because disharmony and the green ray are energetic opposites, the green ray radiated by Emerald gets neutralized in the process of disintegrating disharmony. If the disharmony is strong, the green ray is used up rather quickly. Therefore, if you wish to address not only your physical condition but also its emotional and mental causes, you must wear enough Emerald to maintain a constant saturation of your aura with green ray.

Amount to Wear

The most effective way to maintain Emerald saturation of your aura is to wear a large amount of Emerald. A solid necklace of 30 to 45 carats of therapeutic-quality Emerald will probably maintain saturation of the aura at all times. It will also provide enough Emerald energy to work on the emotional and mental causes of physical conditions.

For a relatively healthy person who wishes to use Emerald for minor disharmonies or preventive purposes, a smaller amount of Emerald will probably be adequate. In this case, a necklace of five or six carats of Emerald harmoniously combined with other uplifting gemstones will likely be enough to saturate the aura. However, it will take much longer to do so than if a larger amount of Emerald is worn, and it won't have enough strength to neutralize large amounts of disharmony or to reach deeply into the emotional or mental bodies.

When you have a serious physical condition or you are experiencing acute symptoms, inner disharmonies are more difficult to abolish. These negative energies resist the entrance of Emerald and other healing energies into your aura. Using higher quality or a larger amount of Emerald, such as that present in a solid necklace, can overcome this resistance more easily. If the disease is serious or life threatening, perhaps as much as 75 or more carats may be necessary.

To maintain a therapeutic level of Emerald energy in your aura, it is important to keep the Emerald necklace either around your neck or within three feet of your body at all times.

"In October 1999, doctors found that my father had a large pancreatic tumor. He was in considerable pain, but his heart condition ruled out both surgery and chemotherapy. Doctors predicted he had two to four months to live. That December he started to wear a solid Emerald necklace, supported by Citrine and Dark Green Aventurine. Within a month he was pain-free without medication. He lived another three years, with no recurrence of pancreas problems, before dying of heart failure."

Alan Coffman, L.Ac.
Licensed Acupuncturist
Madison, Wisconsin

Time Guidelines

Again, once you have taken care of your physical disharmonies with Emerald, you must also resolve their inner causes; otherwise, these inner disharmonies will continue to manifest in your physical body. Perhaps they will manifest in a different location or as a different condition, but they will manifest. Therefore, to fully resolve the inner disharmonies, you should continue wearing enough Emerald to saturate your aura for some time after your physical condition has appeared to heal. People whose physical bodies are overburdened with disharmony should— probably for the rest of their lives—wear enough Emerald to saturate the aura continually and provide enough Emerald energy to work on the underlying, inner causes of their physical conditions.

Co-Workers in Healing

Anyone with any kind of physical disease, especially one involving an organ, can benefit greatly from wearing the strongest combination of physically healing gemstones yet known: Dark Green Aventurine in one necklace and Emerald in another.

For example, Emerald and Dark Green Aventurine can be used together to combat cancer of an organ. The effect of Emerald energy on cancer is one of shock. Cancer is like a living entity. It works to maintain its own life, which exists at the expense of its host. When cancer is introduced to the pure green ray and the energy of Emerald, the cancer entity becomes so shocked that it energetically pulls in and becomes somewhat more compact and isolated. The Aventurine works from the inside of an organ to expel disharmony and to spread healthy, harmonious energy throughout the organ's cells. The Emerald stands at the "doorway" of each cell, directing green ray at the exiting disharmony and disintegrating it. This is the power of the green ray. It is the perfect opposite of cancer.

For more information on the benefits of using Emerald and Dark Green Aventurine together, for both organ diseases and other physical conditions, see *Dark Green Aventurine*, on page 70.

"Six years ago, I started to see a patient with AIDS just as he was entering a hospice. He began taking the AIDS retroviral drug cocktail and wore a solid Emerald necklace 24/7, in combination with Dark Green Aventurine therapy sessions. In six weeks, the measured HIV viral load in his blood showed a decrease equivalent to results typical of taking the AIDS cocktail by itself for a full year. Today he is thriving and healthy and running his own successful business."

Alan Coffman, L.Ac.
Licensed Acupuncturist
Madison, Wisconsin

Emerald Shape

A *rondel* is a sphere that is somewhat flattened on two opposite sides. Therapeutic Emerald is best shaped into rondels rather than spheres. Emerald spheres tend to have a somewhat harsh, searing effect on the aura and body. The rondel shape helps the body regulate the absorption of Emerald energy in the aura, while providing benefits similar to those of gemstone spheres.

The rounded yet irregular form known as rounded chips should be avoided in the case of Emerald. Emerald chips have an irritating effect on the human aura.

Therapeutic-Quality Emerald

Color, brightness, and clarity are of equal importance in therapeutic-quality Emerald. The color green that most closely matches the green of the rainbow is most powerful in Emerald. Therapeutic Emerald is a rich, radiant, pure bright green with good clarity. When the necklace is examined as a whole, it should be free of black flecks or have only a minimal number of them.

One should avoid any Emerald that is cloudy or dull in appearance or noticeably yellow-green or blue-green in color. This is not therapeutic Emerald. The blue in particular is a contaminant that can alter the vibration of Emerald. Not only is it non-therapeutic, but it can actually have harmful effects.

Mineral Composition
$Be_3Al_2(SiO_3)_6 + Cr + V$

A gem variety of beryl, or beryllium aluminum silicate, Emerald derives its rich green color from traces of chromium and sometimes vanadium. Emerald is found in Colombia, Russia, Brazil, Africa, and North Carolina

Emerald Therapy
Green Ray Infusion

Emerald energy and the green ray are infused into the body to uplift its health and neutralize the disharmonious energies that have collected there.

Variation for Localized Conditions
Emerald is placed on a distressed or diseased area to focus the Emerald's benefits on the area.

Variation for Systemic Conditions
Emerald is placed on special points on the abdomen to promote a deep, overall energetic cleansing of the physical body. This variation also gives the body extra energy to help heal a systemic ailment, overcome the flare-up of a chronic systemic condition, or fend off an oncoming acute illness.

Therapy Tools

- One therapeutic necklace of Emerald rondels
- (Optional) Lamp with a halogen or full-spectrum incandescent bulb

Variation for Localized Conditions
Indications

- When you are experiencing any kind of disharmony in a localized area of your body, such as that found in a congested or diseased organ or a tumor
- When you are experiencing acute symptoms or the flare-up of a chronic condition in a localized area of your body

Effects

This variation infuses life-giving Emerald energy and green-ray nourishment into a distressed area of your body. There, it neutralizes the area's negative energies and strongly supports physical healing. This variation is particularly beneficial for areas of high-density disharmony, such as that found in a congested or diseased organ or a tumor.

When you wear an Emerald necklace around your neck, it finds all areas that require its attention and disintegrates their disharmonious energies. When you place the necklace on a specific organ or area, as you do in this therapy, you focus the Emerald's healing work on that area. Using a light source enhances the penetration of the Emerald energy into the body.

Procedure

1. Place the Emerald necklace directly on the area of your body most affected by your condition or on an associated organ. Arrange the necklace into a flat spiral and place it directly on your skin (see Fig. EMR-1).

2. Ideally, expose the Emerald to direct sunlight, either by performing the therapy outdoors, or by performing it indoors in an area where sunlight is shining through an open window. Do not cover the Emerald.

3. If sunshine is not available, do one of the following—
   - The best alternative is to shine a halogen or full-spectrum incandescent bulb directly on the Emerald. Place the lit bulb 6 to 12 inches away from the gemstones. Allow the warmth of the bulb to penetrate the Emerald and warm your skin.
   - Alternately, place the Emerald on your skin and under clothing without using a light source. Therapeutic effects will be considerably milder.

4. When you have completed the infusion treatment, immediately cleanse the Emerald necklace and then place it around your neck (see cleansing instructions on page 397). Wearing a therapeutic Emerald necklace between infusion treatments will strongly support your recovery.

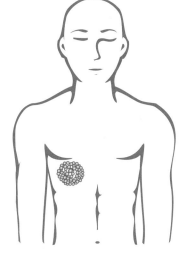

Fig. EMR-1

Caution: Artificial Light and Emerald

Never use artificial light to infuse Emerald energy into your chakras or your head; only sunlight should be used for this purpose. If you wish to perform this treatment on your chakras or head, but no sunlight is available, simply place the Emerald on the treatment area. Again, without sunlight, you will have to keep the Emerald in place much longer to achieve the same effects.

Time Guidelines

Perform infusion treatments once or twice a day for 15 to 20 minutes each. For example, you may place the Emerald on the treatment area and lie in the sun during the day, and then do so again in the evening with or without the artificial light.

If you are performing this therapy without sunlight or a lamp, keep the Emerald on the treatment area for at least one hour.

If your illness is severe, continue the infusion treatments for several weeks after symptoms have abated. Continue to wear the Emerald necklace around your neck for at least several months, and possibly several years, after the improvement of your symptoms. If you are treating acute symptoms or the flare-up of a chronic condition, wear the Emerald necklace until the condition is resolved.

Variation for Systemic Conditions
Indications

- When you have a chronic systemic illness that affects either several areas of your body or your body's overall condition
- When you want an overall energy boost
- When you want to energetically cleanse and lubricate your body
- When you are coming down with a cold or flu but are not yet experiencing acute symptoms
- When you feel "under the weather"

Effects

This therapy infuses life-giving Emerald energy and green-ray nour-ishment into the entire body. An Emerald necklace is folded into a smaller circle and placed on special points on the abdomen. This procedure neutralizes disharmonious energies in the body and enlivens all the organs in the torso, including their internal processes and energy flows. It also gives your body the extra healing energy it needs to overcome a chronic or acute ailment more thoroughly and swiftly. By removing some of your body's disharmonious energies, this therapy may also give you an extra burst of vitality. The infusion of Emerald energy into your abdomen is greatly enhanced by shining light through the gemstones. (see "Caution" on page 66).

Procedure

Ideally, perform this treatment outdoors in the sunlight or indoors with the sun shining through an open window directly on your abdomen. If sunlight is not available, use a halogen or full-spectrum incandescent bulb, as described in Step 5.

1. Determine the size of a circle you will make with the Emerald necklace—
   - Measure the distance between your xiphoid process and your navel (see Fig. EMR-2 for the location of the xiphoid process.)
   - Divide this distance by 3. This number is the diameter of the circle you will make.

   Example: If the distance between your xiphoid and navel is 6 inches, the circle will be 2 inches in diameter.

2. Fasten the necklace's clasp. Fold over the necklace several times to form a neat circle approximately of the size you calculated.

3. Lie on your back with the area between your xiphoid process and your navel uncovered.

4. (*Placement 1*) Position the circle on your abdomen so that its upper edge touches the tip of your xiphoid process (see Fig. EMR-2).

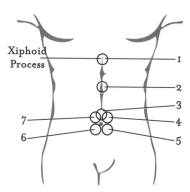

Xiphoid
Process

Fig. EMR-2

5. Allow sunlight to shine directly on the Emerald. Do not cover the gemstones.

   If sunlight is not available, use a lamp. Place the lit bulb 6 to 12 inches away from the gemstones. Allow the warmth of the bulb to penetrate the Emerald and warm your skin.

   In Steps 6–11, each time you reposition the Emerald, adjust the lamp so that its light shines directly on the Emerald.

6. (*Placement 2*) Move the Emerald circle down the midline of your body to halfway between your xiphoid process and navel (see Fig. EMR-2). Make sure the Emerald circle is centered between them.

7. (*Placement 3*) Move the Emerald circle down so that the lower edge of the circle is touching the upper edge of the navel (see Fig. EMR-2).

8. (*Placement 4*) Move the Emerald circle northeast of your navel, keeping the edge of the circle touching the edge of the navel (see Fig. EMR-2).

9. (*Placement 5*) Move the Emerald circle southeast of your navel, keeping the edge of the circle touching the edge of the navel (see Fig. EMR-2).

10. (*Placement 6*) Move the Emerald circle southwest of your navel, keeping the edge of the circle touching the edge of the navel (see Fig. EMR-2).

11. (*Placement 7*) Move the Emerald circle northwest of your navel, keeping the edge of the circle touching the edge of the navel (see Fig. EMR-2).

12. If you are using a lamp, turn it off.

13. When you have completed the treatment, immediately cleanse the Emerald necklace and then place it around your neck (see instructions below). Wearing a therapeutic Emerald necklace between infusion treatments will strongly support your recovery.

Post-Treatment Cleansing of Gems

When you apply the Emerald in the sun, the sunlight cleanses the gems as they work for your body. When you apply the Emerald under artificial light, this cleansing does not occur.

If you can only perform this treatment using artificial light or without access to direct sunlight, immediately after each treatment—

- Rinse the Emerald necklace under alternating hot and cold running water several times.
- Pat it dry with a soft towel.
- Immediately place the Emerald necklace around your neck.

If you are experiencing severe physical disharmony, the Emerald should never leave your aura. In that case, it is best not to lose the Emerald's support by removing it from your aura and placing it outdoors for cleansing. Instead, simply rinse it each day as described above.

Time Guidelines

Keep the Emerald in each placement position (Steps 4–11) for three to four minutes before moving on to the next step. Perform this treatment every other day until your symptoms significantly improve or disappear.

If your illness is severe, wear the Emerald necklace around your neck for at least several months, and possibly several years, after your symptoms have improved. If you are treating acute symptoms or the flare-up of a chronic condition, wear the Emerald necklace until the condition is resolved.

Dark Green Aventurine

Purifying the Physical Body

Dark Green Aventurine initiates a deep purification of the physical body, especially the vital organs. Aventurine energy permeates the body and then focuses on your most distressed organ, filling it with healing energy and encouraging it to release its accumulated disharmony. Once this organ has been uplifted, your next most distressed organ receives Aventurine's attention. Thus, organ by organ, Aventurine helps heal and purify your entire body.

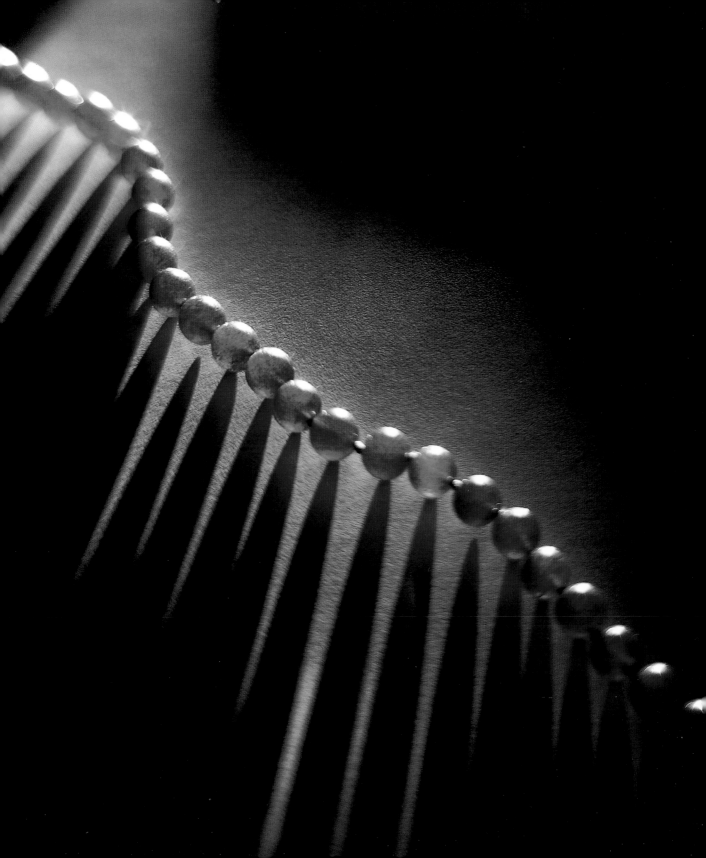

Indications *for Wearing a Therapeutic*
Dark Green Aventurine Necklace

WHEN ONE OR MORE OF THE FOLLOWING APPLY—

YOU ARE EXPERIENCING—

Disease or distress anywhere in the body, particularly in one or more organs

Cancer in an organ*

YOU WANT TO—

Heal or strengthen your weakest or least healthy organ

Increase your overall physical health, harmony, and vitality

Promote the release of certain toxins or disharmonious energies

* To be used as an adjunct to other therapies

CONTRAINDICATIONS

YOU HAVE A HISTORY OF—

Intensive drug use, prescription or otherwise

Exposure to toxic chemicals

Chemotherapy

Note: See Light Green Aventurine, on page 82, as an alternative to Dark Green Aventurine.

Benefits of *Wearing a Therapeutic*
Dark Green Aventurine Necklace

Dark Green Aventurine initiates a deep purification of your physical body, especially its vital organs. It purifies and uplifts the organ that is weakest and has the most limitations.

The Earth produces two basic varieties of green Aventurine: Light Green and Dark Green. The light green variety displays few or no dark green flecks in a light green base. The dark green variety is actually Light Green Aventurine[5] so infused with dark green flecks that it appears dark green. Therefore, the light green variety that contains no flecks radiates one type of energy, and the dark green variety offers two: the light green energy and the energy of the flecks.

Both the light and dark green energies focus their effects on organs. The light green energy uplifts and strengthens an organ by encouraging its healthiest cells to distribute their vitality throughout the organ. The dark green flecks expel the organ's low and disharmonious energies.

Of the two types of Aventurine, Dark Green Aventurine works most deeply—in part, because Dark Green Aventurine offers the effects of both the light and dark green vibrations. Nonetheless, when you wear a Dark Green Aventurine necklace, its primary effects are those of its dark green vibration—that is, it expels the organ's low and disharmonious energies. Dark Green Aventurine not only drives out an organ's disharmony and disease, it strengthens the organ. In Dark Green Aventurine, the light green component takes on a supporting role: it helps vitalize the organ, enabling it to more easily throw off the disharmony being expelled by the dark green vibration.

When you wear either Dark or Light Green Aventurine spheres around your neck, the Aventurine's energy fills your aura and enters

---

5 *See page 82, for more information on the therapeutic benefits of Light Green Aventurine.*

the physical body through your breath. As with anything inhaled, the Aventurine energy first enters your lungs, then your blood stream, and then every cell in your body. This is how the whole body becomes introduced to Aventurine energy. As the particles of Aventurine energy are distributed to every cell in the body, they maintain communication with each other. When enough Aventurine energy has permeated your body, it detects the organ with the most disharmony. Then, all the Aventurine energy already in your body, plus any more that is breathed in, surrounds and begins to enter that organ.

Every organ, even a diseased one, has areas that are healthier than others. It is in these healthier areas that Aventurine's energy first establishes itself. Once Aventurine energy gains a foothold in the organ, it makes room for more of itself to enter by expelling disharmonious energies from the organ. Then it gradually distributes itself as evenly as possible throughout the organ. As more and more Aventurine energy enters the organ, it forces out disease and disharmony while uplifting and strengthening the organ.

With both types of Aventurine, when the target organ is no longer the most disharmonious in the body, the Aventurine energy slowly leaves the organ. Then it finds the next organ with the greatest degree of disharmony and begins to work there. The Aventurine continues this process for as long as you wear it. If you wear Aventurine long enough, it's possible that it will treat every organ, including the organ it originally targeted. The longer you wear Dark Green Aventurine, the stronger and healthier your organs will become. Naturally, this will lead to a strengthening of your entire body.

Dark Green Aventurine can help those who aspire to greater spirituality and yet are unable to keep their attention on Spirit because their awareness is continually drawn to the body's disharmony, pain, or distress. As Aventurine helps your body work through a condition and lifts some of its burden, you will find it easier to expand your awareness to include other areas of life. With this opening of awareness, you may come to terms with the reasons for your ailments and more easily learn the life lessons associated with them.

Contraindication: Drugs and Dark Green Aventurine

Dark Green Aventurine should never be worn by or placed on the body of someone who is taking toxic drugs as part of another therapy, such as in chemotherapy. If the Aventurine is targeting an organ with drug residues, the Aventurine may recognize these residues as disharmonious and work to loosen and dispel them from the organ. If the organ has been accumulating drugs for years, a potentially serious situation may arise. When the Aventurine starts moving these drugs and their energies out of the organ and into the body, they will start circulating there, and the body may not be able to handle the influx and remove them. For people who wish to enjoy the benefits of Aventurine but who are taking toxic drugs or who have a history of taking them, it is best to wear Light Green Aventurine for some time before using Dark Green Aventurine.

Deep Breathing

When an organ is surrounded by Aventurine energy, it recognizes that a change is about to occur and that it will no longer be able to hold onto its disease. Physical matter often resists change, and anything that is diseased is especially resistant to the healing energy of Aventurine. A disease is also like a living entity. It knows that the presence of Aventurine energy is the beginning of its demise, so naturally it will want to push the energy away—and will do so with all its might.

You can help the Aventurine energy enter the target organ by breathing deeply. Deep breaths bring more oxygen to the organ. The Aventurine energy latches onto the oxygen molecules and rides them into the organ. In this way, deep breathing increases the amount of Aventurine energy entering the body. Therefore, when you wear Aventurine, it is advisable to periodically breathe deeply for a minute or two. People with serious organ conditions should breathe deeply as often as possible. When deep breathing, care should be taken not to hyperventilate.

Deep breathing will be most effective when your aura is saturated with Dark Green Aventurine energy. If you are wearing a therapeutic necklace of 10-mm spheres, your aura will probably become saturated

"I've used Dark Green Aventurine with excellent results in cases of pain, inflammation, and congestion. Migraines, uterine cramps, and joint and muscle inflammation have responded to Dark Green Aventurine almost universally."

Dr. Sara Hazel
Naturopathic Physician
Corbett, Oregon

within fifteen minutes. It may take up to forty-five minutes if you are wearing 8-mm spheres.

Children

Young children should generally not wear an Aventurine necklace made of larger than 6-mm spheres, unless the child has a serious condition or the necklace is being used to ease a temporary condition.

Animals

Both Dark and Light Green Aventurine can assist all forms of life, including animals. A collar of Aventurine is a wonderful gift for a dog or cat who is unwell or whose health you wish to fortify.

Powerful Partners: Dark Green Aventurine and Emerald

Anyone with a physical disease, especially one involving an organ, can benefit greatly by wearing the strongest combination of physically healing gemstones yet known: Dark Green Aventurine in one necklace and Emerald in another. When working on healing a physical condition, Emerald and Aventurine are indispensable. Indeed, if all you had were a solid necklace of Emerald and a solid necklace of Dark Green Aventurine, your gemstone "tool box" for physical-body healing would be nearly complete.

Emerald carries the green color ray. The green ray raises the vibrations of the physical body and provides it with powerful nourishment, vitality, and healing. Often those in pain resist the influx of Emerald's green ray nourishment. By focusing on their discomfort and tightening up against the pain, they inadvertently resist the entrance of the green ray. Wearing a Dark Green Aventurine necklace along with Emerald encourages the body to relax and open itself to the green ray's healing vibration.

When you wear Dark Green Aventurine alone, it expels disharmony from your weakest organ. A small amount of this disharmony is neutralized by the Aventurine's own light green vibration. It is then up to your body to eliminate the rest—that is, unless you also wear a necklace of Emerald. The Aventurine focuses the Emerald's green ray on the

"I've had problems with hot flashes for several years. You name it, I've probably tried it—pills, shots, patches. Nothing worked, until I started taking herbs and wearing a Dark Green Aventurine necklace. Previously, I was having hot flashes several times an hour. Now I'm down to one or two a day. Wearing the necklace has made all the difference. The herbs helped, but it was when I started wearing the necklace that I noticed the significant difference."

S.D.
Littleton, Colorado

organ. The green ray not only uplifts the organ; it also neutralizes much of the disharmony expelled by the Aventurine. In this way, Emerald relieves your body of the burden of eliminating much of this disharmony. To support the expulsion of disharmony from your body, you can also perform other therapies that boost your overall vitality and support your organs of elimination.

Because Dark Green Aventurine and Emerald work so powerfully together, people with seriously diseased organs are strongly advised to wear them together. Ideal would be a necklace of therapeutic Dark Green Aventurine spheres and another necklace of therapeutic Emerald. One should continue to wear them both, even if it appears that a healing has taken place. Once the energy of a disease has entered the body, it often lingers—sometimes for an entire lifetime—after the disease's physical manifestation has been cleared.

Time Guidelines

The time it takes for Dark Green Aventurine to complete its work depends on the size and quality of the Aventurine being worn. It also depends on the degree of toxicity in the target organ and the overall level of toxicity in the body.

To illustrate the time it takes for Aventurine to do its work, we can place an organ's disease or the degree of toxicity on a scale of zero to five: zero indicates perfect health, and five indicates a level of toxicity so great that virtually no life is left in the organ. We will also assume that therapeutic, exquisite-quality 10-mm Dark Green Aventurine spheres are being worn.

People whose conditions register one on this scale should wear Dark Green Aventurine continually for one or two months. Individuals in this category include those who are relatively healthy but who have aches and pains or organs that are not as strong as they would like them to be. If Emerald is also worn, the time required can be considerably reduced.

Those with conditions registering two may need to wear Dark Green Aventurine continuously for six months. Those with conditions

"When undergoing intensive chemotherapy, I wore Emerald and Dark Green Aventurine necklaces. Since I had such an aggressive form of cancer, I looked at every possible treatment. I wanted the alternative therapies I chose to have some demonstration of efficacy. With the gems, I felt I was getting additional energy at a time when I was feeling drained. Throughout my treatment, I was able to surf, ride my horse, play with my kids, and do all the normal things entailed in being a mom and a wife. People who were diagnosed with the same cancer are not even here to talk about it now."

Brenda Denslow-Perretta, M.D., FACEP
Portland, Oregon

registering three may need to wear the Aventurine for a year or more. If worn with Emerald, both of these times can be cut in half.

Those whose conditions register four and five must have very toxic bodies for their organs to possess such a low degree of life force. These individuals will need to wear Aventurine continually for at least three to five years. Again, the use of Emerald will greatly reduce this time requirement. Unfortunately, a body that is this toxic may not live that long unless it is supported by other therapies. These could include other gemstone therapies.

Therapeutic-Quality Dark Green Aventurine

To experience its true therapeutic effects, only certain qualities of Aventurine should be used. Again, therapeutic Dark Green Aventurine is composed of dark green flecks in a light green base. Its appearance varies, depending on the character of its light green base, the abundance and distribution of its dark green flecks, and the way these elements interact. The more translucent the Aventurine and the finer its color, the greater are its therapeutic effects. The overall color of the finest Dark Green Aventurine is rich forest-green.

To evaluate Aventurine for therapeutic quality, it must be examined under a microscope. This is required to determine whether the Aventurine has the proper ratio of light and dark green elements. This also ensures that the dark green flecks are not loose clouds or streaks but appear as solid, discrete, fully matured capsules suspended throughout the light green base. Any Aventurine that is muddy-looking or that displays other colors should be avoided.

Evaluating Dark Green Aventurine for therapeutic quality is so complex, that it is necessary to have viewed hundreds of specimens before one can confidently classify a sphere as therapeutic in quality.

Mineral Composition
$SiO_2 + K(Al,Cr)_2(AlSi_3O_{10})(OH)_2$

Dark Green Aventurine is composed of interlocking Quartz grains filled with tiny platelets of a green chromium mica, called fuchsite. Green Aventurine can display *aventurescence*, a glittery effect observed when the stone is rotated in reflected light. Green Aventurine is found in India, Russia, South Africa, Australia, Germany, and Wyoming.

Dark Green Aventurine Therapy
Awakening the Body

Dark Green Aventurine necklaces are placed on the soles of the feet to awaken the entire body to the presence of a disharmonious condition and to provide distressed areas with a steady supply of healing energies. This therapy stimulates the healing of an acute illness, a chronic condition, or any condition that has stalled in its healing.

Therapy Tools

- Two therapeutic necklaces of Dark Green Aventurine spheres of approximately equal length and sphere size (8 mm, 10 mm, or 12 mm)
- Thick, natural-fiber socks

Indications

- When you wish to enlist the aid of your entire body to resolve one of the following—
  - An acute condition, such as a cold, flu, or headache
  - A long-standing chronic condition
  - Any condition that has stalled in its healing
- When you wish to enlist the aid of your entire body to energetically cleanse and heal the weakest organ in your body
- When you desire an overall upliftment of your health

Effects

The application of Dark Green Aventurine necklaces to the soles of your feet awakens your entire body to its weakest area and encourages the body to provide the area with a steady supply of healing energies.

Placing Aventurine on the soles of your feet introduces your body to Aventurine energy in a special way. When you wear Aventurine around your neck, its energy immediately fills your body and then highlights the organ of lowest energy. In contrast, when you place Aventurine on the soles of your feet, the Aventurine energy first collects at your feet and then begins moving up your body in rhythmic waves, with each wave reaching closer to your head. Then, when your entire body has become filled with Aventurine energy, the Aventurine highlights your weakest organ, just as it does when you wear Aventurine around your neck.

The Aventurine also performs a function unique to this therapy: as the Aventurine energy moves up your body, it alerts all the atoms it touches. When all the atoms in your body have been alerted, the attention of every component in your body is directed to the most ailing area. Your entire body becomes aware that a part of it is distressed.

Often, one part of your body will be unaware of the fact that another part is ailing—whether it is with a tumor or a simple bruise. When your body becomes awakened to an ailment or other area of disharmony, it can begin to focus more of its resources on the area, and powerful healing can occur. Your atoms, molecules, and cells begin to contribute their energies to the distressed areas with awareness, willingness, and joy.

If you perform lengthy treatments every day, expect to see some kind of short-term cleansing reaction, such as common cold symptoms.

Procedure

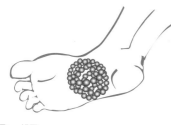

Fig. AVD-1

1. Wash your feet thoroughly with soap and warm water. Then, briskly rub your feet with a rough towel to dry them and to increase circulation. Rub each foot for at least 30 to 60 seconds.
2. Put on thick, natural-fiber socks. These socks should be snug enough to keep the Aventurine necklaces in contact with the soles of your feet throughout the treatment.
3. Place one Aventurine necklace inside each sock. Arrange the Aventurine in a flattened clump over the center of the sole of each foot, making sure that the Aventurine stays in contact with your skin for the duration of the treatment (see Fig. AVD-1).
4. Remove and cleanse both necklaces with running water and then place one necklace around your neck and the other outdoors in

sunlight for 15 minutes maximum. Each time you perform this treatment, alternate the necklace you place outdoors.

Time Guidelines

The first time you perform this treatment, perform it for one hour. Then, each subsequent time you perform it, increase the treatment time by one to two hours. In this way, gradually increase the treatment time until you are keeping the necklaces on your feet for eight hours, such as during a night's sleep. Do not exceed eight hours of treatment. It is important to increase the time gradually and to watch for signs of detoxification. Be aware of how your body is responding to the treatment, and make adjustments accordingly.

Perform this treatment no more than once a day. For acute conditions, perform it every day until symptoms disappear. For chronic conditions, perform it every two or three days until symptoms improve or disappear.

Support from Emerald

While following a regimen involving this Aventurine therapy, wearing an Emerald necklace during and between treatments is highly recommended.

Light Green Aventurine

Uplifting the Physical Body

Light Green Aventurine uplifts and strengthens one's most distressed organ by encouraging the organ's healthiest cells to distribute their vitality throughout the organ. Nonetheless, it promotes a much gentler purification of the physical body than Dark Green Aventurine. Light Green Aventurine is recommended over Dark Green Aventurine only for people with a history of intensive drug use, prescription or otherwise, or who have been exposed to toxic chemicals.

Indications for *Wearing a Therapeutic*
Light Green Aventurine Necklace

WHEN ONE OR MORE OF THE FOLLOWING APPLY—

YOU WANT TO—

Heal or strengthen your weakest or least healthy organ

Gently purify, uplift, and vitalize one or more organs

Release toxic drug or chemical residues from an organ

Note: Light Green Aventurine is recommended over Dark Green Aventurine for people who have a history of drug use, prescription or otherwise, or exposure to toxic chemicals.

Benefits of *Wearing a Therapeutic*
Light Green Aventurine Necklace

A necklace of Light Green Aventurine spheres is most useful for people who require a particularly gentle upliftment of a physical condition. When Light Green Aventurine is worn, its effects are primarily those of Aventurine's light green vibration—that is, it encourages the healthiest cells of the body's most distressed organ to distribute their vitality throughout the entire organ.

No organ is homogeneous in its energetic makeup; there are always some cells or groups of cells whose energies are healthier than others. Cells of low energetic condition are more susceptible to disease— indeed, they can act as the doors through which disease enters an organ. Yet, fortunately, even diseased organs usually contain some healthy, vibrant cells. Light Green Aventurine focuses its energy on the healthiest of these cells. It compels them to spread their healthy energies to adjacent cells, which in turn spread this vitality to their own neighboring cells. As a result, the entire organ gradually gains more vitality and strength.[6]

Releasing Drug Residues

Light Green Aventurine has an important role to play in our society, where so much medicine is chemical in nature. The physical body knows how to rid itself of most toxic foreign substances. Many of these substances cause diarrhea or vomiting as part of the body's effort to expel them. However, when the foreign substance is not overtly toxic— as in the case of most drugs and some chemicals—the body doesn't always know how to deal with it. It doesn't know how to pass the substance

---

6 *For a fuller discussion of how Light Green Aventurine works, see Dark Green Aventurine, on*
   page 70.

"I have had chronic fatigue syndrome with severe upper stomach problems and have tried everything over the years. Within 20 minutes of wearing Light Green Aventurine, my stomach felt significantly better. Over the next month, I wore the Light Green Aventurine around the clock. My stomach problem cleared up completely and hasn't returned."

M.M.
Mt. Clemens, Michigan

"I had used many drugs for an autoimmune problem, so I appreciated the gentle detoxification that Light Green Aventurine provided. I am healthier and feel lighter and stronger than I have in years. What a wonderful healing gift."

M.B.
Los Angeles, California

through the system in order to excrete it. Although a drug may appear to be metabolized, some of the drug's substance or energy often remains in the body.

When the body doesn't know how to get rid of a drug or, in some cases, its residue, the body often encapsulates and isolates the drug after the drug has completed its work. More specifically, if a drug targeted a specific organ, the body's protective mechanism encapsulates what is left of the drug in that organ to protect the rest of the body from the drug's toxicity. If the organ with the encapsulated drug is the same organ being targeted by a Dark Green Aventurine necklace, the Aventurine energy will infiltrate the organ. It may then recognize these drug residues as disharmonious and work to loosen and expel them from the organ.

Now, if the organ has been accumulating drugs for years, a serious situation may arise when the Dark Green Aventurine starts moving these drugs and their energies out into the body. The drugs or their energies will suddenly start circulating in the body, and the body may not know how to remove them. In this case, wearing Light Green Aventurine—especially if it contains some dark green flecks—is more appropriate than wearing Dark Green Aventurine. This is because the light green variety focuses more on uplifting the organ and loosening disharmonious energies than on expelling those energies. Thus, the release of toxic energies into the body will be more gradual, and they won't overwhelm the body.[7]

Emerald and Light Green Aventurine

The process of moving drugs and their energies out of the body can be greatly enhanced by wearing an Emerald necklace along with Light Green Aventurine. However, be aware that Emerald works only on natural toxicity—that is, the toxicity produced by a living organism.

---

7 *See page 105 for information on how wearing a therapeutic Bloodstone necklace can help flush the toxins released by Aventurine in someone whose body is overburdened by drug or other toxic residues.*

Therefore, the Emerald won't disintegrate the energies of the drugs themselves. Instead, it will enhance the overall healing process by disintegrating the disharmony created by the drugs' presence.

Wearing Light Green Aventurine and Emerald together will uplift the toxic organ and encourage the surrounding area to become less disharmonious. This will help the organ, the area, and the whole body to become stronger and better able to deal with the released encapsulations of toxicity.

Caution: Light Green Aventurine and Sunlight

Placing Light Green Aventurine in direct sunlight bleaches the dark green flecks in the gemstones. Therefore, when cleansing Light Green Aventurine outdoors, keep it in a shady spot and no longer than five minutes. Alternately, cleanse it in the rain for at least 15 minutes.

Therapeutic-Quality Light Green Aventurine

The parameters for therapeutic quality in Light Green Aventurine are similar in many ways to those of Dark Green Aventurine. The primary difference is that Light Green Aventurine contains many fewer dark-green flecks than Dark Green Aventurine. Indeed, a proper balance of dark-green flecks in a light green base is crucial to Light Green Aventurine's effectiveness. If more than 25 percent of its surface displays flecks, the effects of Dark Green Aventurine will begin to dominate and therefore undermine the action of the Light Green Aventurine.

The overall color of Light Green Aventurine is pale green with a slight bluish tint. With a light source behind it, the dark green flecks become more apparent, and the gem appears bright, crystalline, and translucent.

The vast majority of Light Green Aventurine available today has been dyed to make it resemble higher-quality Aventurine. Any dye applied to either Light or Dark Green Aventurine makes it non-therapeutic. (See page 78 for more information on Aventurine quality.)

Mineral Composition
$SiO_2 + K(Al,Cr)_2(AlSi_3O_{10})(OH)_2$

Light Green Aventurine is composed of interlocking Quartz grains filled with tiny platelets of a green fuchsite. It is distinguished from Dark Green Aventurine by its fewer number of fuchsite platelets. Light Green Aventurine is found in India, Russia, South Africa, Australia, Germany, and Wyoming.

Light Green Aventurine Therapy
Organ Tonic

Two Light Green Aventurine necklaces are used to gently purge an organ of toxins without causing an imbalance in the rest of the body. This tonic can also be used to help make a relatively healthy organ so strong that it can become virtually immune to disease. One Light Green Aventurine necklace is worn around the neck, and the other is placed directly on an organ.

Therapy Tools

Two therapeutic necklaces of Light Green Aventurine spheres (8 mm or 10 mm)

Indications

- When you are relatively healthy and want to make an organ more resistant to disease
- When you have a family history of a particular organ disease
- When you wish to gently purge an organ of toxins without creating an imbalance in the rest of your body

Effects

This therapy uses two Light Green Aventurine necklaces to make a relatively healthy organ almost impervious to disease. One necklace is worn around the neck, and the other is placed on an organ to direct the effects of the first necklace to the organ. Using Light Green Aventurine this way is particularly helpful in cases where a family history of organ disease is present. For example, if your family has a history of liver disease, you can use this as a preventive therapy to increase your liver's resistance to illness.

This tonic also gently and gradually purges an organ of toxic residues, such as those left by certain drugs. This gradual release cleanses the organ without overtaxing your elimination system.

Even a diseased organ contains vibrant and healthy cells. When you place Light Green Aventurine on any organ, the Aventurine's energy initiates the spread of the healthy cells' vitality to neighboring cells until the whole organ attains greater vitality. The longer and more often you perform this therapy, the stronger the organ becomes.

Procedure

Note: Exposing the Light Green Aventurine to direct light, even sunlight, is *not* recommended for this therapy.

1. Place a Light Green Aventurine necklace around your neck.
2. Place another Light Green Aventurine necklace in a neat pile or flat spiral on your skin over the organ you wish to treat (see Fig. AVL-1).
3. If you wish to secure the Aventurine to your body for some time, place the gemstones on your skin and then place a light cotton cloth over the gems. To secure the gems to your body, tape the cloth to your skin with non-plastic first aid tape. Avoid letting the glue from the tape touch the gems.

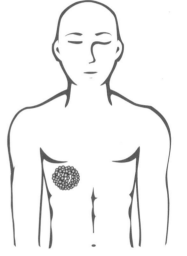

Fig. AVL-1

Time Guidelines

The first time you apply the Light Green Aventurine to the organ, keep it there for 30 minutes. Then, double the application time on each successive day. Thus, on the second day, apply the Light Green Aventurine for one hour; on the third day, apply it for two hours; on the fourth day, apply it for four hours; and so on. In this way, gradually increase the application time until you can bandage the Aventurine over the organ for several days at a time.

Post-Treatment Cleansing of Gems

Immediately after completing a treatment, it is important to cleanse the gems of any disharmonious energies released by the body in the course of treatment. See Appendix A: "Care and Cleansing of Therapeutic Gems," on page 397, for cleansing instructions.

Malachite

Harmonizing the Body

Malachite promotes harmony and improves communication throughout your physical body. As Malachite's energy flows through you in a rhythmic, wave-like motion, it erodes discordant energies and alerts your entire body to its own disharmonies. Malachite's waves awaken every cell to what is happening in every other cell, so that your body can rally its own healing forces to combat disease and restore harmony. As isolated and diseased areas come back into harmony with the rest of the body, the body begins to function like a fine-tuned instrument.

Indications for *Wearing a Therapeutic*
Malachite Necklace

YOU ARE EXPERIENCING—

Physical pain or tightness

Congestion or stagnation

A chronic injury

Any kind of physical illness

YOU WANT TO—

Enlist all of your body's resources to resolve a physical condition

Develop a body that functions like a fine-tuned instrument

Bring your body to the next level of health by alerting it to any hidden disharmonies

Improve communication and cooperation among all parts of your body

Benefits of *Wearing a Therapeutic*
Malachite Necklace

Malachite promotes harmony and improves communication through-out your physical body. Its soothing energy moves down and up the inside of your body in rhythmic waves, alerting your body to its own disharmonies and healing ever more deeply-seated areas of distress. As more of these areas are restored to health, the strength of Malachite's flow increases.

Physical disharmony can occur when parts of the body do not know what other parts are doing. If your body has no awareness that some of its parts are not working well together or that disharmony is brewing, it cannot call on its forces to fix the problem. This situation is much more common than might be expected and underlies many of the conditions people experience.

Malachite lets every cell of the body know what is happening in every other cell. When one part of the body knows what is happening in another part, it becomes easier for the body to call all its resources together to combat a disease. Let's say, for example, that your liver has a cyst tucked away in it and that your mind has no awareness of it. The rest of your body may also have no idea it is there. Malachite can help the physical body discover such a cyst. Once alerted to the existence of the cyst, your body's survival mechanism will naturally call on your immune system, eliminative organs, and whatever other systems are needed to start working on that cyst.

Malachite's energy moves down and up the inside of the body in a movement that resembles waves. This wave-like motion is key to its effects. Malachite spheres start emitting their waves when the spheres are awakened by your aura. Then the waves move down and up your body in a soothing, rhythmic flow. As they move through you, the Malachite waves gather information about your body and start alerting

"I recently put on my Malachite neck-lace after not having used it for many months. During the next four days I made a dietary adjustment, treated myself to a Citrine therapy, and selected a homeopathic remedy to upgrade my overall health. I attribute all these steps and the resulting bene-fits to the influence of the Malachite."

Herbert Wheeler, M.T.
Medical Technologist
Ft. Lauderdale, Florida

the body to its disharmonies. The action of the waves also erodes the energetic surfaces and edges of these disharmonious areas, assisting in their resolution.

Everyone who wears therapeutic Malachite experiences different effects. This is because the side effects of its wave-like motion can be felt in many different ways. In some people, Malachite breaks up stagnant fluids and releases congestion; in some, it increases circulation; and, in others, it opens chakras. Some people say it opens the brow chakra, and they give credit to Malachite for the spiritual experiences that result. Malachite's wave-like motion simply stirs and breaks up anything in the way of establishing and increasing harmony through-out the body.

When Malachite has awakened the body in its unique way, it is possible that you will come to a deeper knowingness and understanding of your physical condition. You may even realize that you have the potential to heal in areas where you thought health was no longer possible. All of this will result from all parts of your body becoming aware of all other parts.

In a sense, Malachite enables your body to hear that its disharmonious areas are out of tune with the rest of your body, thus prompting your body to work to bring them back into harmony. Malachite's goal is to have every cell playing a note of a harmonious chord. The subtle music emanating from someone who has worn Malachite spheres for a long time is beautiful. This music is the vibration of harmony expressing itself in subtle sound. When all your cells are in harmony, no note cancels out or dampens the sound of any other note. You ring with subtle, harmonious music.

Malachite Framed in Metal

When any form of Malachite is framed or mounted in metal, the metal inhibits the Malachite's emanations. It is through Malachite's wave emanations that it produces its healing benefits. Consequently, if you wear Malachite mounted in metal and want to experience its full healing effects, you will be disappointed. The minor effects that you may experience when Malachite is even partially encased in metal come from the waves reflecting off the open face of the Malachite and into your aura. This is usually an indirect, haphazard kind of wave motion, and it is not necessarily soothing.

Therapeutic-Quality Malachite

Therapeutic Malachite displays crisp, straight black or dark-green bands in a light green base. These bands form a bull's-eye on opposite sides of each sphere. Malachite spheres with irregularly shaped or muddy bands are much less effective than those with sharp, distinct bands. Indeed, the greater the contrast between the dark bands and light green base, the greater the Malachite's therapeutic effects.

Bead Orientation

Therapeutic Malachite necklaces should be strung with the spheres' drill holes piercing the center of each sphere's bull's-eye. This way of stringing facilitates the down/up wave motion of Malachite. If all the drill holes were positioned so that the bull's-eyes faced in random directions, the down/up wave motion would be erratic. The wave emanations of the Malachite would radiate in the various directions that the bull's-eyes were pointing. This would not only make the necklace non-therapeutic, but would be disruptive to the wearer.

Mineral Composition
$Cu_2(CO_3)(OH)_2$

Malachite, or copper carbonate hydroxide, is formed when hot carbonated water reacts with copper. Malachite's green color comes from its copper content. Malachite is found in Russia, Romania, Africa, France, England, California, Nevada, Utah, Pennsylvania, Tennessee, and the southwestern U.S.

Malachite Therapy
Dissolving Disharmony

This Malachite therapy awakens the entire body to the presence of distress or disease in a particular area. A Malachite necklace is placed on an ailing area to help dissolve the area's deep-seated disharmonies, to bring the area into greater harmony with the rest of the body, and to improve communication throughout the entire body.

Therapy Tool

One therapeutic necklace of Malachite spheres (8 mm or 10 mm)

Indications

- When you are experiencing any of the following in a localized area of your body—
  - Disease
  - Congestion
  - Swelling and inflammation
  - A chronic injury
- When an area of your body seems heavily burdened
- When you feel that an area of your body is out of harmony with the rest of your body

Effects

Wherever you place Malachite on your body becomes the epicenter of the Malachite's wave emanations. Placing Malachite on an ailing part of your body awakens your entire body to the presence of distress or disease in the area. This awakening gives your body the opportunity to marshal its forces to resolve the condition.

Malachite's wave-like motion stirs and breaks up anything in the way of establishing and increasing harmony, both within the distressed area and between the area and the rest of your body. The Malachite gradually wears away physical and energetic blockages and eliminates stagnation. In this way, the Malachite soothes and helps heal the area while bringing it into greater harmony with the rest of your body. With increased harmony, all parts of your body will know what is happening in every other part, making it much easier for your body to call its forces together to combat any injury or illness.

Procedure

Place the Malachite necklace in a neat pile directly on your skin on the area you wish to treat (see Fig. MLC-1).

If you wish to secure the Malachite to your body so that you can move around during your treatment time, place the gemstones on your skin and then place a light cotton cloth over the gems. To secure the gems to your body, tape the cloth to your skin with non-plastic first aid tape. Do not let the glue from the tape touch the gems.

Time Guidelines

For the first treatment, keep the Malachite in place for 20 to 30 minutes. You may increase the length of subsequent treatments up to one hour. Perform treatments once or twice a day, as needed.

Post-Treatment Cleansing of Gems

Immediately after completing a treatment, it is important to cleanse the gems of any disharmonious energies released by the body in the course of treatment. See Appendix A: "Care and Cleansing of Therapeutic Gems," on page 397, for cleansing instructions.

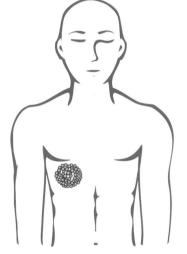

Fig. MLC-1

Bloodstone

Strengthening the Immune System

Bloodstone strengthens your immune system and keeps it alert and responsive to your body's needs. Bloodstone's energy empowers certain microorganisms in your bloodstream that are vital to optimal immune function. This empowerment uplifts the overall quality of your body's energy, making your body an incompatible environment for infections of all kinds. Bloodstone also removes burdens from your immune system as it facilitates the removal of toxins and enhances your cells' absorption of nutrients.

Indications *for Wearing a Therapeutic*
Bloodstone Necklace

YOU ARE EXPERIENCING—

An acute ailment, such as a cold or flu

Allergies

Environmental sensitivities

Weak or sluggish immune system

An immune system disorder or dysfunction

Chronic fatigue syndrome

Fibromyalgia

Overall toxicity, particularly in the blood

Difficulty absorbing nutrients

YOU WANT TO—

Bolster your immunity to infection

Strengthen your entire immune system

Benefits of *Wearing a Therapeutic*
Bloodstone Necklace

Bloodstone strengthens your immune system and keeps it alert and responsive to your body's needs. Bloodstone's energy empowers certain microorganisms in your bloodstream that are vital to optimal immune function, making your body an incompatible environment for infections of all kinds. Bloodstone also facilitates the removal of toxins from your body and enhances your cells' absorption of nutrients.

To understand Bloodstone's special role in boosting immune function requires an understanding of certain components of the blood and their role in promoting health. Today, microbiologists are describing newly discovered sub-cellular components essential to the body's healthy functioning. Bloodstone has a natural affinity with certain of these components. Through its effects on them, Bloodstone profoundly benefits the immune system.

When you wear a necklace of Bloodstone spheres, Bloodstone energy collects in certain sub-cellular components in your blood that we may call *mutable bodies*. These microscopic, plant-like organisms are part of your immune system's early-warning mechanism and are essential for life. Mutable bodies have both physical and more purely energetic components. The center of a mutable body is comprised of energy with a higher vibration than physical matter, thus allowing the center to transcend certain physical laws. This center is surrounded by a layer of physical vibrations, which manifest as protein molecules and can be compared to a plant's cell wall. The dual nature of the mutable bodies—i.e., their physical and nonphysical components—allows them to provide a vital service to the immune system.

Mutable bodies share certain characteristics of plants. Just as plants absorb both nutrients and toxins from the soil in which they are planted, mutable bodies absorb nutrients and toxins from the blood.

Like plants, mutable bodies also convert metallic forms of nutrients into colloidal forms. Vitamins and minerals occur naturally in both metallic and colloidal forms in the plants we eat, but the body can use only the colloidal forms for nourishment. Not only do mutable bodies convert metallic nutrients into their colloidal forms, they also deliver these nutrients directly to the cells that need them. Mutable bodies also absorb toxins, such as heavy metals and toxic chemicals, from your blood and cells. These toxin-laden mutable bodies then exit your body through your organs of elimination.

Any change occurring in your body, no matter how small, is reflected in the vibratory quality of your blood. A change in blood quality can be caused by many things, such as the ingestion of a certain food, a sad or happy thought, a trauma, a therapy, or an infection. Mutable bodies, which live in your blood fluid, are sensitive to the vibrations of their environment. Changes that significantly alter the chemistry and vibrations of your blood affect them directly. When such a change occurs, the mutable bodies' walls mutate to reflect the change. For example, when you have a healing or joyful experience, your body's vibration rises. In response, the mutable bodies' walls change to reflect the higher vibration. This allows their centers to express more of their energies through the walls. The resulting infusion of higher energy into your bloodstream leaves you feeling vital, uplifted, and energized.

The ability of mutable bodies to reflect their environment is key to how they work for the immune system. Another example of how mutable bodies reflect changes in the blood is their response to a bacterial invasion. In this case, the mutable body walls quickly take on the appearance and characteristics of the invading bacteria. The result is that, in the early stages of an infection, your blood will appear to contain more bacteria than it actually does. This illusion of bacterial abundance is normal and, in fact, essential to your health—it alerts your immune system to the infection much more swiftly than if only "real" bacteria were present.

When your body has successfully overcome the infection, the mutable bodies respond by resuming their plant-like forms. This is important, because it is only when mutable bodies are in plant-like form that they can bring nutrients to your cells, remove toxins, pass higher energies into your body, and alert your immune system to new invaders.

A healthy immune-system response depends on the optimal functioning of the mutable bodies. If they are weakened or otherwise unhealthy, the immune response becomes compromised, and illness can set in more easily. Mutable bodies can become unhealthy when your body is constantly overworked, excited, agitated, stressed, or dosed with caffeine.

These stresses cause the mutable bodies to become overreactive and change form at the slightest change in blood vibrations. This, in turn, confuses the immune system and makes it respond unnecessarily. The immune system becomes like a group of firefighters who continually respond to false alarms; eventually, they stop paying attention and can miss a real fire. The immune system can start to ignore certain warnings and even certain kinds of infections. Furthermore, when mutable bodies are overreactive, the blood becomes filled with an excess of disguised mutable bodies, and not enough plant-like ones are available to perform their essential jobs. The resulting dysfunctions can include premature aging, low energy, allergies, environmental sensitivities, and diminished organ function.

Enter Bloodstone. Although anything beneficial to the body can encourage mutable bodies to return to their original, plant-like forms, nothing does this as effectively as Bloodstone. Bloodstone helps mutable bodies reverse their overreactivity and better discriminate between a real need to mutate and a false one.

The Bloodstone energy itself also distinguishes necessary mutable body "disguises" from excessive, unwarranted, or worn-out ones. Bloodstone energy collects around the mutable body walls. There, it clears away any unnecessary vibrations and dissolves the unnecessary disguises, allowing the mutable bodies to return to their plant-like forms. In this way, Bloodstone relieves your immune system of the burden of eliminating the excess mutations so that it can focus its energies on resolving the real infections.

"I began to develop a bladder infection that was quickly becoming painful. I put the Bloodstone necklace around my neck and drank lots of water. Within two hours, all the symptoms were gone. I now put on my Bloodstone at the first sign of any cold, flu, or other viral or bacterial symptoms."

M.E.
Portland, Oregon

Bloodstone energy also fortifies mutable bodies in their plant-like form, making them robust and strong. Specifically, it strengthens their walls and the very nature of the mutable bodies themselves. Bloodstone empowers them to serve your immune system in a more proactive way and makes your body much less susceptible to infection. When enough mutable bodies are empowered, the overall vibration of your body is uplifted. This uplifted vibration is incompatible with that of bacteria, viruses, and other infectious agents, such as parasites. Existing infections die off, and external agents receive the message that they are not welcome. At the same time, your body becomes able to rid itself of toxins more easily.

How to Wear Bloodstone

It is particularly beneficial to wear a Bloodstone necklace so that it touches your skin. If Bloodstone is worn over clothing and not touching the skin, it will take much longer to work. This is because of the somewhat unique way in which Bloodstone works. When Bloodstone touches the skin, some of its energy radiates into the aura, but most moves directly into the body, where it starts working on the blood.

Flushing Toxins

If you are wearing Bloodstone and have a significant infection of parasites, yeast, viruses, or bacteria, much dead matter can build up in your body as these microorganisms die off. Such a buildup can be noxious to the body; dead parasites, in particular, can be quite toxic. Therefore, it is essential to keep your bowels moving during the time you are wearing Bloodstone. If drinking extra water isn't adequate to prevent constipation, temporarily use additional fiber or herbal laxatives and supplements that support the liver and organs of elimination.

Preventive Therapy

Because wearing Bloodstone can help keep your immune system alert and resistant to infection, it can be helpful to wear a Bloodstone necklace when visiting a foreign country or places where contagious disease is present, such as a hospital.

Supporting Aventurine's Work

Bloodstone can support the work of Dark Green Aventurine, which strongly encourages the body's organs to release stored toxins. Bloodstone can help flush the toxins released by Dark Green Aventurine in someone whose body is overburdened by drug or other toxic residues. Wearing a necklace of Bloodstone spheres whose size is nearly equal (within 2 mm) to those of the Aventurine can help the body handle the release of toxins more safely and efficiently. The Bloodstone will cause the mutable bodies to reveal their plant-like forms, which will readily absorb any toxins that Aventurine is releasing.[8]

Therapeutic-Quality Bloodstone

The color of therapeutic Bloodstone is a distinct, rich, and consistent dark green. Therapeutic Bloodstone also contains red flecks and, occasionally, flecks of orange or yellow. Of these colors, red represents the highest quality, orange is next best, and yellow the next. Ideally, the flecks are distinct and appear either as tiny pinpoints or larger patches and do not dominate the green color. The presence of shiny pinpoints that look like translucent crystalline structures is beneficial. White flecks or patches are not desirable. Bloodstone spheres that are bluish or muddy or in which green does not dominate are not therapeutic.

Bloodstone is best evaluated in direct sunlight, where one can assess the color, translucency, and flecks most accurately. The higher the quality of the Bloodstone, the more effective it is at enhancing the mutable bodies' ability to absorb toxins and transform vitamins and minerals in the blood into bioavailable forms.

Mineral Composition
$SiO_2 + FeO_2$

Bloodstone is green chalcedony, a form of Quartz composed of masses of minute Quartz crystals. Its red spots are bits of iron oxide. Bloodstone occurs in Australia, Brazil, China, India, and Wyoming.

---

8 *See page 73 for more information on Dark Green Aventurine's ability to expel toxins from organs.*

Bloodstone Therapy
Strengthening Localized Immune Response

Bloodstone is placed on an ailing area to boost the body's immune response there. The Bloodstone's energy also facilitates the transfer of nutrients to the area and the removal of toxins or metabolic wastes. In the process, the Bloodstone helps bring the area into greater harmony with the rest of the body.

Therapy Tools

One therapeutic necklace of Bloodstone spheres (8 mm, 10 mm, or 12 mm)

Indications

- When any part of your body has an infection
- When an area of your body is holding toxins or has accumulated metabolic wastes; symptoms may include—
  - Weakness
  - Arthritic joints
  - Sore muscles
  - Gouty conditions
- When you are participating in a cleansing or detoxification program

Effects

Whenever Bloodstone is placed on your skin, some of its energy radiates into your aura, but most moves directly into your body through your skin. Once inside your body, the Bloodstone energy returns *mutable bodies* to their plant-like forms.[9] As your blood circulates, it passes the area where the Bloodstone has been placed. There, it picks

---

9 *See page 101 for more information on mutable bodies.*

up the Bloodstone energy and spreads it throughout your body and bloodstream. This is true whether you wear Bloodstone around your neck or place it somewhere else on your body.

When you place Bloodstone on a particular area as you do in this therapy, and not around your neck, the Bloodstone's energy alerts the plant-like bodies to pool in the placement area. Even as the blood circulates, the plant-like forms linger there as if held by a magnet. Because the blood continually circulates, this pooling will occur within minutes. Once the mutable bodies have collected in the placement area, they begin to focus their nutrient-transfer and toxin-absorption mechanisms there. This can be particularly helpful for areas that have collected toxins or metabolic wastes, such as in sore muscles, arthritic joints, or areas suffering from gout. After some time, some of the mutable bodies will circulate away from the area: the toxin-laden mutable bodies will move to your organs of elimination; and some of the nutrient-rich mutable bodies will move to other cells that need them. This process will continue as long as you keep Bloodstone on the area.

If the area has an unresolved infection, Bloodstone will provide an added benefit. The mutable bodies that Bloodstone calls to the area will start to reflect the area's vibrations, and the immune system will respond by pooling white blood cells, or leukocytes, in the area to address the unresolved infection.

Circulation tends to keep the blood's energies homogeneous throughout the body. Particular areas may also have their own unique vibrations. However, in a relatively healthy person, the vibratory quality of any given area does not differ much from the body's overall vibrations. However, when an area is sick or injured, its vibrations can be very different from those of the rest of the body. If the area's vibrations have strayed too far, the mutable bodies may not respond on their own to an infection or blood-chemistry change there. Placing Bloodstone on the area will alert the mutable bodies, and they in turn will respond by mutating into whatever forms are required to achieve balance in the area. This process also improves the vibrational homogeneity between the local area and the rest of the body.

Placing Bloodstone on the liver supports it during an internal cleansing program.

Procedure

Place the Bloodstone in a neat pile or flat spiral directly on your skin on the area you wish to treat (see Fig. BLD-1).

If you wish to secure the Bloodstone to your body so that you can move around during your treatment time, place the gemstones on your skin and then place a light cotton cloth over the gems. To secure the gems to your body, tape the cloth to your skin with non-plastic first aid tape. Avoid letting the glue from the tape touch the gems.

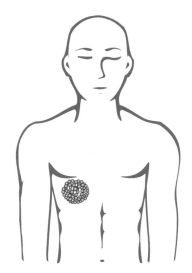

Fig. BLD-1

Time Guidelines

For the first treatment, keep the Bloodstone in place for 30 minutes. You may increase the length of subsequent treatments up to one hour. Perform treatments once or twice a day, as needed.

Post-Treatment Cleansing of Gems

Immediately after completing a treatment, it is important to cleanse the gems of any disharmonious energies released by the body in the course of treatment. See Appendix A: "Care and Cleansing of Therapeutic Gems," on page 397, for cleansing instructions.

Emotional Healing and Upliftment

Ruby

Roselle

Rhodonite

Mother of Pearl

Although the following gems are categorized elsewhere, they also offer significant healing benefits for emotional issues and conditions. Therefore, see also:

Aquamarine • Carnelian
Green Tourmaline • Lapis Lazuli
Lavender • Pink Tourmaline
Quartz • Rhodochrosite

Ruby

Healing the Emotions

Ruby helps heal and open the heart. It illuminates the emotional level of life and reveals the divine love at the core of every molecule in creation. Ruby and the red ray it carries restore emotional fluidity by relaxing undesirable patterns and dissolving congestion in the emotional body. Ruby teaches you to become a vehicle through which divine love and joy can enter your life and touch those around you.

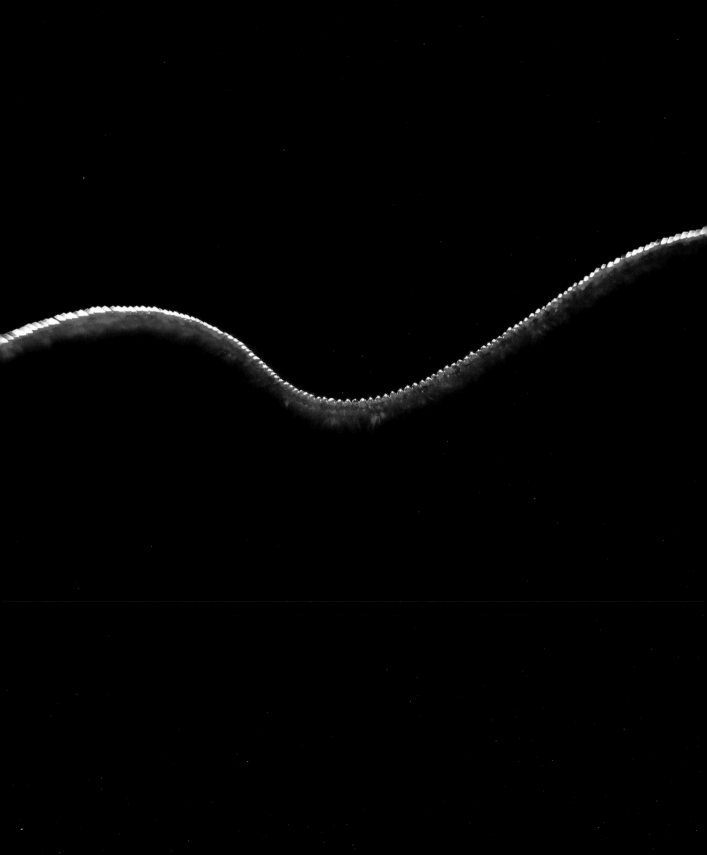

Indications *for Wearing a Therapeutic*
Ruby Necklace

YOU ARE EXPERIENCING—

Apathy or disconnection from others

Wounds of the heart

Depression

Emotional congestion or exhaustion

A physical condition that is being fed or exacerbated by emotional issues

Any unwanted condition of the muscles or physical heart (only as an adjunct to other treatments)

Tight or closed heart chakra

YOU WANT TO—

Experience and express more divine love

Open and develop your heart

Become more emotionally alive, aware, and balanced

Understand the true nature of love

Benefits of *Wearing a Therapeutic*
Ruby Necklace

Ruby helps heal and open the heart. It is the carrier of the pure red ray of the life force.[10] Like all color ray gemstones, Ruby's energy is a unique combination of the color ray it carries and its mineral essence—in this case, corundum. Thus, the way Ruby expresses the red ray is different from any other source of red ray, red color, or red light.

Ruby's domain is the heart. Its greatest effects are on the emotional level of being. It heightens your awareness of divine love and enhances your ability to experience and express it. Ruby illuminates the emotional level of life and reveals the divine love at the core of every molecule in creation.

Ruby teaches emotional mastery. Such mastery implies emotional balance, understanding, and the ability to regulate how much emotion you want to exhibit in a given situation. Yet this is not all that Ruby teaches. The emotional mastery Ruby teaches is total awareness of your emotional being.

The kind of love Ruby teaches is not human love, for human love implies needs and expectations. People need human love, yet this kind of love alone does not sustain us. We also need divine love. Divine love gives us the freedom to be who we truly are and who we want to be. This freedom nourishes us and our relationships. It gives us space to grow. Ruby's love implies freedom. It is a noble and powerful love. It turns your attention to that which is greater than yourself.

Unfortunately, many people have difficulty understanding the difference between human and divine love. Even those who understand the concept often have no real idea of how to open their hearts and express divine love. The necessity of divine love may make sense

---

10 *See page 40 for more information on the vital role of color rays in restoring and maintaining health.*

intellectually, but when it's time to express divine love to others, they're not sure where to begin. Ruby teaches this. Ruby will open your heart and give you a taste of divine love. Then it will teach you how to become a vehicle through which divine love and joy can flow. This love will then touch others around you, even if they are not wearing Ruby themselves.

Ruby brings powerful healing to the emotions. Emotional disharmony is often caused by congestion in the emotional body. Such congestion interrupts the natural flow and expression of emotions. This can lead to all kinds of unwanted emotional conditions, such as depression and emotional burnout. When you wear Ruby, the red ray identifies and collects in any areas of emotional congestion and then loosens and dissolves this congestion. This allows powerful emotional healing to take place.

Congestion in the emotional body also blocks the flow of life force to the physical body and feeds it with disharmonious energy. When Ruby dissolves emotional congestion, any physical condition caused by it will cease to be fed with disharmonious energy and will start to heal. For example, emotional congestion associated with the stomach may be causing chronic stomach distress; when the emotional congestion is resolved, the stomach will no longer be fed with disharmonious energy, and a true healing of the stomach's distress will be possible. Furthermore, when Ruby's red ray collects in congested areas of the emotional body, it also directs red ray to corresponding areas in the physical body and dissolves congestion there, thereby further supporting physical healing.

Wearing Ruby helps your mind see and understand the connection between emotional causes and physical symptoms. When this under-standing dawns, you will have taken a major step toward truly resolving a physical condition—for when you know and understand the reason for a certain condition, you are better prepared to resolve it.

Wearing Ruby allows the red ray and the feeling of love to flow through your heart chakra and filter into your physical body. Ruby also opens and aligns the heart chakra and strengthens its regulatory ability. When this happens, more life force can flow both into and

"Life speeds up for me when I wear Ruby. When emotional situations show up, I'm not deluded about what the real issues are. Ruby shows me clearly what I have to address. I move quickly beyond the emotional issue with the help of Ruby."

Margie Mulholland, L.M.T.
Louisburg, North Carolina

through your emotional body, bringing with it greater harmony, balance, and emotional fluidity.

Ruby also enhances the mind's ability to orchestrate a better relationship between your emotions and physical body. It empowers your mind to create the opportunities for you to become more attuned to your emotions. This is useful, because your mind is primarily responsible both for bringing things into your life and for removing them.

When you begin to wear Ruby, your mind will see that your heart is opening and that you are preparing to accept greater knowledge of your emotional world. As Ruby gives its love, and you accept and become accustomed to it, your heart will open even more. The more your heart opens and the more love enters you, the more love Ruby will give.

Love is the force and power behind one's strength, willingness, and ability to make positive changes. If you truly want to change and are willing to make the effort, Ruby can be a great tool. It can help you open to the infinite source of divine love. This will help you make the changes you wish to make and grow into the person you wish to be.

Ruby and the Muscular System

Each of the seven color rays of the life force is particularly healing and nourishing to certain aspects of the physical body. The red ray nourishes and supports the muscles, tendons, and fascia. Consequently, wearing Ruby can help strengthen these parts of the body and resolve certain conditions associated with them.

Ensuring Balanced Change—Ruby Combinations

The red ray flows strongly through Ruby. Indeed, the force of its flow is stronger than the flow of any other color ray through its corresponding gemstone. For this reason, wearing a solid Ruby necklace by itself can flood you with so much red ray that your physical and subtle bodies could become severely imbalanced. Therefore, Ruby is the only color ray gemstone that should not be worn by itself as a solid necklace without proper preparation.

"Ruby has given me the knowledge that what I seek is within my own heart, and it is there I will find the answers to my questions about love and life. I've come to realize that love never dies. Its transforming power is with me always."

N.O.
Greensboro, North Carolina

The ideal way to prepare for wearing a solid Ruby necklace is to wear Ruby in a properly designed combination necklace that contains other balancing gemstones. After wearing such a combination necklace for at least several months, you can start wearing a solid Ruby necklace.

To ensure that your balance is maintained, whenever you wear a solid Ruby necklace, you should also wear a separate, solid necklace of therapeutic Quartz spheres. Quartz gently attracts all seven color rays in balance, and can thus help prevent any color-ray imbalances that might result from wearing a solid Ruby necklace.

Amount to Wear

The size, amount, and quality of Ruby worn determine how much force Ruby puts behind the changes it initiates. Five or six carats of .20- to .33-carat Ruby spheres begin to open the heart immediately and direct the red ray onto emotional congestion. This amount of Ruby allows for gentle and balanced, yet effective, work. Because this amount is too small to create a solid necklace, it requires that the Ruby be included in an optimally designed combination necklace containing other appropriate gems.

Ten or twelve carats of therapeutic-quality Ruby spheres have very strong effects. Within minutes, this amount of Ruby not only directs red ray onto congestion but begins to fill you with the energy of divine love. It can also saturate your aura with red ray, causing disharmonious emotional patterns to relax, break up, and release their hold on your physical patterns.

Beware of wearing more than 30 carats of Ruby, since such a large amount might cause imbalances, particularly in the ratios of color rays within you. The force of the red ray behind this much Ruby is too powerful for most people, unless they have been wearing Ruby for a long time and just need some extra Ruby energy to make additional changes.

Therapeutic-Quality Ruby

Ruby crystals occur naturally in different qualities of color and clarity. The purer these qualities are, the more powerful are Ruby's effects. Judging therapeutic quality in Ruby requires exceptional care and the consideration of many factors.

Therapeutic-quality Ruby is at least somewhat translucent, true red and free of black inclusions to the naked eye. Non-Ruby inclusions can be identified under a microscope and should be avoided as much as possible, since they restrict Ruby's effects. Their area of influence is greater than the physical space they occupy; an inclusion affects the Ruby surrounding it in a radius equal to the inclusion's diameter.

In order for Ruby's energy to touch and stimulate the heart, it must carry the brightness of true red. Dark, burgundy-colored Ruby has a heavy energy that cannot reach above the lower chakras; the darker the color, the heavier the energy. On the other hand, Ruby that is too light or pinkish in color is immature and lacks the strength required to be therapeutically effective.

The precision of Ruby's shape is crucial. Because Ruby energy radiates from the bead's outer surface, poorly shaped rondels or spheres will make Ruby's energy flow into the aura in an inconsistent manner.

When Ruby is cut into spheres or rondels, they are covered in a red oily polish. This polish should not be rubbed off, because the oil actually helps preserve the integrity of the physical crystal, which is very brittle. Fortunately, Ruby's energetic function is unaffected by this polish.

Mineral Composition
Al_2O_3

Ruby is a variety of corundum, which, after Diamond, is the hardest material known. Pure corundum is colorless, but even tiny amounts of additional elements can create a wide range of vivid colors. When a small amount of chromium replaces part of the aluminum, corundum is tinted red and called Ruby; all other corundums are called Sapphire. Ruby is found in Burma, Sri Lanka, Thailand, Kampuchea, Australia, and Africa.

Roselle

Purifying the Emotions

Roselle initiates a deep purification of the emotional body, thereby helping release the emotional limitations that hinder personal growth and happiness. Roselle's energy enters the wave-like flows in the emotional body. There, it dislodges suppressed and unacknowledged feelings, gently transforming them into flowing energy that can be released through healthy emotional expression. This purification removes the emotional causes of physical illness and helps you grow more in touch with your true emotional nature.

Indications *for Wearing a Therapeutic*
Roselle Necklace

YOU ARE EXPERIENCING—

Difficulty expressing your emotions

Feeling emotionally flat, closed, or shut down

A physical condition being exacerbated by an emotional issue

YOU WANT TO—

Release, express, and resolve suppressed emotions

Acknowledge and understand any suppressed or hidden feelings

Promote the healthy expression of your emotions

Be more in touch with your feelings

Let go of emotional burdens or heaviness

Benefits of *Wearing a Therapeutic*
Roselle Necklace

Roselle, the spherical form of Rose Quartz, initiates deep emotional purification by helping you release the emotional limitations that hinder personal growth and happiness. Roselle energy helps you express, release, and resolve suppressed emotions.

Repressed or unacknowledged feelings impede emotional and physical health. These unexpressed emotions place pressure on your physical body and can eventually manifest as disease. Like locked doors within your being, suppressed emotions obstruct your experience of greater self-awareness and self-understanding.

Roselle helps you unlock these doors and then gently stimulates your heart to open so that you can express the feelings hidden there. Roselle does not heal emotions, but rather helps you resolve and let go of them. It will help reveal long-forgotten emotions that have been pushed deep within as a result of many kinds of conditioning. These forgotten emotions may even include love, joy, or happiness, as well as more difficult ones, such as fear, anger, and grief.

Roselle works in two phases. In the first phase, it stirs suppressed emotions, allowing you to acknowledge, understand, and then feel them. In the second phase, it encourages you to express these feelings, resolve and let go of them, and then move on. As long as you wear Roselle, it releases more and more deeply embedded collections of suppressed emotions. Roselle also initiates an energetic stability in your physical body to help prepare it for this emotional outflow.

Roselle can help people with many kinds of emotional conditions—from those with only slight emotional problems to those whose emotional state is so disharmonious that, by society's standards, they are considered emotionally ill. Roselle can help the emotionally ill regain some strength and hope.

Although its action is subtle, Roselle is very effective and should not be overlooked, especially if you are experiencing any emotional disharmony whatsoever. Because Roselle can show people so much about themselves, it is a helpful addition to any counseling or self-help program.

Using Roselle with Consciousness

Roselle's effects can be made stronger and more significant if it is used consciously as a therapeutic tool. Roselle is best utilized when worn or applied with the clear intention of moving beyond the particular emotional limitations that keep one from taking the next step in one's personal growth.

Even if you don't feel you have an emotional problem, it can be an interesting experience in self-awareness and self-understanding to wear Roselle and observe which emotions start coming up and which emotions you try to suppress. This experience might also help you recognize which mental attitudes are causing you to suppress particular emotions.

When Releasing Emotions

When you are releasing painful emotions, you may find it comforting to remove your Roselle necklace, hold it in your hands, and cry. You may also find that you want to hold the Roselle over one of four chakras, depending on where the Roselle feels most comforting: the stomach, the heart, the throat, or near your eyes over your brow. The chakra to which you are naturally drawn will probably be the one that is calling most strongly for the Roselle energy to help complete its release.

Roselle and Ruby

When you wear therapeutic Roselle and Ruby together, Ruby gives additional light and life to Roselle's effects. If you are having trouble expressing or letting go of your emotions, Ruby's powerful love will give you the confidence you need to do so. It will help you realize that

"I wear Roselle daily. It keeps me heart-centered, empathetic, and in touch with what is at the heart of the matter for my clients and for me. I am kinder and not as easily upset with things when I wear Roselle. I take things in stride."

Beth Doyle, M.A., L.P.C.
Salem, Oregon

you will still have love and be loved if you express the feelings you have been suppressing.

Roselle and Rhodochrosite

Wearing Roselle for several weeks can prepare you to wear Rhodochrosite, which can strongly break up emotional patterns and cleanse and rebuild your entire emotional being.

Contraindication: Roselle and Gold

Roselle should never be worn touching gold. The combination of Roselle and gold is disharmonious. Although gold can be beneficial in many situations, its energy tends to lock in one's state of consciousness and close the heart. These effects are in direct conflict with the action of Roselle. Roselle's energy also enlivens and strengthens gold and makes its effects more erratic and unstable.

If you wear gold with Roselle, your emotions will be stimulated and grow out of proportion. For example, if the amount of your suppressed anger could be compared to the size of a sparrow, the combination of Roselle and gold will expand your anger to the size of an elephant. Such over-stimulated emotions will surround you like a bubble in which you can become lost.

Amount to Wear

People will tend to be attracted to the Roselle sphere size that is most comfortable for them. It is best to begin by wearing a necklace of either 8-mm or 10-mm Roselle spheres. After several months—or when you feel that you have resolved certain emotional blocks and issues but still have more to work on—you can move on to the next larger size. Continue this process until you reach 12-mm spheres or the largest sphere size that is comfortable for your neck.

Therapeutic-Quality Roselle

Therapeutic-quality Roselle is translucent but not to the point of being optical in quality. It is neither cloudy nor clear. Its consistency and color resemble a rose mist that permeates the entire sphere. Very minor inclusions within Roselle are part of its nature and do not diminish its therapeutic effects. However, any dullness, cloudiness, uncharacteristic color, dark inclusions, surface fissures, gouges, or poor drill holes hamper Roselle's effectiveness. Large drill holes diminish the strength of Roselle's radiance. Smaller drill holes allow Roselle's energy to penetrate the aura more quickly.

Non-dyed vs. Dyed Roselle

Only natural, gem-quality Roselle should be used therapeutically. Roselle is by nature a delicate light pink. To the untrained eye, this natural pink color may appear somewhat pale, especially when compared to dyed Roselle. Nearly all the Roselle spheres available today have been dyed in an attempt to make them look like gem-quality Roselle. Natural Roselle of a fine pink color is rare.

Although dye might make the Roselle appear higher in quality, it is a harmful irritant, which inhibits Roselle's action. Natural Roselle calms and soothes the emotions; the soothing, massaging motion of its energy allows hidden feelings to emerge. Dyed Roselle, on the other hand, expresses an irritating energy. This energy can be so strong that, when worn, dyed Roselle can make you feel like crying or expressing anger. You may think that the Roselle is helping you to release suppressed emotions. On the contrary, the interaction of the dye with the Roselle energy creates an irritation that causes unnecessary upset. Dyed Roselle can also place stress on the chakras, which will brace themselves in self-protection against the energy of the dyed Roselle.

To guarantee that a Roselle necklace is free of dye, it must be examined under a microscope.

Therapeutic vs. Optical Quality

Optical-quality Roselle has slightly different effects from optimal therapeutic-quality Roselle. Optical Roselle's energy is more abrupt, even harsh. It can tear into the wearer's energetic fabric, ripping open "containers" of suppressed emotion.

For this reason, optical Roselle can be used for short periods when someone has an immediate need to understand his feelings about an issue. This may be the case when someone must make an important decision, or when finding clarity has become difficult because a situation has become emotionally overwhelming. Optical-quality Roselle will cut through the grief, anger, frustration, or other emotion so that the person can examine his true feelings.

Optical Roselle should not be worn for more than one or two days at a time, and often five to 15 minutes are sufficient. It is best applied under the care of a professional gem therapist or a well-trained layperson.

Mineral Composition
SiO_2

Roselle is Rose Quartz. Its pink to rosy-red color is unique among minerals and is caused by traces of titanium or manganese in silicon dioxide. Rose Quartz occurs in Brazil, Madagascar, Maine, South Dakota, Japan, India, Africa, Russia, and Germany.

Roselle Therapy
Releasing Stress in the Heart

This technique restores the heart chakra's natural flexibility and responsiveness by releasing the energetic knots and blockages that have collected there. A Roselle necklace is held in the palm of each hand to promote a rhythmic unwinding of the heart chakra.

Therapy Tools

Two therapeutic Roselle necklaces of equal length and sphere size (8 mm, 10 mm, or 12 mm)

Indications

- When your heart chakra feels painful, tight, stuck, closed, or unresponsive
- When you are having inappropriate emotional responses—for example, you are not opening your heart in situations where it's appropriate to be vulnerable or loving; or you are not protecting yourself in potentially negative or emotionally damaging situations
- When you are not having success with other therapies for opening or healing your heart chakra
- When you want help addressing the energetic entanglements underlying a physical heart condition

Effects

Releasing Tangled Energies

When you hold Roselle in the palms of your hands, a flow of Roselle energy is initiated, forging a direct connection between your heart and palm chakras. The Roselle energy moves back and forth, from palm to palm, through your heart chakra. This flow of Roselle energy encourages your heart chakra to relax and let go of any unwanted energies that have become entangled there. With the release of these trapped energies, your heart chakra's natural elasticity is restored, and the chakra is better able to open and close as needed.

As the Roselle energy flows back and forth through your heart chakra, the chakra begins to unwind in a circular motion. This motion may be clockwise, counter-clockwise, forward, backward, or in several directions at once. At first, the motion's rhythm will be rather quick, and the motion may change directions often. Then the unwinding will gradually slow down, until a slow, steady rhythm between the hands, heart, and Roselle becomes established.

Much of the release of trapped energies will occur during the busy unwinding period. Strengthening and healing will take place when the slower rhythm has become established. You may or may not feel the unwinding process. Sometimes your palm chakras must be awakened, opened, or cleared before the flow of Roselle energy can occur. If so, the unwinding will first occur only in your palms.

Supporting the Physical Heart

Any area of physical pain, including an injured or diseased heart, tends to wind itself up to protect itself from further pain. This occurs on an energetic level. Unfortunately, the resulting knots of energetic tension can interfere with the area's physical functioning. Therefore, any influence that can unwind and release these knots will be beneficial. This Roselle therapy can do just that. It can help an ailing heart to relax, unwind, and release the tangled energies contributing to its illness. This, in turn, will allow more healing energies to enter it. On a physical level, this will improve the circulatory system's access to the heart and thus allow more nutrients to enter and more metabolic wastes to be removed. On an energetic level, the relaxation will allow life-giving energy to flow into the heart.

Fostering Heart Chakra Flexibility

Today, many people are working on opening their chakras, particularly the heart chakra. An open heart is a good thing at the right time and place, but there are also times when the heart chakra must be able to close. A healthy heart chakra can breathe—that is, expand and contract, or open and close—as needed. Ideally, the heart should be able to open in situations where it is appropriate to be open, loving, or vulnerable, and it must be able to close in negative environments or whenever it needs protection. A heart that is constantly open can be easily hurt. This technique fosters healthy flexibility in the heart chakra.

Procedure

1. Sit comfortably at a table.
2. Place a Roselle necklace in the palm of each hand. If possible, form each necklace into a spiral. Gently close your fingers over the Roselle.
3. Rest your elbows on the table and move your arms and hands into the following position (see Fig. ROS-1)—
   - Hold your palms up with the Roselle resting in them.
   - Bend your elbows, and hold your palms about 12 to 18 inches away from your body and 12 to 18 inches apart from each other. Position your hands at the same height as your heart chakra. If you wish, use pillows to support your arms.
   - Fine-tune your position. Try to sense the optimal distance to hold your hands away from your heart and away from each other, and position them there. This distance will vary slightly from person to person.
   - Although lying down is not recommended, if you must lie down during this treatment, do your best to position your hands and arms as described. Use pillows for support.
4. Close your eyes, relax, and feel the Roselle energy in your palms. Then feel the energy moving back and forth, from one hand to the other, through your heart.

Caution: Heart Discomfort

Although it is natural to feel some slight discomfort as a result of the unwinding, if your heart begins to feel too uncomfortable, stop the treatment immediately.

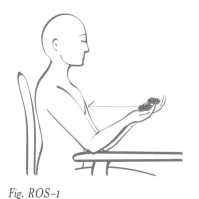

Fig. ROS-1

Time Guidelines

Perform Step 4 for 15 to 20 minutes. If you sense that energy is building in your heart chakra and not being released, continue the treatment for another 30 to 60 seconds. If it still doesn't release, stop the treatment and resume it later that day or the next. You can perform this technique daily.

Post-Treatment Cleansing of Gems

Immediately after completing a treatment, it is important to cleanse the gems of any disharmonious energies released by the body in the course of treatment. See Appendix A: "Care and Cleansing of Therapeutic Gems," on page 397, for cleansing instructions.

Rhodonite

Emotional Transformation

Rhodonite transforms and stabilizes your emotions. It soothes and brings order to feelings that are scattered, imbalanced, or ungrounded. Through its steady upliftment, Rhodonite gradually transforms your emotional foundation, making it more solid, healthy, and secure. At the same time, it uplifts your physical body by slowly and gently raising the quality of its energy. Rhodonite broadens your perspective and deepens your understanding of your emotions, helping you become more balanced, mature, and strong.

Indications for *Wearing a Therapeutic Rhodonite Necklace*

WHEN ONE OR MORE OF THE FOLLOWING APPLY—

YOU ARE EXPERIENCING—

Emotional instability

Grief

Anxiety or depression

Irritability

Not feeling grounded

Frequent hysteria

"Hair-trigger" emotions

Emotional exhaustion

YOU WANT TO—

Build a more solid and secure emotional foundation

Experience emotional stability during challenging times

Foster a state of greater emotional calm and peacefulness

Better understand your emotions

Meet life with more grace and balance

Benefits *of Wearing a Therapeutic*
Rhodonite Necklace

Rhodonite stabilizes your emotions. It soothes and brings order to feelings that are scattered, imbalanced, or ungrounded. Through its steady upliftment, Rhodonite gradually transforms your emotional foundation, making it more solid and secure. When your emotional foundation is improved, your body and emotions can find harmony with each other and respond to life situations in appropriate, healthy ways.

To build a strong emotional foundation, Rhodonite first establishes a new connection between your physical and emotional bodies. This uplifts the vibratory quality of your physical body and provides your emotional body with a secure footing on which to make positive changes. Then Rhodonite helps organize and ground your emotions so that they become more orderly and balanced.

Rhodonite forges a connection between your body and emotions in two ways. First, it builds an energetic connection between your physical spine with its counterpart in your emotional body. This awakens your physical spine's cells and allows more oxygen to enter your sacrum, resulting in a phenomenon called *sacral breathing*. This breathing vitalizes the organs near your sacrum, nourishes and heals the reproductive organs, and encourages greater synchrony and cooperation between your body and emotions. Second, Rhodonite builds an energetic matrix between your physical and emotional bodies. This matrix supports the building of a stronger, healthier, and lasting connection between them.

The construction of this matrix is also the first step in transforming your emotional foundation. The matrix forms the basis of a new, more solid foundation in which emotions can become more organized and grounded. When a mason lays a brick patio, he places boards on their edges to create a form in which he places the bricks. These boards are like Rhodonite's energetic matrix, and the bricks are like your emotions. Rhodonite builds its matrix in great detail, creating a mold for each individual emotion, or brick.

Each emotion you experience potentially serves as a brick in your emotional foundation. Each has an optimal place in your foundation, where it contributes most to the foundation's stability. A healthy emotional foundation consists mostly of positive, well organized and compartmentalized emotions.

However, when your foundation is improperly laid, your emotions tend to float around like balloons with no place to land, and emotional imbalances result. These ungrounded emotions fly, sometimes wildly, in the energetic currents of your emotional body. Such balloon-like emotions are anxious to be expressed. Thus, people whose emotional foundations are not laid properly and who have many ungrounded emotions tend to be emotionally reactive. They frequently lash out in anger, jealousy, or impatience; they may also be hypersensitive or cry easily.

Rhodonite rebuilds your emotional foundation in a way that allows all your emotions to find their proper places in your emotional being. Rhodonite energy seeps into your emotional foundation, where it dissolves old "mortar" and loosens and frees the bricks that are improperly placed. Then, as the Rhodonite energy builds the energetic matrix that will become your new foundation, it starts to give your balloon-like emotions ballast. When your new matrix is completed, Rhodonite encourages disorganized, ungrounded, and balloon-like emotions to settle into to their proper places in your new foundation and contribute to its stability.

The changes required to rearrange and transform an emotional foundation, though healthy and desirable, can sometimes feel disruptive and uncomfortable. Rhodonite eases this process by speeding it up. Its energy also does much of the work that would normally be done by the emotions themselves, thus saving you from suffering the same intensity of emotion that would otherwise be required.

When emotions have settled into their proper places, they become part of your foundation—and therefore part of your strength. When

"Rhodonite seems to loosen my most stubborn misplaced emotions—and does so with a precision more exact and thorough than any emotional therapy I've ever experienced. Rhodonite has helped me become emotionally more solid and flexible."

L.D.
Mill Valley, California

your feelings are more organized, you can understand and come to grips with them more readily. You naturally place new emotional experiences in their optimal places and are less likely to suffer emotional flare-ups. Because your emotions aren't flying out ahead of you and clouding issues, you can also deal with situations more maturely and objectively. You greet life's unexpected experiences with more grace and stability. Indeed, you become more balanced, mature, and strong.

Healing Grief

During the process of grieving, emotions become like unruly balloons. They fly around wildly, overwhelming one's sense of balance. This is natural. When you have lost a loved one or have experienced a painful major change in your life, your emotional foundation must adjust, because your essential life circumstances have changed. The bricks that once comprised your emotional foundation must rearrange themselves to suit your new circumstances.

Health professionals recognize four stages in the grieving process: shock, protest and denial, disorganization, and recovery. This painful but necessary process dissolves the mortar between the bricks in your emotional foundation. It also temporarily transforms the "bricks" into "balloons," so that they can be rearranged. As the grieving cycle is completed, the balloons fall to the ground again, where they find new places in your emotional foundation and become more brick-like. This is why it is necessary to fully experience all stages of grieving—it prevents you from dragging an old foundation into the future and allows you to forge a new foundation on which to build a new life.

Rhodonite can support the grieving process by ensuring that you experience all stages of the process as quickly and comfortably as possible. Although Rhodonite cannot completely avert the pain of grief, it can accelerate the rebuilding of your emotional foundation. Its energy does much of the work that would normally be done by the emotions themselves. By wearing Rhodonite, you will not have to suffer the same intensity of grief that would otherwise be required to build a new foundation.

"A young woman had been suffering from recurring panic attacks. On one occasion, her panic was so intense that she didn't feel safe leaving her bedroom. A friend drove her to my office for a treatment. I had her put on a Rhodonite necklace, and within minutes she was much calmer and later left my office in a balanced state. When I ran into her two months later, she reported that she had had no further panic attacks and was preparing to move to Los Angeles to pursue a new career."

Alan Coffman, L.Ac.
Licensed Acupuncturist
Madison, Wisconsin

Becoming Heart-Centered

Rhodonite can be especially helpful for people who are consciously working to become heart-centered. For such people, a clear physical-emotional connection is particularly important. Unfortunately, many people who are striving to become more heart-centered incorrectly interpret heart-centered to mean emotionally centered. They wrongly believe that their emotions are the source of truth, and they base decisions primarily on how they feel. Wiser decisions can be made by giving equal weight to input from the body, emotions, mind, and intuition. Rhodonite helps people master the shift to a more balanced, heart-oriented view by helping them put their emotions in proper perspective.

Roselle, Ruby, and Rhodochrosite

Once you have gained greater emotional stability, you can take further steps toward emotional well-being by wearing a therapeutic necklace containing Roselle, Ruby, or Rhodochrosite. It is best to continue wearing the Rhodonite necklace at the same time. The Rhodonite will help you maintain your stability as you experience the changes initiated by these other gemstones.

Time Guidelines

Emotional rebuilding takes time. It also takes time for Rhodonite to construct its energetic matrix. Therefore, it is important to maintain continual contact with the Rhodonite for at least the first three weeks of wearing it, and possibly longer. To do this, you can wear it during the day and keep it within three feet of your body at night. This will probably allow enough time for the matrix to be built and for some emotional rearranging to occur.

After wearing Rhodonite for this initial period, you will enter the second, and equally important, phase of Rhodonite therapy. In this phase, your emotional body will have become strong enough to start working fully on its own. You will know you've entered this phase when you feel that you need to take a break from Rhodonite. Then it will be time to remove the Rhodonite and wear it only intermittently. Ideally, during this time, you should keep the Rhodonite exposed to the air near your bed. This will allow you to maintain an energetic connection to the necklace at night while you are sleeping. Depending on the size of your home, this connection will probably remain intact during the day as you move about your house, and it will disengage when you leave. Do not put the Rhodonite in plastic. As it does with all gemstones, plastic cuts off the flow of Rhodonite's energy and would disrupt your connection with the Rhodonite. If you begin to feel emotionally wobbly or unstable, or if you find yourself getting easily upset, it is time to wear Rhodonite continually again. You may also want to wear it again simply for the emotional support it provides or when you need help getting through a temporary situation that is emotionally challenging.

Therapeutic-Quality Rhodonite

All therapeutic Rhodonite contains areas of rich medium- to dark-pink. Some has clearly-defined streaks and patches of black, and some has softer areas of white and yellow. In therapeutic Rhodonite, none of the non-pink colors make the pink appear muddy.

Five Categories of Rhodonite

Rhodonite is different from most other therapeutic gemstones, in that different colorations of Rhodonite produce slightly different benefits. Each of the four colors found in therapeutic Rhodonite—pink, black, white, and yellow—corresponds to a mineral element in Rhodonite, and each has a specific job in producing Rhodonite's effects. Pink Rhodonite highlights your emotional aspect and establishes the physical-emotional connection through the spine. It is primarily responsible for sacral breathing. The yellow and white elements work together to rebuild the emotional matrix—specifically, yellow dissolves old "mortar," and white builds the new matrix. Black grounds your emotions and helps bring them into the new matrix.

Mineral Composition
$MnSiO_3$

Rhodonite is a manganese silicate that is formed in metamorphic rock and hydrothermal deposits where mineral-rich fluids have been superheated within crystallizing magma. Rhodonite is found in Canada, Australia, China, Germany, Romania, Italy, Russia, South America, Mexico, Colorado, and Montana.

Therapeutic-quality Rhodonite can be divided into five basic categories, based on the ratio of colors found in each category:

Category 1

In this category, the black element covers as much as 50 to 75 percent of each sphere. The spheres also contain enough well-defined pink areas to maintain a good emotional-physical connection. The pink is clearly visible, and some white and yellow may also be present. This category of Rhodonite is deeply grounding and therefore helpful for stabilizing imbalanced, volatile, or out-of-control emotions.

Category 2

In this category, the black element covers 30 to 50 percent of each sphere. The remainder is predominantly pink with traces of white and yellow. This Rhodonite puts equal emphasis on grounding the emotions and rebuilding a new emotional foundation. It is useful for people who are emotionally strained and having difficulty maintaining their balance but who can also afford to put some attention on rebuilding a new emotional foundation.

Category 3

This Rhodonite is predominately pink and contains 15 to 30 percent black. The pink element is brightest and richest in this category and brings healing energy to the emotions. The black element is still a significant force, but the emphasis on grounding is not as strong as in Category 2. This Rhodonite is appropriate for those who are emotionally struggling, yet coping. It helps reestablish emotional stability as it rebuilds a better emotional foundation.

Category 4

The Rhodonite spheres in this category are also predominately pink and contain only three to 15 percent black. They display more white than yellow, and the white element is obvious to the eye. This category builds a strong bridge between the emotional and physical bodies, allowing emotions to be expressed more fully and clearly. The white element helps stabilize the desirable emotions in the newly-developing emotional foundation. The yellow element dissolves whatever has been holding undesirable emotions in the old foundation. This category has just enough black to settle down unsteady emotions so that they can become established in the new foundation. Category 4 is recommended for people who are not currently overwhelmed by any emotions but who wish to make some significant changes in their emotional ways.

Category 5

In this category of Rhodonite, the spheres are almost entirely pink, with some white and only occasional traces of black or yellow. Hence, it provides no additional ballast to the emotions. The amount of white and yellow can be similar to that of Category 4, although Category 5 may contain a little more white. In this category, these colors also support the new structure of the emotional foundation and keep it in place. The pink nurtures the emotions and maintains a strong connection between the physical and emotional bodies. This allows feelings to come through cleanly, purely, and with control. This Rhodonite is most appropriate for emotionally healthy people who wish to improve the emotional foundation they already have.

Rhodonite Therapy
Emotional Regulation Therapy

This therapy improves the chakras' ability to regulate the healthy flow and expression of emotions. Placing Rhodonite on the chakras clears, soothes, and stabilizes the chakras and restores harmony among them.

Therapy Tool

One therapeutic necklace of Rhodonite spheres (8 mm or 10 mm)

Indications

- When you wish to better regulate your emotions
- When you are feeling irritable, overreactive, hyper-sensitive to others, unstable, or biochemically out of balance, such as when hormones surge
- When you continually feel low on energy, alternate between states of high and low energy, have mood swings, or crave stimulants
- When wearing a Rhodonite necklace does not provide you with enough emotional stability and support

Effects

Your chakras play a vital role in your emotional well-being. Among other functions, they regulate the channels through which your emotional energy flows to your physical body for expression. This Rhodonite therapy restores harmony among your chakras so that they can better regulate the flow of your emotional energy. By treating your chakras, you also treat all the emotional-physical channels throughout your body.

The channels themselves are vibrational in nature. They can be imagined as tiny tubes connecting each cell in your physical body with its counterpart in your emotional body. Through them, your physical cells receive emotional energy. This flow of energy is important. To maintain health, your emotions should help fuel everything you do, whether it's a casual hobby or a large responsibility.

When all these channels are working properly, each chakra expresses a subtle sound, or note, that harmonizes with the notes played by all the other chakras. This harmony among your chakras denotes accord between your body and emotions. Mild positive emotions, such as contentment, peace, and quiet happiness, keep the chakras' music on key. Stronger emotions, whether positive or negative, change the chakras' notes. If the emotions are strongly negative, the notes can change significantly. Then it takes some balancing and recentering for you to reestablish the harmonious music among your chakras.

Maintaining harmony among your chakras helps you keep your emotional balance. Chakras whose vibrations are off-key cannot properly regulate the cellular channels between your physical and emotional bodies. Many things can happen as a result. For example, channels in certain areas can become blocked, thus cutting off your body from its source of emotional fuel and information. When your chakras are off-key, you can also become irritable, overreactive, hypersensitive, or emotionally unstable, or you can experience a biochemical imbalance. You might also experience low energy, have mood swings, or crave stimulants.

This Rhodonite therapy helps restore harmony to your chakras. It also helps release any unnecessary energies from the chakras and imparts a healing, soothing, and supportive influence to each chakra on which it is placed. When your chakras are operating in harmony, you can more easily acknowledge, feel, and balance your emotions. Your chakras also become better regulators of your cellular channels.

Placing the Rhodonite on the root chakra first promotes emotional stability in the physical body.

Procedure

1. Lie down on your back.
2. Bunch a Rhodonite necklace in your hand, and hold it on your root chakra (see Fig. RDN-1 for an illustration of chakra locations). Keep it there for at least several minutes.

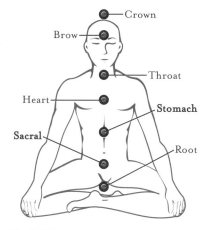

Crown
Brow
Throat
Heart
Stomach
Sacral
Root

Fig. RDN-1

3. Be alert to your intuitive sense of when to remove the Rhodonite from the chakra.
    • If, after several minutes, the chakra seems to be soaking in the Rhodonite energy and wants to retain the Rhodonite, keep it there for a few minutes longer. Then go to Step 4.
    • If you sense a pull-away—that is, an increasing pressure or discomfort or simply an urge to remove the Rhodonite—go to Step 4.

4. Choose the next chakra for treatment, and move the Rhodonite to that chakra—
    • If you sense which chakra wants the Rhodonite next, move the Rhodonite to that chakra.
    • If you do not sense which chakra wants the Rhodonite next, lift the Rhodonite off the chakra and hold it 12 to 18 inches above your heart chakra. Try again to sense a pull-in to another chakra. If, after 30 seconds or so, you still don't feel a pull-in, use your intuition to choose another chakra for treatment.

5. Hold the Rhodonite in the center of the next chakra for at least several minutes.

6. Repeat Steps 3–5 until you have treated all the chakras that have called for treatment. You may find that some chakras want to be treated more than once or that a certain chakra does not want any treatment. Trust your intuition about which chakras are requesting treatment.

Post-Treatment Cleansing of Gems

Immediately after completing a treatment, it is important to cleanse the gems of any disharmonious energies released by the body in the course of treatment. See Appendix A: "Care and Cleansing of Therapeutic Gems," on page 397, for cleansing instructions.

Mother of Pearl

Emotional Fulfillment

Mother of Pearl stirs and awakens the primordial memory of your origin in the infinite ocean of divine love. It stirs this memory in your thoughts, your feelings, and in every cell of your physical body. As your memory opens, this divine love flows into you, repairing the deep wounds created by unfulfilled needs. Mother of Pearl's energy sings the song of motherly love as it imparts the feeling of being cradled in a loving mother's arms.

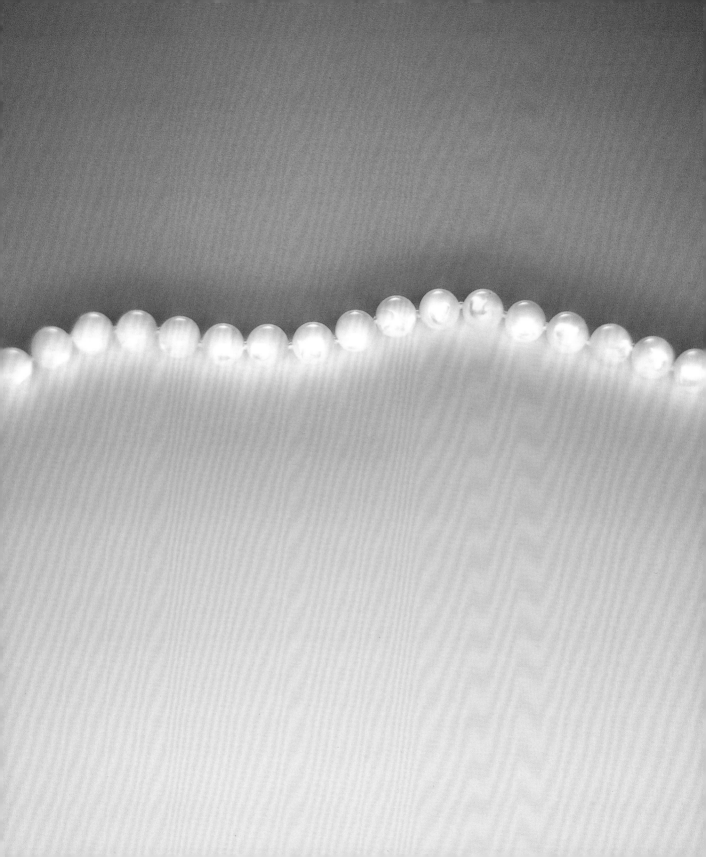

Indications *for Wearing a Therapeutic*
Mother of Pearl Necklace

WHEN ONE OR MORE OF THE FOLLOWING APPLY—

YOU ARE EXPERIENCING—

A sense of abandonment

Unfulfilled emotional or physical needs from childhood

Difficulty feeling or expressing love

Out-of-balance emotions

YOU WANT TO—

Feel calmed and soothed

Feel nurtured by motherly love

Be reminded of the ocean of divine love within you

Be protected from certain negative energies

Note: Mother of Pearl is highly beneficial for children.

Benefits of *Wearing a Therapeutic* *Mother of Pearl Necklace*

Mother of Pearl stirs and awakens the primordial memory of your origin in the infinite ocean of divine love. It stirs this memory in your thoughts, your feelings, and in every cell of your physical body. As your memory opens, this divine love flows into you, repairing the deep wounds created by unfulfilled needs.

Every cell in your physical body and every aspect of your mind and emotions has a primordial memory. Mother of Pearl stirs the forces that have kept this memory hidden. It is the memory of the time you were part of the sea—the unbounded spiritual ocean where all souls dwell.

As Mother of Pearl stirs your mind, it also enlivens the memories of recent dreams, making their symbols clearer and more easily understood. It also stirs your mind to look within and beyond itself to deeper levels of your being. As Mother of Pearl stirs your emotions, they become more balanced and harmonious. The sharpness of negative emotions, such as a sharp temper or the pang of fear, is smoothed and calmed. If you have difficulty expressing positive feelings, such as love, these feelings become stronger, more defined, and easier to express.

In your physical body, Mother of Pearl produces an overall calming effect as it gently stirs the life energy of your cells. Like waves lapping the shore, this stirring is steady, relaxing, and rhythmical. Overactive mechanisms throughout the body are calmed, and the flexibility of your cells increases, improving their ability to accept oxygen and life force.

All human beings have a natural, innate need to be cared for, nurtured, and loved. These needs are first felt in the womb and are most apparent in infants and young children. Even if most of our needs were well met when we were children, we do not stop having these needs as we get older. They are part of our very fabric. As infants,

"At night, when I'm tired and spiritually at a low, I put on my Mother of Pearl and feel as though I'm enveloped in a soft blanket. I feel tension leave my body and peacefulness enter."

T.E.
Dallas, Oregon

"As long as I can remember, I've been a body in perpetual motion—a typical Type A personality. Relaxation was just a word to me; my body was never allowed to truly experience it. I've been wearing a Mother of Pearl necklace for several months now. I'm still in perpetual motion, chasing my son and maintaining a busy household, but now I feel calm and peaceful inside. I'm a different person, and I like myself a lot more."

N.B.
Stone Mountain, Georgia

we need to be loved and nurtured in order to survive. As we grow older, these needs are not as critical for our physical survival, but they are absolutely essential for our emotional survival. As we grow into adulthood, our mothers are no longer there to fulfill all our needs for love and nurturing, and often life does not fulfill them either.

All unfulfilled needs become like holes in the fabric of one's being. These holes can have many sources, such as a scarcity of attention received in childhood; not receiving the education one wanted; inadequate food, shelter or clothing; or the absence of a relationship that fulfilled the need for love. When Mother of Pearl's energy has saturated the aura, it detects these holes. There, its vibration sings of the source of infinite love. Its song stirs within every part of us the memory of this source—the primordial ocean of love out of which we all grow. As our memory opens to this ocean, its love flows into us and helps repair the holes created by unfulfilled needs.

Sometimes, before these holes can be mended, you must acknowledge them and cry many tears. Mother of Pearl can help you with this part of your healing. It bestows the feeling that you are resting in the arms of a loving mother. Thus, Mother of Pearl helps those who need some motherly love, whether or not they are aware of that need. At the same time, it brings the security of knowing that the Mother within is always in your heart, ready to give you all the love, support, and comfort you need.

Protection from Negative Influences

Like a protecting mother, Mother of Pearl can help safeguard you from negative influences. When certain harmful frequencies enter your aura, Mother of Pearl either scatters or absorbs them. These include the frequencies of other people's negative thoughts and emotions, as well as electromagnetic radiation and the harmful emissions of televisions, radios, and microwave transmitters. Although this protection is a side effect of Mother of Pearl's energy, it is a profound one and begins to take effect within minutes of donning a Mother of Pearl necklace.

Protection for Children

Because of its protective properties, Mother of Pearl is an ideal gemstone for young children. A child's inner being is delicate and precious; it is the foundation upon which he will build the rest of his life. In addition to his need for physical protection, a child's inner nature must be shielded and allowed to grow unharmed.

Mother of Pearl does not protect a child from the emotions that are important for him to experience. For example, a parent's discipline may be needed to teach a valuable lesson. However, if a parent or anyone oversteps the boundaries of healthy discipline into destructive anger, Mother of Pearl will deflect the energy of this anger away from the child. Thus, it can deflect the brutal thoughts and emotions that accompany abuse. If the child is wearing Mother of Pearl at the time, although he may cry and appear shaken, the inner core of his being will be protected.

Therapeutic-Quality Mother of Pearl

Mother of Pearl's shimmering, reflective quality helps its energy quickly enter the aura. The more opalescence Mother of Pearl possesses, the more deeply it can work—be it physically, emotionally, or mentally—and the more clearly you will receive its benefits.

The energy of most gemstones is disrupted by chemical alteration. Mother of Pearl is unusual, in that bleach empowers and has a brightening effect on its energy.

"I wear Mother of Pearl when I am having difficulty feeling loving. It has brought out more sweetness and helps me be more loving and patient with my clients."

Dr. Laura Schneider, L.Ac.
Naturopathic Physician
Milwaukie, Oregon

Mineral Composition
$CaCO_3$ with organics and H_2O

Mother of Pearl is the iridescent substance that forms the lining of the shells of some freshwater and saltwater mollusks. Mother of Pearl is composed of alternate layers of the aragonite form of calcium carbonate, and conchiolin, a protein component of mollusk shells. It is found in Sri Lanka, Philippines, China, Japan, Australia, the Persian Gulf and the Mississippi River.

Karmic Healing
and Resolution

Rhodochrosite

Carnelian

Opalight

Although the following gems are categorized
elsewhere, they also offer significant healing
benefits for issues and conditions associated
with karma and the causal body.
Therefore, see also:

Aquamarine

Lavender • Quartz

Rhodochrosite

Developing Inner Freedom

Rhodochrosite helps develop inner freedom by neutralizing the destructive behavioral patterns that restrict personal growth and undermine physical health. Rhodochrosite's energy comes like a storm: it destroys negative patterns, sweeps away emotional clutter, and works with you to build healthier patterns. By helping you resolve inner conflicts, Rhodochrosite encourages all aspects of your being to work together with a unified focus. It imparts self-confidence as it helps you realize your power to transform your own life.

Indications for *Wearing a Therapeutic Rhodochrosite Necklace*

WHEN ONE OR MORE OF THE FOLLOWING APPLY—

YOU ARE EXPERIENCING—

Unhealthy emotional patterns or habits hindering your health and happiness

A pattern of destructive, unhealthy, or dead-end relationships

Patterns of negative experiences, such as repeated accidents

Low self-confidence

Feeling of being in a rut

Feeling emotionally "cluttered"

Difficulty moving forward or taking action because of conflicting needs

YOU WANT TO—

Break free from negative or restrictive behavior patterns

Encourage new, healthier, and more uplifting behavior patterns

Experience greater self-confidence

Resolve inner conflicts

Benefits of *Wearing a Therapeutic Rhodochrosite Necklace*

Rhodochrosite helps develop inner freedom by neutralizing the destructive behavior patterns that restrict personal growth and undermine physical health. First, Rhodochrosite neutralizes destructive emotional patterns. Then it cleanses any disharmony caused by the neutralization of the destructive patterns. Finally, its energy helps you rebuild a healthy, solid, and efficient emotional foundation. These three functions—neutralizing, cleansing, and rebuilding—all work together to promote inner freedom.

To understand how Rhodochrosite works requires some understanding of the energetic makeup of patterns. Behavioral patterns manifest in the subtle bodies as what appear to be thin lines. A closer look reveals that these lines are made of blocks positioned one after the other. One block is a certain cause, the next block is your response to that cause; the next block is a similar cause, the next is your response, etc. The more often you respond in the same way to a particular cause, the longer a particular pattern line becomes. As soon as you finish reacting to a certain cause, the next cause block starts to form. As soon as a new cause block is completed, it develops something like a magnetic charge that draws to it the response characteristic of that particular pattern line. The longer a pattern line is, the stronger its magnetic charge and the more strongly it directs you to react in the same way.

Of course, not all behavior patterns are negative or undesirable. Rhodochrosite affects only undesirable pattern lines. It changes the magnetic charge of the cause block at the end of an undesirable pattern line—ideally drawing a different, healthier response. When you first wear Rhodochrosite, you might find that you have a greater awareness of your undesirable actions and that these actions no longer feel like your most comfortable response to a certain situation. In other words, you may feel as though you've outgrown a particular response. For a while, you may continue to react as you always have. However, as time goes on, you will naturally begin to respond to the same cause in a different way. This will be the beginning of building a new, more uplifting and harmonious pattern.

Emotional patterns resemble an incorrectly assembled puzzle that has been sitting around and collecting dust between its pieces. When the puzzle is shaken up, the dust flies. Emotional patterns behave in a similar way. When unhealthy emotional patterns are formed, they tend to collect miscellaneous and undesirable energies—in other words, emotional "dust." When Rhodochrosite is worn, its energy sweeps across your emotional fabric, shaking up these unhealthy patterns and cleansing the dust from them.

When the dust has cleared, your emotional strengths will be revealed. These are the strengths that have been buried beneath the dust of emotional confusion and the needless emotional energies that clutter one's life. This dust obscures emotional clarity and undermines clear emotional expression. When Rhodochrosite has cleared away the dust and debris, it rebuilds the puzzle so that all the pieces fit together correctly.

Rhodochrosite is a tool that can change your life. When patterns are highlighted, worked on, and given perspective by Rhodochrosite, they can provide the lessons needed to master life. Working with therapeutic-quality Rhodochrosite will give you the opportunity to arise newborn in a new arena, where you can be the master of your own destiny.

The Influence of Patterns on Health

Emotional patterns feed energy into the physical body like lasers. The amount and type of energy fed depends on the attitude or feeling associated with the pattern. If the attitude is one of hurt, anger, fear, or anything else negative, then this is exactly what will be aimed at the physical body. If enough of these negative emotional energies are fed into the body, a weak spot will develop, and physical disharmony and disease will result. Rhodochrosite can help you stop feeding your physical body with disharmonious energies by resolving the underlying negative patterns and by creating new, positive patterns.

Rhodochrosite will also make pattern lines more flexible. When pattern lines become rigid, they restrict the flow of life force to related areas in the physical body, thereby weakening the areas. When you wear Rhodochrosite, your pattern lines will begin to loosen until they move with your breath, thus allowing more life force to flow wherever it is needed.

Self-Confidence

Rhodochrosite mobilizes, encourages, and motivates you to change your patterns. At the same time, its energy instills you with self-confidence. As your patterns begin to change, you will become stronger. The realization that you can change your emotions, patterns, and reactions—and with them, your life—will also give you tremendous self-confidence. Some people who wear Rhodochrosite feel this greater self-confidence almost immediately. Others may need to experience several behavioral changes before this new confidence is felt. Consequently, at first they may be a little unsure of themselves. Continuing to wear the Rhodochrosite will eventually build their self-confidence.

Healing Inner Conflict

At every moment, each of us is subject to the myriad influences, perspectives, and desires of our inner and outer aspects. Somehow we must manage the simultaneous demands of our physical, emotional, karmic, mental, and intuitive bodies as they strive to be expressed through our consciousness and actions. We manage this task by sorting through all these influences and categorizing them in some way. When, for some reason, our consciousness cannot categorize all these influences, inner conflicts develop. As the years go by, this collection of uncategorized influences grows, leading to a perpetual state of unresolved conflict. This conflict manifests as areas of tightness and stiffness in the physical body.

"My early childhood was lived with a schizophrenic mother. Needless to say, even as an adult, my first response to anything unpredictable was fight or flight. Wearing Rhodochrosite is like wearing an "Aha!" necklace. Now, when something happens, I see my pattern and then have a choice whether to change it. I believe that, after years of therapy, using this gem is what helped me shift to living a happier and healthier life."

D.G.
Oak Park, California

Rhodochrosite helps the physical body resolve the conflicts created by all the inner and outer influences trying to manifest through it. It encourages the physical and subtle bodies to work together with a singular focus as an integrated whole. In this way, Rhodochrosite affects the way we express ourselves and the very way we live.

Focusing Rhodochrosite with Mental Intention

A mental declaration of the specific reason you are wearing Rhodochrosite will strongly focus the gemstones' action on the patterns associated with that issue. For example, you could mentally declare that you are wearing Rhodochrosite to change the patterns affecting your digestive system. You should periodically remind yourself of your intent as you wear the necklace. This will enhance the action of the necklace for your intended purpose.

If no mental direction is given, the Rhodochrosite will work in a somewhat holistic manner. It will find the longest pattern lines with the most emotion and negative attitudes associated with them, and it will work on those first.

Time Guidelines

During the initial phase of working with Rhodochrosite, it should be worn 24 hours a day. At night, you can wear it or keep it close to you in bed. As long as the Rhodochrosite stays within your aura, it will continue to work for you.

This initial phase may take two to six months. By then, you will have attained greater emotional balance. Enough pattern lines will have been resolved, and enough new ones will have been formed that you may feel like you are starting a new life. You will have a new attitude about yourself and your health. Also, by this time—if other therapies have been properly supporting your physical body—you will probably feel much better physically and have made much progress in your physical healing. All these changes will indicate that the initial phase of Rhodochrosite's work is completed.

In the next phase, continue to wear the Rhodochrosite for at least a few hours every day. If you wish, you may keep it next to you while you sleep, so it can continue working with you through the night.

Rhodonite and Rhodochrosite

It is no coincidence that Rhodonite and Rhodochrosite have similar names. Wearing Rhodonite can help balance Rhodochrosite's power. When you are undergoing the great changes that Rhodochrosite can initiate, Rhodonite can establish a foundation of emotional and physical stability.

Necklace Length

For maximum effectiveness, Rhodochrosite should be worn in a necklace that falls near the heart.

Therapeutic-Quality Rhodochrosite

Rhodochrosite occurs in a wide range of clarity from opaque rock to opalescent gem. If you imagine this range as a vertical line, at the very top is Rhodochrosite that is so translucent that the entire sphere displays opalescence; at the bottom is Rhodochrosite that is so rock-like and dense that its vibrations cannot reach beyond the physical level. Rhodochrosite that is rock-like or that contains rock matrix or any other foreign material, such as brown or black spots or blemishes, is not therapeutic.

Although therapeutic Rhodochrosite exhibits a wide range of clarity, its color falls within a relatively narrow spectrum—from watermelon- and rose-pink on one end to orange-pink on the other. The deeper and more vibrant the color of the Rhodochrosite, the more powerful its effects will be.

Therapeutic-quality Rhodochrosite can be divided into four quality grades: Fine, Very Fine, Exquisite, and Exquisite-Plus:

Mineral Composition
$MnCO_3$

Rhodocrosite is manganese carbonate with traces of iron, calcium, magnesium, zinc, or cobalt. It is usually found in nodes or veins associated with silver, copper, iron, or lead sulfides and where mineral-rich fluids have been superheated within crystallizing magma. Rhodochrosite is found in Argentina, Spain, Saxony, Australia, New Jersey, and the western U.S.

Fine

Fine-quality Rhodochrosite displays the minimum parameters for therapeutic quality and thus will support Rhodochrosite's therapeutic mission. It contains some white bands or spots and some mildly translucent areas.

Very Fine

Very Fine has fewer white bands or patches of white than Fine quality and is clearly translucent or even somewhat opalescent.

Exquisite

Exquisite-quality Rhodochrosite has very few bands or patches of white. It is opalescent and translucent.

Exquisite-Plus

Exquisite-Plus is free or nearly free of white and is in an altogether different league. It is the most translucent and opalescent. The crystalline matrix of Exquisite-Plus Rhodochrosite is a whisper of physicality. It does not recognize the difference between the physical, emotional, and mental bodies and therefore works with each of them equally and with the knowledge that each is a part of your whole being. Other therapeutic-quality Rhodochrosite must focus on one level at a time, whereas Exquisite-Plus can work on all aspects at once.

To produce the most profound changes, therapeutic-quality Rhodochrosite spheres 8 mm or larger are required. Smaller sizes will take longer to initiate Rhodochrosite's effects, and the effects may not be as deep or far-reaching.

When working with Rhodochrosite, high quality is essential; the higher the quality, the better the results. Indeed, the more translucent the Rhodochrosite, the faster and more powerfully it will work.

Rhodochrosite Therapy
Inner-Conflict Resolution

A Rhodochrosite necklace is placed on a localized area of pain, tightness, injury, or other disharmony to help the body resolve the underlying inner conflicts associated with the area. By clearing these inner conflicts, this therapy sets the stage for a deeper physical healing to occur.

Therapy Tool
One therapeutic necklace of Rhodochrosite spheres (8 mm or 10 mm)

Indications
- When any area of your body is painful, injured, tight, or otherwise disharmonious
- When an inner conflict appears to be negatively affecting your physical and emotional health

Effects
A healthy life requires that we manage the simultaneous demands of our physical, emotional, mental, and spiritual selves as they strive to be expressed. We manage this, often unconsciously, by sorting through all these demands and influences and categorizing them in some way. Yet, when these various influences overwhelm our ability to sort out and categorize these demands, inner conflicts develop. As the years go by, this collection of uncategorized influences grows and tends to manifest as areas of tightness, stiffness, and sometimes pain in our physical bodies.

Indeed, every disharmonious manifestation or condition in the body has some element of inner conflict associated with it. These unresolved conflicts tend to perpetuate a condition and act as obstacles to its healing. This Rhodochrosite therapy helps painful, tense, or injured areas resolve the conflicts created by the inner and outer influences trying to manifest through the area. When these conflicts are resolved, healing can occur more swiftly, easily, and permanently.

When you place Rhodochrosite on the body, the Rhodochrosite highlights and then accentuates the conflict associated with the placement area. This accentuation temporarily increases the feeling of tension in the area that has been generated by its improperly filed, uncategorized energies. This heightening of tension strongly encourages the body to finally resolve the conflict and thereby sets the stage for a deeper and more permanent healing to occur.

Procedure

1. Place a Rhodochrosite necklace in a neat pile on the area you wish to treat (see Fig. RCR-1).
2. Be alert to a sense of increasing energy or tightness in the area. This feeling results from Rhodochrosite highlighting and accentuating the conflict associated with the area.
3. When this feeling reaches a peak, remove the Rhodochrosite. You may experience an insight regarding the conflict.
4. Move the Rhodochrosite to another area of your body that you feel is related to the conflict. Allow your intuition to guide your choice. You may sense that the Rhodochrosite "wants" to move to a certain area, or you may feel an energetic or biomagnetic pull to a certain area.
5. Repeat Steps 2–4 once. When the feeling of energy or tightness reaches a peak in the third placement area, remove the Rhodochrosite from your body.

Time Guidelines

If you don't experience the increased energy or tension peaking in the treatment area, keep the Rhodochrosite on each area for 10 to 15 minutes. Place the Rhodochrosite on a maximum of three different areas per treatment. The larger the Rhodochrosite and the higher its quality, the faster this therapy will work and the stronger its effects will be.

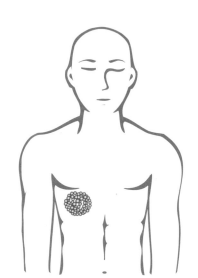

Fig. RCR-1

Post-Treatment Cleansing of Gems

Immediately after completing a treatment, it is important to cleanse the gems of any disharmonious energies released by the body in the course of treatment. See Appendix A: "Care and Cleansing of Therapeutic Gems," on page 397, for cleansing instructions.

Carnelian

Revitalizing Your Being

Carnelian nourishes and vitalizes your entire being, bestowing you with optimism and enthusiasm for life. The orange ray carried by Carnelian deeply relaxes your mind, emotions, and physical cells so that they can release their disharmony and disease. Carnelian enhances mental clarity and positive emotions, promoting a brighter outlook and an appreciation for your life lessons. By teaching you to balance your higher and lower energies, Carnelian helps bring your aspirations and current life path closer together.

Indications *for Wearing a Therapeutic Carnelian Necklace*

YOU ARE EXPERIENCING—

Lack of inspiration or enthusiasm for life

Pessimism or depression

The depressive effects of a traumatic experience or loss

Mental fog

Low energy or sluggishness

Emotional extremes

Onset of an acute infectious illness, such as a cold or flu

Frequent colds, especially with swollen glands

Any unwanted condition of the immune, endocrine, or lymphatic systems

Hormonal imbalance

Chronic fatigue syndrome or fibromyalgia

YOU WANT TO—

Experience greater optimism, vitality, and joy in living

Support your immune system

Support the resolution of a hormonal imbalance

Increase your mental clarity

Have extra support during a cleansing or detoxification program

Benefits of *Wearing a Therapeutic* *Carnelian Necklace*

Carnelian carries the orange color ray. The orange ray nourishes and vitalizes your entire being, bestowing optimism and enthusiasm for life. At the cellular level, the orange ray motivates cells to achieve greater health. On the whole-person level, it inspires you to make the changes that will move you toward your life's goal or dream.[11]

When you wear a necklace of Carnelian spheres, their orange-ray energy radiates into your aura. From there, the orange ray is breathed into your lungs and distributed throughout your body via the blood and lymph.

The orange ray is a key ingredient for life, especially for the life of the cells. Each individual cell bathes in glory in the presence of the orange ray. Cells need all seven color rays for life. However, when given even a little extra orange ray, they react the way you might when you soak in a hot bath after a hard day's work—you rest and relax, and although you continue to function, you let go of your troubles. Carnelian and the orange ray help your cells let go of their disharmony and disease. They stir and dislodge disharmony so that your body can release it.

Emotions also relax in the presence of the orange ray. This relaxation manifests as calmer, more balanced emotions. Excess emotions are checked, and deficient emotions are brought to life, while others are soothed and smoothed. Negative emotions are not in harmony with the orange ray. Therefore, when Carnelian is worn, negative emotions are dulled, dissipated, or canceled out. Carnelian also helps you express positive emotions more easily.

Carnelian accentuates your memories of joyful and positive experiences. It also highlights positive reasons for living. Carnelian

---

11 *See page 40 for more information on the vital role of color rays in restoring and maintaining health.*

"Stomach cramping had become chronic as a result of metal toxicity. Constant pain made my emotions slump, and I became depressed. Then I began to wear Carnelian. While helping me detox the metal, Carnelian also filled me with positive emotions. It was as if the sun was finally shining after a long and dreary season, and I was able to manage the pain more effectively."

Susan Gold
Holistic Health Counselor
Bonita, California

"After giving birth, I was at a low point from depression, weight gain, and confusion about how to proceed in my life. Longstanding migraines, endometriosis, and digestive problems also plagued me. Since starting to wear Carnelian six months ago, I haven't had a migraine, nor any endometriosis pain or digestive problems. I sleep better. I have energy and am making better choices. My life is starting to look like I once envisioned it, centered around wellness and peace."

D.F-G.
Miami, Florida

helps you appreciate all the gifts of life. When you wear Carnelian, even in the midst of unhappiness and negative circumstances, the good things are highlighted.

Carnelian stimulates, sharpens, and enhances mental functions. It improves mental clarity, memory, and the ability to see things from a higher viewpoint. When you first wear Carnelian, it stirs up the clouds that inhibit mental clarity. Consequently, you may notice that your clarity seems to decrease, and your sinuses and lymph glands may become somewhat clogged. This effect won't last long. Carnelian teaches the body to metabolize these clouds. As more and more clouds are metabolized and eliminated, your clarity will increase and then surpass what you experienced before putting on the Carnelian. You will also gain the strength to help you accept the many changes this increased mental clarity will initiate in your life.

Carnelian will benefit anyone who is deficient in the orange ray. An orange-ray deficiency frequently manifests as weakness in the immune, endocrine, or lymphatic systems. It can also manifest as an imbalance between lower and higher energies, and this may express itself as a disparity between one's dreams and aspirations and one's actual life direction. When you wear Carnelian, the lower and higher energies in your body will come into greater harmony with each other. This will encourage your aspirations and current life path to come closer and closer together. As your life begins to move in the direction you desire, you will be infused with a new sense of vitality and joy for living.

Carnelian and the Lymphatic and Endocrine Systems

Each of the seven color rays of the life force is particularly healing and nourishing to certain aspects of the physical body. The orange ray nourishes and supports the lymphatic system, soft connective tissue, endocrine system (glands), and adipose tissue. Consequently, wearing Carnelian can help strengthen these parts of the body and resolve certain conditions related to them.

Time Guidelines

It is best to wear Carnelian continually, especially if you are wearing it to increase your mental clarity.

Therapeutic-Quality Carnelian

Carnelian's quality is easy to judge with the naked eye. A microscope is not necessary and a light table may even be deceiving. With Carnelian, color is more important than clarity. Nonetheless, to be therapeutic, Carnelian must be free of any rock matrix or non-Carnelian inclusions. The Carnelian should not appear muddy or dull. Cracks, even small ones, should be avoided, because they disrupt the emission of the Carnelian's frequency.

The color of a Carnelian sphere as it is visible to the naked eye in sunlight is a true representation of the energy it will give to its wearer. To judge Carnelian's true color, it must be held up in ambient sunshine outdoors and not directly in front of the sun. In this respect, Carnelian is different from some other gemstones: any light source placed directly behind Carnelian makes it appear lighter than it really is. Carnelian color should be as consistent as possible throughout the sphere and, ideally, true to the pure orange seen in a rainbow.

Such Carnelian is not plentiful. For many people, this optimal Carnelian color may actually provide too strong an influx of orange ray. Therefore, in most cases, using the Carnelian with a slight hint of red coloring is recommended; it emanates a degree of orange ray that is in balance for most people. The more commonly available, dark red-orange is not therapeutic.

Well-formed spheres and neat drill holes are also vital to Carnelian's effectiveness. Irregularly shaped or improperly drilled spheres diminish the strength with which Carnelian can express its frequency into the aura.

Mineral Composition
$SiO_2 + FeO_2$

Carnelian is a semi-transparent to translucent chalcedony, a cryptocrystalline member of the Quartz family. Its orange color comes from traces of iron oxide. Carnelian is found in Brazil, India, and Uruguay.

"I am 45 years old and the mother of eight children. I've had a problem with my weight since childhood. Some months ago, I began a raw foods diet and have also been wearing Carnelian. The necklace has helped me clear away the clouds and stay focused on my weight and spiritual issues. I've lost over 100 pounds and feel like it's just the beginning of my journey."
T.E.
Dallas, Oregon

Carnelian Therapy
Revitalizing and Cleansing Infusion

Carnelian energy and the orange ray are infused into a localized area of the body to vitalize the area's cells and encourage them to release their disharmony, toxicity, or disease. This treatment is especially effective for ailing organs. It also excels as an adjunct to an internal cleansing or detoxification program.

Therapy Tools

One or two therapeutic necklaces of Carnelian spheres (8 mm, 10 mm, or 12 mm)

Indications

- When you are performing an internal cleansing or detoxification program
- When an organ or other area of your body (particularly the endocrine glands, lymphatic system, soft tissue, or skin) is ailing, weak, or toxic
- When a stubborn or persistent condition is not responding favorably to other therapies

Effects

In this therapy, you place one or more Carnelian necklaces on an ailing or toxic area of your body. The orange ray carried by Carnelian deeply relaxes and vitalizes individual cells in the area. At the same time, the Carnelian stirs and dislodges the cells' disharmonious energies, thus allowing the cells to release their disharmony and toxicity.

Performing this therapy in sunlight enhances the penetration of Carnelian energy into your body. The more often you perform it, the deeper the Carnelian's energy penetrates. This therapy can be performed without sunlight; however, the effects will be considerably milder.

Procedure

1. Ideally, position yourself so that the area you wish to treat is exposed to direct sunlight, even if it is just the sunlight coming through an open window on a sunny or cloudy day.

2. Place one or two Carnelian necklaces directly on your skin on the area you wish to treat. Cover as much of the area as possible with Carnelian (see Fig. CRN-1).

   - If you are performing this treatment as part of a cleansing or detoxification program, place the Carnelian on your weakest organ or on the primary organs involved in elimination—that is, your kidneys, liver, or intestines.

   - If you do not have access to sunlight, and you wish to secure the Carnelian to your body so that you can move around during treatment time, place the gemstones on your skin and then place a light cotton cloth over the gems. To secure the gems to your body, tape the cloth to your skin with non-plastic first aid tape. Avoid letting the glue from the tape touch the gems.

3. Between treatments, wear a Carnelian necklace around your neck for ongoing support.

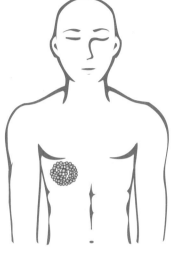

Fig. CRN-1

Time Guidelines

When performing this treatment in sunlight, keep the Carnelian in place for 30 minutes. When performing it on a cloudy day or without sunlight, keep the Carnelian in place for at least 60 minutes. Perform this treatment once a day.

Post-Treatment Cleansing of Gems

Immediately after completing a treatment, it is important to cleanse the gems of any disharmonious energies released by the body in the course of treatment. See Appendix A: "Care and Cleansing of Therapeutic Gems," on page 397, for cleansing instructions.

Opalight

Resolving Karma

Opalight helps resolve the karma, or past entanglements, that perpetuate physical conditions in the present. By shining its light on your aura, Opalight reveals which of your conditions are most deeply rooted in the past and therefore are probably your most serious. It brings their underlying issues to your attention so that you can take steps to resolve them. Opalight's calming effect on the aura can help you sleep, thereby encouraging karmic resolution in the dream state.

Indications *for Wearing a Therapeutic*
Opalight Necklace

WHEN ONE OR MORE OF THE FOLLOWING APPLY—

YOU ARE EXPERIENCING—

Insomnia from an overactive mind

A physical condition that you suspect is being perpetuated by a karmic pattern

YOU WANT TO—

Understand the karmic issues underlying a physical condition

Resolve the karmic issues underlying a physical condition

Experience more restful sleep

Benefits of *Wearing a Therapeutic*
Opalight Necklace

Opalight helps resolve the karma, or past entanglements, that perpetuate physical conditions in the present. Opalight studies your aura, learning all that your aura will reveal to it about your past, present, and future and about how every aspect of your being is affecting your physical body. Opalight then highlights certain areas of your aura to let your highest self know of the current condition of your physical body.

The condition of every cell in your body has been dictated by your past actions, or karma. Consequently, what you do in the present has the power to change your condition in the future. Opalight can bring your awareness to areas of your body with conditions whose causes are most deeply rooted in the past. These conditions are often the most difficult to resolve and usually are the most serious. When you wear Opalight, these areas are revealed as the darkest areas in your aura. Not all the dark areas that Opalight highlights reflect physical ailments. Some reflect mental or emotional conditions that are either affecting the physical body or may do so in the future.

Opalight brings your attention to the areas of greatest need. Attention holds the hand of light, and light holds the hand of love. Therefore, when you place your attention on these deeply rooted conditions, light and love enter the area. Light is the healing force, and love acts like a liquid catalyst for change.

Opalight helps bring you into the present by helping you release past situations that are holding you back. It also highlights the positive qualities and conditions that have grown out of the past. In this way, Opalight can help you feel that things are not as bad as they may seem, and this is comforting and encouraging.

When part of the mind has false concepts about the physical body, it inhibits the body from healing and making other positive changes.

Consequently, the mind's attitudes about a certain condition could impede its resolution. If your mind has false concepts, Opalight will quiet the part of your mind that harbors these concepts and prevent them from affecting your physical body. For example, the Opalight might learn from your aura that you have a hip ailment because of a certain situation in the past. Yet your mind might attribute the ailment to something else altogether. The Opalight will quiet the part of your mind that harbors the incorrect concept and will work on bringing the truth to your awareness. When Opalight quiets part of the mind, vast portions of the mind remain available, giving you the opportunity to start using other, clearer parts of the mind.

Opalight brings light, love, and attention to areas of need. Yet that is where its work stops. If you insist on not seeing what it has illuminated, it cannot convince you to look. Nevertheless, as long as you wear Opalight, it will continue to shine its light and draw attention to those areas.

Resolving Karma During Sleep

When Opalight energy fills your aura, it acts like a filter to diffuse, calm, and soothe any harsh or rough energies contained there. This effect can help you become calmer and can even help you sleep.

Since much resolution of past entanglements is best accomplished in the dream state, this calming effect supports Opalight's work. When the body is asleep, it is much easier to focus light, and thus love, on the darkest areas of the aura. As the days pass, you may start to wake up with an uncanny knowingness that something has been resolved during the night or that it's time to take a particular action. For example, you may realize that you need to see a doctor for a certain condition, or you may wake up knowing that a particular condition is related to a past situation. This knowledge will feel so natural that you may not be consciously aware that something from the past has been resolved or that something new has been learned. This knowledge will simply have become part of you. Therefore, even if you don't wear Opalight during the day, you may wish to wear it at night when you sleep.

"Of all the remedies I have tried, only Opalight allows me to enjoy a completely restful sleep. This experience has shown me that gemstones have profound effects and can produce powerful change in the body."

Dr. Lance Morris
Naturopathic Physician
Tucson, Arizona

Aid for Insomnia

Because of Opalight's ability to help people sleep, it can be an effective aid for insomnia. Be aware, however, that if the insomnia is caused by an external substance such as drugs, caffeine, or certain foods Opalight can do little to assist. Artificial stimulants supersede Opalight's calming and soothing qualities. It can be very helpful, on the other hand, if you cannot sleep because of natural causes. Then, Opalight's calming effect may be just strong enough to allow your own natural sleep abilities to take over.

Opalight's Supporting Role

Whenever you work with Opalight, it is important to work with other kinds of treatments as well, especially if the condition you are treating is serious. Opalight therapy is only a supplementary protocol; it is not sufficient to heal a disease completely. Disharmonious situations invariably have mental, emotional, and physical roots in addition to karmic ones, and these must be addressed. Your physical body also must be supported as it is making its necessary changes. Although Opalight is only a piece of the therapeutic puzzle, it can help resolve certain conditions that have previously resisted other treatments.

Therapeutic-Quality Opalight

Spheres of therapeutic Opalight are variegated in color, combining areas of cream, tan, brown, and sometimes opalescent gray. The most effective Opalight necklace has the greatest variation of color from cream to brown. When Opalight spheres are used singly, independent of a necklace structure, the different colors of Opalight have somewhat different effects. However, when Opalight beads are strung into a necklace, the energies of the individual spheres combine to form the energy that is Opalight, regardless of the quantity of each color in the necklace. As long as the necklace contains an obvious amount of brown, tan, cream or white, and one or two opalescent specimens, the energy of an Opalight necklace is unified.

"Opalight is one of the necklaces that I use quite frequently. It helps me on nights when I have difficulty sleeping and seems to induce a deeper sleep. I have recommended this to a number of different people who have found it helpful for insomnia."

Patrick Weber, M.D.
Pine Ridge, South Dakota

Mineral Composition
SiO_2

Opalight is a form of chalcedony, or cryptocrystalline Quartz, colored by trace amounts of other elements.

Opalight Therapy
Karmic Resolution Technique

Placing an Opalight necklace on an ailing area of the body helps reveal and resolve the karma, or influences from the past, that is contributing to the area's current condition.

Therapy Tools

- One therapeutic necklace of Opalight spheres (8 mm or 10 mm)
- Non-plastic first aid tape
- Small piece of lightweight cotton cloth

Indications

- When you wish to do any of the following—
  - Help resolve the karma involved in an unwanted physical condition
  - Better understand how past influences have shaped a current condition
  - Gain insight into what is needed to resolve an unwanted physical condition
- When a physical condition has been resistant to treatment
- When any part of your body is feeling weighed down or burdened

Effects

Opalight reveals the energetic imprint of a past experience that has contributed to or manifested as a physical condition. This facilitates the resolution of both the physical condition and the associated karma.

Every experience that affects you in some way leaves a vibratory mark, or imprint, on your being. The quality of this mark depends on the nature of your response to the experience. Experiences that evoked the strongest and most negative responses leave their marks at the lowest level of vibration. Experiences that were essentially positive— ones that inspired you or taught you a valuable lesson—naturally uplift you and leave a vibratory mark even higher than the overall vibrations of your body. Neutral experiences leave no mark.

Low vibratory imprints are incompatible with the rest of your body. Their presence can irritate the body so much that a variety of physical symptoms and conditions can manifest. This is why the karma under- lying a negative past experience often manifests as a physical ailment or other condition.

When you place Opalight on an ailing area of your body, the vibrations of the past experiences in the area connect with the vibrations of the Opalight. The Opalight energy then establishes a resonance with these old vibrations. This helps bring the energy of the situation to the surface so that you can address and resolve its associated karma.

When you perform this therapy, you can expect the old experiences corresponding to the treatment area to become re-enlivened in your life. The people associated with the experiences might enter your thoughts or communicate with you; dreams about the experience or issue might become more prominent or vivid; your thoughts might gently and naturally turn to the issue; or you might have strong emotional releases. Any of these experiences will be part of the natural healing process that results from this therapy.

Often the truth about a certain condition is hard to accept consciously. This technique is performed overnight, because during sleep you are especially receptive and open to truth. By wearing Opalight at night, much resolution can occur in sleep.

Procedure

1. Wear a therapeutic Opalight necklace around your neck for several days. This therapy will be effective only if you do this before going on to Step 2.
2. Place a notepad and pencil by your bedside.
3. Get in bed, and prepare to sleep for the night.

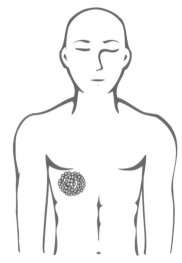

Fig. OPA-1

4. Place the Opalight necklace in a neat pile on the area you wish to treat (see Fig. OPA-1). Place the gemstones directly on your skin, and then place a light cotton cloth over the gems. To secure the gems to your body, tape the cloth to your skin with non-plastic first aid tape. Avoid letting the glue from the tape touch the gems. It is all right if the Opalight falls off onto the bed during the night.

5. Record all your dreams and insights, and interpret them as best you can. Use your own meanings for dream symbols.
   • If you wake up during the night, record your dreams on the notepad.
   • Otherwise, record your dreams in the morning, including any additional ones you may not have recorded during the night.
   • During the day, write down any intuitive insights or unique daydreams you experience.

6. In the morning, remove the Opalight necklace from your body, cleanse it, and wear it around your neck during the day.

Time Guidelines

Repeat this entire procedure for three consecutive nights.

Post-Treatment Cleansing of Gems

Immediately after completing a treatment, it is important to cleanse the gems of any disharmonious energies released by the body in the course of treatment. See Appendix A: "Care and Cleansing of Therapeutic Gems," on page 397, for cleansing instructions.

Opalight's Supporting Role

When performing this therapy, it is important also to work with other treatments, especially if the condition you're treating is serious. Although resolving the karmic entanglements involved in a condition can be a major step toward its resolution, it may not be sufficient to heal a disease completely. Disharmonious situations invariably have mental, emotional, and physical roots in addition to karmic ones, and these must be addressed.

Mental Clarity
and Expansion

Blue Sapphire

Sodalight

Lapis Lazuli

Although the following gems are categorized
elsewhere, they also offer significant healing
benefits for mental issues and conditions.
Therefore, see also:

Aquamarine • Carnelian
Green Tourmaline • Lavender
Pink Tourmaline • Quartz

Blue Sapphire

Healing the Mind

Blue Sapphire heals, nourishes, and brings order to the mind. Its energy permeates the fabric of the mind, clearing out mental "garbage," teaching mental discrimination, and bringing clarity and perspective to thoughts. The blue ray carried by Blue Sapphire disintegrates disharmony in the physical head and profoundly benefits all functions centered there, including the eyesight and hearing. Blue Sapphire expands mental potential and enhances the ability to distinguish between one's mind and one's higher self.

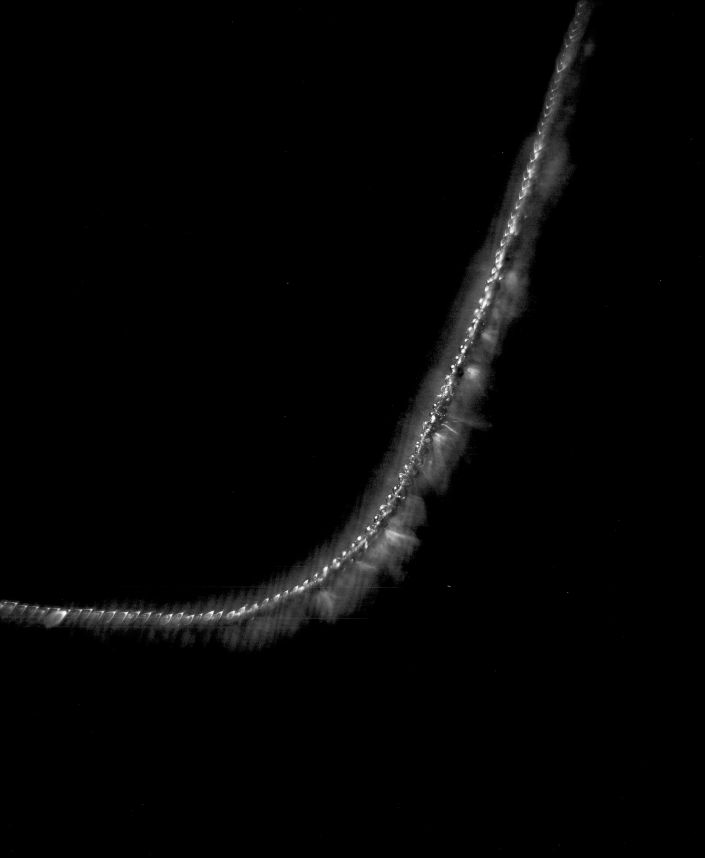

Indications *for Wearing a Therapeutic*
Blue Sapphire Necklace

YOU ARE EXPERIENCING—

Mental fog or confusion

Difficulty focusing your attention

Many negative thoughts or a negative attitude

Distress in the physical head, such as in the eyes, ears, or sinuses

Dysfunction in your vision or hearing

An unwanted condition of the vascular system, nerve sheaths, cerebrospinal fluid, sense organs, or brain

YOU WANT TO—

Experience more mental clarity, flexibility, and orderliness

Expand your mind to its full potential

Improve your memory

Clear out mental clutter

Broaden your perspective

Benefits of *Wearing a Therapeutic* *Blue Sapphire Necklace*

Blue Sapphire is the gemstone bearer of the blue color ray. Its effects are a combination of those of the blue ray and the energy of Sapphire's mineral composition, corundum. Blue Sapphire nourishes the mind and puts thoughts in order and perspective. The blue ray it carries disintegrates disharmony in the physical head, thereby clearing the pathways for healing energies to enliven all the functions centered there.[12]

Blue Sapphire can help you gain self-mastery—that is, mastery of your mind, emotions, and physical body. To understand how Blue Sapphire does this, it's necessary to understand certain aspects of the mind. The mind is complex and comprised of many levels, or areas. Thoughts are formed at the highest level of the mind—that which is closest to your purely spiritual aspect. There, thoughts are generated continually; indeed, a new thought is born every moment. Ultimately, you have the power to discriminate and choose which thoughts you wish to have. This is an important choice, because your thoughts feed and otherwise profoundly affect your emotions and physical body.

Consequently, learning mental discrimination is essential. This discrimination is the ability to choose which thoughts you would like to entertain, empower, and express. It is also the ability to choose which thoughts you would like to ignore and let flow out into the ethers, so that they never manifest or affect anything. Blue Sapphire can teach such mental discrimination.

Blue Sapphire's first step is to bring some orderliness to the mind and thoughts. When your thoughts are in order, your thinking becomes clearer and memory improves. This allows you to give more attention to genuinely important thoughts. The number of useless

---

12 *See page 40 for more information on the vital role of color rays in restoring and maintaining health.*

thoughts we have during the day is astounding. Sapphire promotes useful thoughts and useful thinking. When thoughts are in order, it is also easier to distinguish between true and untrue thoughts, complete and incomplete thoughts, and balanced and imbalanced thoughts—both in oneself and in others.

When your thoughts are in order and you are thinking clearly, your life also falls into order. This is because the state of your mind is always reflected in your emotional and physical bodies. Your thoughts, attitudes, and concepts shape your physical body and all within it. Indeed, one of the mind's functions is to orchestrate the experiences of the emotional and physical bodies. When the mind is more orderly, this orderliness is reflected in these aspects. Conversely, when the minds suffers from any type of dysfunction, inevitably a dysfunction will occur somewhere in the emotional or physical body.

Negative and unconstructive thoughts, attitudes, and prejudices act like garbage in our system. They offer no upliftment, and their impulses contribute to a downward spiral of health. When someone allows mental garbage to flow through his or her mind, this garbage often collects in the head, causing the physical brain and all the head's functions to become malnourished, strained, and stressed. If, for example, the eyesight, hearing, or pituitary gland is malfunctioning in some way, it probably means that mental "garbage" has accumulated in the head.

The blue ray carried by Blue Sapphire is nourishment for the head and mind. It also disintegrates any negativity or disharmony—in other words, garbage—that has accumulated in the head. This is parallel to the way Emerald's green ray disintegrates physical-body disharmony.

We have all heard that thoughts can cure. The key lies in being able to determine which thoughts will act as medicine for a certain condition and which ones will feed the condition with disharmonious energy. It is also important to know which thoughts can cancel out and stop the flow of disharmonious thoughts. Finally, it is essential to know which thoughts will resolve the condition and raise you to the next level of understanding or health. Blue Sapphire can open all

"Shortly after I had a stroke, I started wearing Blue Sapphire at the suggestion of my doctor. I had some loss of sight and shaking on one side of my body. Within a week, all that cleared up. Even my doctor, who understands how this gem works, is surprised and delighted."

S.A.
Washington, D.C.

these levels of understanding—and this can cause fundamental changes, not only in your consciousness and attitudes but also in your health.

Your thoughts and concepts also strongly influence your emotions and emotional expressions, perhaps even more than they do your physical body. For example, if you think a certain situation will make you afraid, you will feel fear; or if it makes sense to your mind that a situation should make you feel loving, you will feel love. Consequently, when Sapphire puts the mind in order, the emotions naturally become more organized, more orderly, and more easily understood. Expressing the emotions you want to express also becomes easier.

The blue ray carried by Sapphire also helps bring your attention to your mind. When you wear a therapeutic Blue Sapphire necklace, the Sapphire energy enters your physical body through your throat chakra. Then it rises and fills your head, nourishing your brain and mind. The more nourishment your mind receives, the more it grows and expands in self-awareness. Interestingly, the more expanded your mind becomes, the more nourishment it requires; even the most brilliant mind must be fed or it will lose its vitality. Blue Sapphire supplies the mind with this essential nourishment.

Blue Sapphire increases mental flexibility. In the process, it loosens concepts and attitudes that are hardened, crusty, and stone-like. Because they are so ingrained, such concepts can keep you stuck in a certain state of consciousness. When these concepts are made more flexible, change of any kind becomes less traumatic and more attainable.

Blue Sapphire as a Spiritual Tool

One of the greatest obstacles to spiritual unfoldment is an inability to distinguish between one's mind and one's true spiritual identity. The mind is so sophisticated that it effectively creates its own center of intelligence. Sapphire can help make you aware that this intelligence—with its glorious ability to expand its consciousness and provide wondrous, life-altering experiences—is not the true Self. Sapphire helps us learn that we are not our minds and that each of us is a pure spiritual being. When the mind becomes more orderly through the use

"The first time I wore Blue Sapphire, it immediately cleared my mind. More options presented themselves in my thinking, as though the Sapphire were helping to expand the foundation of the thought process itself. The lag time between looking for an answer and becoming aware of it seemed shorter."

Warren Gold
Holistic Health Counselor
Bonita, California

of Sapphire, doors will open and opportunities will be presented. If taken, these opportunities will foster even more mental orderliness and lead to experiences of greater spirituality in daily life.

Blue Sapphire and the Vascular System

Each of the seven color rays of the life force is particularly healing and nourishing to certain aspects of the physical body. The blue ray nourishes and supports the vascular system, nerve sheaths, cerebrospinal fluid, sense organs, blood, and brain. Consequently, wearing Blue Sapphire can help strengthen these parts of the body and resolve certain conditions associated with them.

Time Guidelines

How consistently you should wear Blue Sapphire depends in part on your purpose for wearing it. If you are using Blue Sapphire to remove disharmony in your head, to improve your eyesight or hearing, or to resolve imbalances in the brain, it should be worn continually without interruption for at least several months. This is also true when you are using Blue Sapphire to clear mental garbage. The process is comparable to taking out the household garbage—it re-accumulates quickly and, if not removed, starts to overflow.

If you are using Blue Sapphire simply to organize your mental processes, you can wear it for shorter periods without losing ground. The Sapphire will pick up its work and begin organizing your thoughts wherever it last left off.

Amount to Wear

The best way to wear Blue Sapphire is in a short necklace of 3-mm to 4-mm rounded Sapphires with a total necklace weight of 30 to 50 carats. A short necklace is one that lies close to the throat. The blue ray enters the body through the throat chakra, and the Sapphire energy rides on the blue ray. Such a necklace allows both the blue ray and the Sapphire energy to enter your throat chakra easily and to produce strong, immediate effects.

"After one and a half years of wearing Blue Sapphire, I am a different person. It has changed the very way I think. In the past, I set myself up to fail in various ways. Now, as old concepts and attitudes break up, I feel free to discover who I really am and to dream bigger, more fulfilling dreams. I feel less limited in what I can achieve in my life."

Judith Greenwood, L.M.T.
Richardson, Texas

This amount of Blue Sapphire actually provides more energy than is needed by your physical head, and the excess will flow out through your brow chakra. Whenever a color ray flows out through your brow, your attention flows with it. This encourages you to become more aware of things beyond the physical arena. Thus, when your physical sight and hearing become clearer through the use of a 30- to 50-carat Sapphire necklace, so will your inner sight and hearing. Wearing a smaller amount of Sapphire—even one to two carats—will have some beneficial effects, but only if the Sapphire is properly combined in a necklace with other harmonious, supporting gemstones.

Care must be taken not to wear too much Blue Sapphire, thinking that more is better. It is important to avoid wearing more than one solid necklace of Sapphire or a solid necklace that falls significantly below the throat chakra. Wearing rounded Blue Sapphires larger than 5 mm can also be detrimental. Relatively large amounts of Sapphire can sometimes have wonderful influences on the mind, but your body and emotions will resist the overly rapid changes initiated by the Sapphire. This resistance can imbalance and scatter your mind and can cause great mental confusion. Also, the more Blue Sapphire you wear, the more accumulated mental garbage will be stirred up. If more garbage is released into your system than the Sapphire or your body can handle, your body will become stressed and imbalanced in its efforts to metabolize the garbage. Therefore, it is best not to wear too much Blue Sapphire.

Therapeutic-Quality Blue Sapphire

Not all Blue Sapphire is pure enough to emanate the energy required to produce Blue Sapphire's therapeutic effects. Blue Sapphire that is itself filled with flaws, contaminants, and impurities cannot be expected to clear impurities from the mind and head.

Four primary factors determine Blue Sapphire quality: color, clarity, consistency, and a trait called gem *candescence*.

An accurate assessment of Blue Sapphire's color and clarity requires a microscope. Ideal Sapphire is a rich, true blue—neither too pale nor

Mineral Composition
Al_2O_3 + Fe + Ti

Blue Sapphire is a variety of corundum, the hardest material on Earth, after Diamond. When a tiny amount of iron and titanium replaces part of the aluminum in pure corundum, the crystal is tinted blue. Blue Sapphire is found in Burma, Sri Lanka, Thailand, Kampuchea, India, Australia, Montana, and Africa.

too indigo. Only a microscope, which allows you to see how light passes through the gemstone, can reveal Blue Sapphire's true color. A microscope also lets you see whether the gem contains even the slightest black tinge. This is essential, because any black coloration is a severe contaminant that nullifies all of Blue Sapphire's effects. Even a wisp of black renders Blue Sapphire non-therapeutic.

The greater its clarity, the more energy a Blue Sapphire can radiate. Common inclusions found in Blue Sapphire are impurities, such as rock matrix, white clouds, and a toxic yellow discoloration that renders the Sapphire non-therapeutic.

Consistency is also an important element in a therapeutic Blue Sapphire necklace. Inconsistency in the color, clarity, or size of spheres within a necklace creates a distraction, which the Blue Sapphire energy must first overcome before it can do its work. This is one reason why most Blue Sapphire necklaces are not therapeutic or are much less therapeutic than their other quality parameters might indicate.

Gem candescence is an optical quality possessed by some Blue Sapphire. A bead displaying gem candescence looks like a drop of liquid Blue Sapphire. In the Sapphire in which it is found, gem candescence is an intense outpouring of the blue ray, making the Sapphire look like its own source of pure blue light. Its liquid appearance is an energetic quality that allows the Sapphire energy to access the mind instantly. All other factors being equal, gem-candescent Blue Sapphire is many times more powerful than Blue Sapphire without gem candescence.

Blue Sapphire Therapy
Eye Treatment

A Blue Sapphire necklace is placed over the eyes to soothe eyestrain and to improve vision.

Therapy Tools
One therapeutic necklace of Blue Sapphire rondels

Indications
- When you wish to relieve strain or fatigue in your eyes
- When you wish to improve your vision

Effects
When mental "garbage" collects in the head, all the functions centered there become malnourished, strained, and stressed. This includes eye function. The blue ray carried by Blue Sapphire disintegrates this mental garbage and disharmony while nourishing all parts of the head and enlivening their functioning.

In this therapy, you place Blue Sapphire on your eyes, where it helps loosen and neutralize mental garbage and any other disharmonious vibrations that are burdening and straining them. As a result, this therapy soothes tired and strained eyes and helps improve vision.

Procedure
1. Lie down on your back. Ideally, position yourself so that your eyes are exposed to sunlight, even if it is just the sunlight coming through an open window on a sunny or cloudy day. Sunlight enhances the penetration of Blue Sapphire and blue ray energy into your body.

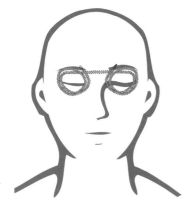

Fig. BSP-1

2. Close your eyes.

3. Place the center of the Blue Sapphire necklace over the bridge of your nose and arrange the two ends into spirals over each eye. Lay the two parts of the metal clasp on your cheeks or above your eyebrows. Avoid placing the metal directly on your eyes (see Fig. BSP-1).

Caution

Do not shine artificial light directly on Blue Sapphire. If sunlight is unavailable, this therapy can be performed in ambient artificial light.

Time Guidelines

When performing this treatment in direct sunlight, keep the necklace in place for 15 minutes. When performing it without sunlight, keep the necklace in place for at least 60 minutes. This therapy can be performed daily.

Post-Treatment Cleansing of Gems

Immediately after completing a treatment, it is important to cleanse the gems of any disharmonious energies released by the body in the course of treatment. See Appendix A: "Care and Cleansing of Therapeutic Gems," on page 397, for cleansing instructions.

Sodalight

Purifying the Aura

Sodalight purifies your aura, making it a cleaner, more harmonious atmosphere in which to live. To do this, Sodalight absorbs and neutralizes the clouds of mental disharmony that pollute the aura, bog down the mind, and make you feel burdened. Sodalight also clears your physical body of the negative mental energies that disrupt the body's functioning and perpetuate disease. Purifying your body and aura with Sodalight restores your physical vitality and helps reveal your true nature, strengths, and life's purpose.

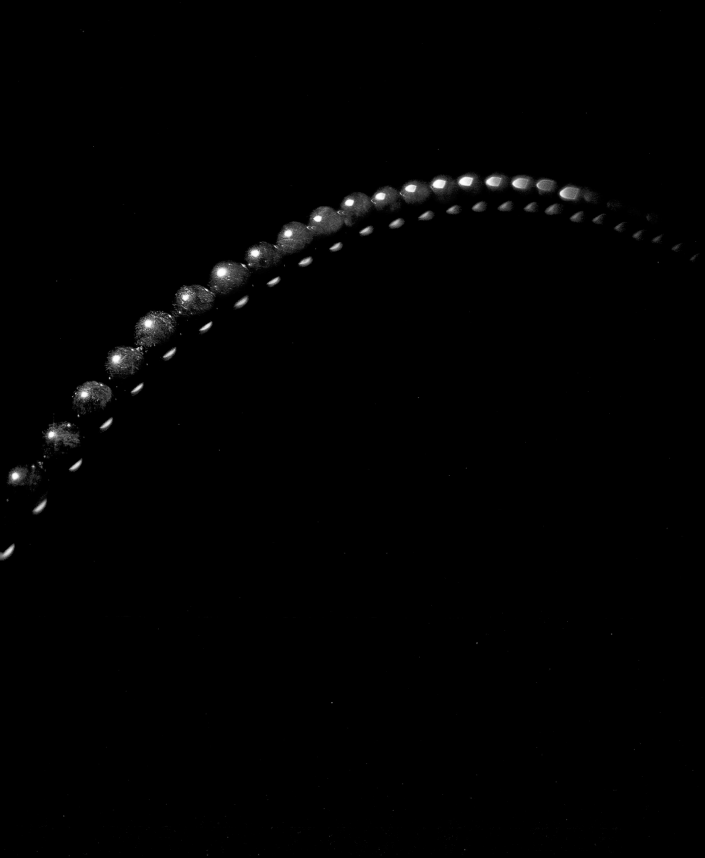

Indications *for Wearing a Therapeutic*
Sodalight Necklace

YOU ARE EXPERIENCING—

Mental cloudiness or fogginess

Feeling bogged down, burdened, or overwhelmed

General sluggishness or depression

Extreme emotional sensitivity or a tendency to overreact

Persistent painful memories interfering with your day-to-day functioning

Insomnia

Attention deficit disorder

Difficulty defining your own goals

Difficulty distinguishing between your own thoughts, feelings, and desires and those of others

Any unwanted condition of the skeletal system, including the bones, ligaments, joints, or cartilage

YOU WANT TO—

Experience greater mental clarity

Develop more positive mental habits

Strengthen your bond with a pet

Protect yourself from the negative thoughts or emotions of others

Benefits of *Wearing a Therapeutic*
Sodalight Necklace

Sodalight purifies your aura, making it a cleaner, more harmonious atmosphere in which to live. Just as planetary health requires a clean atmosphere, your personal health requires that your aura be as clear as possible of disharmonious energies. An aura clouded with negative and disharmonious energies burdens you, while a clean aura supports balance and harmony within you. Sodalight also frees your physical body of the negative mental energies that impede the body's functioning and interfere with the expression of its true energetic nature.

Negative thoughts, attitudes, and concepts emanated by the mind collect in the aura as clouds of disharmony. Wearing a necklace of Sodalight spheres removes these clouds. It also removes the other non-life-giving energies that tend to accumulate in the aura, polluting it and bogging down your mind, emotions, and body. Sodalight absorbs and neutralizes these undesirable energies. Like the sun shining on the Earth after clouds have dissipated, the light of the life force can then shine more brightly through your inner aspects to your physical body.

When these mental clouds have dissipated, you will feel as though you have been relieved of a great weight. You will also begin to see your mental habits more clearly. With this new clarity, you may come to recognize the burdensome effects of negative thinking. If you have many negative thoughts in a day, hopefully you will commit yourself to developing new, more positive mental habits. Sodalight does not remove the cause of the negativity; it simply removes the clouds. If you do not change your negative mental habits, and you stop wearing Sodalight, eventually your aura will become as polluted as it was before you wore the Sodalight.

Wearing a necklace of therapeutic Sodalight also gradually clears your physical body of the excess mental energies that have infiltrated it.

These energies disrupt metabolic functions and perpetuate physical ailments of all kinds. Sodalight lifts the mental weight from your body, helping to restore its vitality and reclaim its true nature.

To accomplish this, Sodalight strengthens the energy flows throughout your body. It spurs your body's energies into motion, enhancing their movement through all your energy meridians. If the meridians' flows are blocked or congested, Sodalight clears them and prompts them to move; if they are over-stimulated, it helps them calm down. Sodalight works with all your energy flows at once, strengthening them and urging them to find balance with each other. Like a swiftly moving river pushing away debris, these stronger flows enable your body to easily slough off unwanted energies.

Your emotions are even more susceptible to excess mental clutter than your physical body. People whose emotions are clouded with excessive mental clutter may have super-sensitive emotions or respond to events with unexpected outbursts. They may react to life emotionally, express strong emotions, or lose control of their emotions. Wearing a Sodalight necklace will gradually clear the emotions of excess mental clutter, allowing them to become more balanced. People who continually feel overwhelmed or burdened, often for no clearly defined reason, will benefit greatly from wearing Sodalight.

When unnecessary mental energies clutter your memory, its "filing" mechanism gets disturbed, and painful memories cannot be properly stored or retrieved. Instead of retreating to the background, as they should, these improperly stored memories impinge on the person's awareness. As the Sodalight purifies your aura, obstructions to your memory are gradually removed, and painful recollections are able to find their proper places.

Mental clutter inhibits the mind's ability to focus and give undivided attention to tasks; it also makes it easy for the mind to fall into ruts. Sodalight energy cancels out and obliterates mental clutter.

When your aura is cleaner, you can see yourself more clearly—your true nature, your strengths and shortcomings, and the direction in which your life is headed. You more easily recognize your true thoughts, feelings, and goals. Therefore, Sodalight is especially beneficial for people who have difficulty distinguishing between their own thoughts, emotions, and goals, and those projected onto them by others. When you see yourself more clearly, you can choose to enhance your positive attributes, work on your shortcomings, and more clearly define your life's direction.

Attention Deficit and Related Disorders

Mental clutter can make us easily distracted and cause difficulty in focusing. Thus, children with attention deficit disorder that has been caused or exacerbated by mental clutter may benefit from wearing Sodalight.

Because of the mind's special relationship to the brain, the mind tends to deposit a great deal of mental metabolic waste, or "garbage," there. In children, a variety of things can cause mental waste to accumulate in the brain—for example, too much visual stimulation from excessive television viewing, or the discomfort caused by parental bickering.

To learn subjects such as reading and math, the mind requires a proper connection to the body. Mental clutter can interfere with this connection. When a child's brain is cluttered with too much mental "metabolic" waste, and the mind-body connection is impaired, many problems can result. These problems can include difficulty focusing the attention, poor memory, ear infections, and vision problems. The child may also develop dyslexia, a reading disability in which the brain has difficulty translating written images into meaningful language.

You can use a necklace of therapeutic Sodalight to help clear a child's mental clutter and help unravel an inappropriate blending of the mind and body. This can be beneficial in certain cases of attention deficit disorders.

Cleansing Your Home Atmosphere

The energies of a family's thoughts, both positive and negative, are collected and contained within the walls of the family home. As students of the Chinese art of feng shui are aware, energy currents in a home can have a significant impact on the quality of its inhabitants' lives.

"Although I was a successful physician and mother, I was always fighting to prove I could do anything. I was always responding to others' challenges rather than going after what I wanted. In fact, I didn't know what I wanted, and I felt crushed by the burden of other people's expectations. Now those things are no longer an issue. Sodalight helped me get clear about what I want and to redirect my stubbornness to follow my own heart."

Dr. Cari Nyland
Naturopathic Physician
Corbett, Oregon

Sodalight can benefit the atmosphere of any home by clearing its accumulated thought energies. Rounded Sodalight easily absorbs the imbalanced, disharmonious thoughts that collect there and works at improving the home's atmospheric balance.

The atmosphere of every home is unique. To help Sodalight learn the nature of your thought energies, wear it around your neck for at least a few days. Then remove the Sodalight from your aura and place it on the mantle or in some other place where it is exposed to your home's atmosphere. Sodalight does not need to touch the soil to affect a home environment.

Helping the Earth's Atmosphere

When you wear Sodalight in spherical form, many negative energies are absorbed from your aura that otherwise would have been released into the Earth's atmosphere. Therefore, the more that people wear Sodalight, the less mental pollution the Earth will be forced to assimilate and the healthier our planet's atmosphere will be.

Sodalight's Protection

Sodalight can protect you from the negative thoughts, emotions, or other energies directed at you by others. This includes unwelcome prayer. When worn, Sodalight can soak up these energies as they enter your aura.

Enhancing Human-Animal Relationships

Sodalight has a special affinity with animals. Hence, you can use Sodalight to improve your connection with the animals you love and to enhance your ability to communicate with them. Sodalight can build a bridge of awareness between your two souls. When you and the animal wear Sodalight together, the love bonds between you will become more solid, real, and tangible. Your telepathic connection will also grow. Your sense of togetherness and oneness for a common purpose will deepen, even if that purpose is nothing more than enjoying life and the outdoors together.

To experience these benefits, simply wear a Sodalight necklace and place a collar of Sodalight around the animal's neck. For a horse, you can secure a necklace of Sodalight to its halter or bridle. Keep the Sodalight on both you and the animal at the same time. If you remove your Sodalight, keeping it on the animal will be of no value.

To be most effective, a human/animal work team must perform together on many levels—physical, emotional, mental, and intuitive. If you are part of a human/animal work team—such as in the mounted police or in an army canine unit—you can use Sodalight to help develop your team in both spirit and practice. Wearing Sodalight when you first form your team will create strong inner links between you. You can wear the Sodalight while you are working together and occasionally overnight. When your team has fully formed, it is best to wear the Sodalight together only occasionally. This will allow you to spend time growing as individuals, which is also important in maintaining a healthy team.

Making Sodalight Yours

Because the energetic charge of each person's thoughts is unique, Sodalight works with each person in a unique way. To be most effective for you, Sodalight gets to know your unique charge and your overall vibratory picture. Consequently, a Sodalight necklace works best if only one person wears it.

Sodalight and Blue Sapphire

Wearing a Blue Sapphire necklace along with a Sodalight necklace will help clear mental clutter and reestablish a healthy mental-physical connection. The Sodalight will clear the physical body of mental clutter and help untangle any inappropriate blending of the mind and body. The Blue Sapphire will help the mind make the proper connections to the body. Blue Sapphire also clears mental clutter. However, unlike Sodalight, Sapphire directly addresses the causes of mental disharmony, which are found in the mind itself. Sodalight works mostly on the physical body and the aura.

"I gave a Sodalight necklace to a patient whose major complaint was that she had no energy to get things done. Before wearing it, this patient couldn't get out of her own way. She talked too much. She thought too much. She used all her energy for other people. After wearing the Sodalight, she began to allow changes to happen. She stopped accumulating everyone else's 'stuff' and started to focus on her own work and her own healing. She found a job with better hours and better pay. She felt better about her relationships, which in the long run allowed her to be more helpful to her friends and family. The Sodalight was enormously helpful to her."

*Dr. Evan Fleischmann
Naturopathic Physician
Chestnut Ridge, New York*

Sodalight and Metal

Sodalight strengthens all the energy flows in your body. Wearing base metals, such as those often used in jewelry, can cut off or inhibit these flows. Therefore, when wearing Sodalight and jewelry at the same time, some people may experience pain in their fingers and wrists. If this happens, simply remove your rings, bracelets, and wristwatches while you are wearing Sodalight. Some people may also need to remove their eyeglasses to allow the body's energy flows to move more freely about the face. Although gold, silver, and copper are less apt to have this effect, it is good to be aware of any possible conflicts.

Time and Other Guidelines

Sodalight produces its greatest effects when it touches the atmosphere while it is being worn. Therefore, it is best worn over, rather than under, clothing. Its strength and effectiveness also increase steadily the longer it is worn. Therefore, if Sodalight is worn constantly—for example, for five weeks—its work will be much stronger than if it were worn for only five days.

If you cannot wear Sodalight during the day, you can sleep with your necklace at night. You can either wear it around your neck or keep it in the bed with you. Be aware that Sodalight cannot absorb disharmonious energies when it is covered by leather or any man-made material, including plastic. Therefore, placing Sodalight under your pillow will work only if your pillow is made entirely of cotton, down, or some other natural material. If placed under a pillowcase made of polyester or some other synthetic fabric, the Sodalight will not be effective.

Storing Sodalight

To minimize the tendency for Sodalight to turn white over time, it should be stored in a special container. The ideal container is a wooden box, lined on the bottom with fresh or dried moss over a one-inch layer of garden soil. If you must store or transport Sodalight in a plastic bag, fill the bag with a copious amount of dried sphagnum moss, which can be purchased inexpensively at a garden-supply store. The moss will absorb the gas given off by the plastic so that the Sodalight doesn't have to. It will also help the Sodalight maintain its Earth-energy connection, which will keep the Sodalight working at full capacity even if whitening does occur.

Therapeutic-Quality Sodalight

Therapeutic-quality Sodalight spheres are a deep, rich blue, with relatively consistent color throughout the entire sphere. When the highest-quality Sodalight is first fashioned into spheres, it has only a faint suggestion of white streaks or clouds. If more than 10 percent of the sphere's surface is white, its therapeutic effectiveness is diminished.

Therapeutic Sodalight may also have tiny—sometimes microscopic—pinpoints of various other colors, such as black, gold, orange, and silver. Sodalight's nature is to purify the human aura and body by absorbing energies that do not fit its wearer's overall vibratory picture. A moderate amount of these additional colors, or elements, allows the Sodalight to respond to a wider spectrum of these energies. However, if these colors cover more than five percent of the sphere's surface, the sphere will lack the ideal proportion of essential and nonessential Sodalight components, rendering it non-therapeutic.

Exquisite-quality Sodalight may display its crystalline nature as reflective facets of dark blue or black. If the Sodalight is somewhat translucent, the facets may appear to be contained inside the sphere. Therapeutic Sodalight should not be so transparent or gem-like as to encroach on the properties of Indigo.

Sodalight is yet another gemstone that is commonly dyed. Dye hides any white streaks or clouds and prevents the Sodalight from expressing its healing energy. It also clogs the stone's pores and thus inhibits its ability to absorb disharmony. Consequently, Sodalight that contains any dye is non-therapeutic.

Mineral Composition
$Na_4Al_3(SiO_4)_3Cl$

Sodalight, or sodium aluminum silicate chloride, is crystallized in magmas in the Ural Mountains of Russia, Mt. Vesuvius in Italy, Norway, Germany, Brazil, South Africa, Bolivia, Canada, Maine, and Montana.

Sodalight Therapy
Emotional Pain Resolution

This technique uses Sodalight to clear mental clutter and confusion from a heart that is experiencing emotional pain. Relieved of its mental burden, the heart experiences greater peace, and its healing is accelerated.

Therapy Tools
One therapeutic necklace of Sodalight spheres (8 mm or 10 mm)

Indications
When you have emotional pain centered in your heart chakra and are experiencing any of the following—
- You have been obsessing about an emotionally painful situation
- You have been trying to heal or resolve a particular emotional issue for a long time without making much progress
- You want to understand the true reasons for your emotional pain

Effects
A heart can feel emotional pain for any number of reasons, but the mind often compounds the pain by burdening the heart with its attitudes, concepts, expectations, needs, and sense of what is fair. If an aching heart could free itself of the mind's influence, it would feel only a fraction of the pain, and the true cause of the pain would become easier to pinpoint and understand.

This Sodalight technique clears the mental clutter that burdens the heart and exacerbates emotional pain. It clarifies the causes of emotional pain and thus helps bring greater peace to the heart. By fostering greater clarity in the heart, this technique accelerates the heart's healing.

Procedure

1. To bring forward the pain in your heart, think about the circumstances and individuals involved with it. Open up to the pain so that you feel it strongly. Face it as fully as possible. This may take some courage.

2. Hold a Sodalight necklace in a pile in your hand, and place your hand over your heart chakra, so that the Sodalight touches your body, ideally on your skin (see Fig. SOD-1). Center the gemstones on the pain.

   If it helps, gently press the Sodalight into your body, or use it to massage the painful area by moving the Sodalight in a small circular motion.

3. As you tune in to the pain, pay attention to how the feeling changes. Allow any new understanding to enter your awareness. Notice how you become more at peace with the pain.

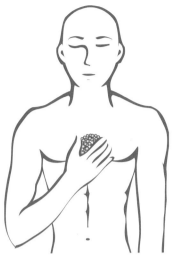

Fig. SOD-1

Time Guidelines

The clearing of mental clutter associated with emotional pain can sometimes happen very quickly. If you are truly ready to change, let go of the pain, and acknowledge and resolve the related issues, this clearing can happen rapidly. Clarity, relief, and a huge step in healing can occur within a few minutes. In this case, only one treatment may be enough. However, for issues that are deeply rooted or that are associated with complex mental influences, you may need to perform this therapy daily for a while.

For acute pain, such as that experienced during grieving, perform this therapy for 5 to 10 minutes several times a day until the pain subsides.

Post-Treatment Cleansing of Gems

Immediately after completing a treatment, it is important to cleanse the gems of any disharmonious energies released by the body in the course of treatment. See Appendix A: "Care and Cleansing of Therapeutic Gems," on page 397, for cleansing instructions.

Lapis Lazuli

Harmonizing Heart and Mind

Lapis Lazuli harmonizes your heart and mind as it forges stronger bonds between them. When your mind is attuned to your emotions, it is enriched and made more fruitful; when your emotions are illuminated by your mind, they become more clearly understood. With heart and mind working in harmony, mastery of any area of life becomes more attainable. Lapis Lazuli empowers you to envision and then live your dreams with vitality and a fearless, adventuresome spirit. Its royal blue color stirs memories of the infinite source of life within.

Indications *for Wearing a Therapeutic*
Lapis Lazuli Necklace

YOU ARE EXPERIENCING—

Conflict between the dictates of your heart and mind

Lack of self-confidence

Difficulty envisioning your dreams or putting them into action

Sluggish energy

Imbalanced energy flows

YOU WANT TO—

Harmonize your thoughts and feelings

Heighten your mental awareness

Better understand your emotions

Bring an emotional perspective to creative or analytical projects

Balance and vitalize the flow of energy throughout your body

Feel more empowered and cultivate a more fearless, adventuresome spirit

Achieve greater mastery of a specific area in your personal or professional life

Benefits of *Wearing a Therapeutic Lapis Lazuli Necklace*

Lapis Lazuli harmonizes your heart and mind as it forges stronger bonds between them. The energy radiated by Lapis can help you experience the energy and power you possess within. This power is greatest when the energies of your mind and heart come together—in other words, when your emotional and mental bodies are working in harmony. Lapis improves the connection, communication, and understanding between your heart and mind. When the mind is attuned to your emotions, it becomes richer, more fruitful, and bountiful. When feelings are illuminated by the mind, emotions are better understood. A strong connection between the heart and mind opens many possibilities. It expands your horizons and your potential.

When you wear Lapis Lazuli around your neck, it gradually and systematically identifies all the significant power points in your body. These points include your acupuncture points, chakras, and, to a lesser extent, your energy meridians. The Lapis then helps these points achieve equilibrium—points with excess magnetic energy are drained, and deficient points are filled with Lapis energy until they can regain their own strength. This promotes healing of the physical body and its energy flows at a fundamental level.

The energy of Lapis' royal blue color can affect people deeply. This is because its color touches the optic nerve in an unusual way. Your optic nerve picks up impressions of what you see with your physical eyes as well as what you see in your dreams and inner visions. All these impressions stimulate the optic nerve. The energy of Lapis and its royal blue color impresses the optic nerve in a way that reminds your brain of a primordial memory—the memory of that which links you to your divine source.

For this reason, people are comforted and inspired by Lapis' royal blue color. These feelings are often felt within moments of connecting

"All my life, I've been described as being very analytical, very passionate, and not very balanced. Wearing Lapis immediately calmed my thinking, and I became more stable emotionally. I was able to focus on the differences between my mind and heart and to appreciate their differences without either of them pushing for control."

M.R.
Holborn, Great Britain

Mineral Composition
$Na_3Ca(Si_3Al_3)O_{12}S$

The gem variety of lazurite, Lapis Lazuli is a sodium and aluminum mineral of great complexity. Lapis Lazuli occurs in only a few major deposits around the world, including in Lake Baikal in Siberia, Ovalle in Chile, and the Kokcha Valley of northern Afghanistan.

with Lapis' energy. When you feel comfortable, you feel freer—and with freedom comes confidence. This confidence gives you courage and the fearless, adventurous spirit needed to realize your dreams and to master life.

It takes practice to become a master, yet the potential to do so is available to everyone. Lapis Lazuli can help you attain mastery, perhaps more so than any other gemstone. This might be mastery of bread baking, piano playing, or of spirit itself. To become a master, first you must see your goal and then you must feel that you have attained it. Lapis can help you have these feelings. Lapis can help you see your goals and dreams and give you the courage to attain them. If you continue to wear Lapis, it will also help you to realize these dreams.

Necklace Length

When worn as a necklace, Lapis produces its greatest effects when the necklace falls directly over the heart or as close to the heart as possible.

Lapis Lazuli Tisrati

Placing Lapis Lazuli around the head in a tisrati can result in profoundly heightened mental awareness. To form a tisrati, encircle your head with the necklace so that it lies across your brow chakra and just above your ears. Fasten the necklace at the back of your head with a natural-fiber tie, allowing the excess to fall straight down toward your spine.

Therapeutic-Quality Lapis Lazuli

Lapis Lazuli's therapeutic effectiveness depends on the character of its color and the amount of pyrite it contains. The richer and deeper its royal blue color and the less white it contains, the more powerful the Lapis is. Therapeutic Lapis contains a substantial amount of golden pyrite flecks but not to the point of overpowering the blue areas.

Lapis occurs in a wide continuum of quality, and the very finest quality is quite rare. Lower-quality Lapis is usually dyed to enhance its color and make it seem higher in quality. Unfortunately, any dye applied to Lapis Lazuli clogs its pores and renders it non-therapeutic.

Lapis Lazuli Therapy
Inquiry Technique

Lapis Lazuli is placed over the brow chakra to produce a heightened state of awareness, in which answers to important questions can be learned.

Therapy Tool
One therapeutic necklace of Lapis Lazuli spheres (8 mm or 10 mm)

Indications
- When you seek guidance regarding a difficult decision or life circumstance
- When you have a question, and a heightened state of awareness would increase your ability to discover the answer

Effects
When Lapis Lazuli energy enters your head through your brow chakra, a profoundly expanded state of awareness results. This heightened state can offer you the wisdom and knowledge that can serve as the source of answers to many questions.

Procedure
1. Wear a therapeutic Lapis Lazuli necklace around your neck for at least one hour.
2. Formulate the question you wish to ask. Make it clear and focused.
3. Remove the Lapis Lazuli necklace from around your neck.
4. Place the necklace in your palm. Find a section of four to six spheres to which you feel especially drawn. Make sure that at least a few of these spheres contain some gold flecks.
5. While continuing to hold the rest of the necklace in your palm, grasp the section of four to six spheres between the fingertips of your thumb, index finger, and middle finger (see Fig. LAP-1)

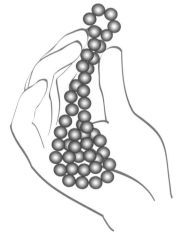

Fig. LAP-1

Fig. LAP-2

6. Gently press these Lapis spheres to your brow chakra (see Fig. LAP-2).

7. Close your eyes, and take a minute or so to settle your mind.

8. Now imagine the Lapis spheres' energy flowing through your brow into your head. Feel your head filling with this energy.

9. When the Lapis energy reaches the back of your skull, allow the question to enter your thoughts. (It may take up to five minutes for the Lapis energy to reach the back of your skull.)

10. Place your attention inside the Lapis spheres resting on your brow chakra. Keep your attention there.

   If you are patient and open, your answer will come. It may appear in any number of ways: a scene may unfold in your mind's eye, an insight may come to you in a flash, you may hear the answer, or you may simply know it.

Time Guidelines

Practice this technique for at least 5 minutes and up to 15 minutes.

Post-Treatment Cleansing of Gems

Immediately after completing a treatment, it is important to cleanse the gems of any disharmonious energies released by the body in the course of treatment. See Appendix A: "Care and Cleansing of Therapeutic Gems," on page 397, for cleansing instructions.

Higher Consciousness and Spiritual Awakening

Aquamarine

Lavender

Indigo

Amethyst

Purple Rainbow Fluorite

Citrine

Aquamarine

Illumination

Aquamarine opens your awareness to the inner ocean of knowledge, wisdom, and creativity. It brings deep relaxation and liquidity to your mind and body while heightening your awareness of truth at every level of existence. Aquamarine illuminates the hidden causes of your life situations so that you may better master their lessons. Its youthful essence renews your spirit and nourishes you from a wellspring of spiritual energy.

Indications *for Wearing a Therapeutic* *Aquamarine Necklace*

WHEN ONE OR MORE OF THE FOLLOWING APPLY—

YOU ARE EXPERIENCING—

Difficulty understanding yourself

Inability to deeply relax

Intense emotional or physical pain

Grief

Physical rigidity or inflexibility

Crystalline deposits, such as those that occur in the joints

Edema, sluggish circulation, or water retention

YOU WANT TO—

Heighten your awareness on all levels

Enhance your creativity

Promote fluidity in your mind, body, and emotions

Gain insight into your own nature

Transcend a spiritual plateau

Deeply relax your mind so it will be more open to truth

Understand the underlying causes of an illness

For pregnant women:	When you want to connect more deeply with your unborn child
For terminal patients:	When you want to ease the transition to the end of life

Benefits of *Wearing a Therapeutic*
Aquamarine Necklace

Aquamarine opens your consciousness to your inner ocean of knowledge, wisdom, and creativity. Its energy illuminates the hidden causes of physical, emotional, and mental conditions so that you may better master their lessons. Aquamarine's light blue color deeply relaxes the body and mind and helps you let go of any resistance to the truth within. As a source of spiritual nourishment, it imparts youthful energy and brightens your aura, as it brings energetic liquidity to all aspects of your being.

Aquamarine developed on Earth, not just as a product of the planet's evolution but as the result of a grand evolution constantly occurring on all levels of life. Pure Spirit is the fountainhead of the life force. It is also the source of another stream of energy that flows through the inner dimensions to the physical plane. This stream is often referred to as the Healing Waters, the Nectar of the Gods, or the Fountain of Youth. As it flows through the inner planes, it changes color and consistency. When it reaches the physical plane, it manifests as the gemstone Aquamarine.

Because Aquamarine exists on every level of reality, it is able to heighten your awareness of truth on all these levels: physical, emotional, mental, and spiritual. It also opens your awareness to the ways in which the realities or truths on these levels can sometimes seem to conflict with one another.

Simply having Aquamarine in your aura will begin to open your awareness on all levels. To understand how Aquamarine does this, you can compare yourself to a mansion with several floors. The floors of the mansion are like your inner levels. Aquamarine works to open more and more doors within this mansion and turn on the lights within its rooms. In this way, Aquamarine increases your awareness of your own inner dimensions. When you wear a necklace of therapeutic Aquamarine, you become more aware of things hiding in the recesses of your emotions, memory, and mind and thus gain insight into who you are and what your true potential is.

As your awareness grows and you gain a greater understanding of yourself, several things will start to happen. Opportunities on all levels of life will present themselves. You will also begin to understand life better, and this will allow you to work in greater harmony with your true self and with all of life.

Aquamarine works in stages: it will show you only enough about yourself to stimulate your growth to the next level of awareness. At each new level, you will be shown a little more. Aquamarine will continue this cycle for as long as you wear it. The amount of truth Aquamarine can reveal at each stage is limited only by the depth and brilliance of its blue color. Therefore, the deeper and brighter the Aquamarine's natural color, the more it can give.

Accepting Truth

Because Aquamarine opens the awareness so powerfully, some people feel uncomfortable when they first wear it. If you are not quite ready to accept a certain truth about yourself, you may resist what the Aquamarine has helped to reveal, and you may become uncomfortable or cranky. If this happens, you can regulate the Aquamarine's intensity of work by adjusting how often you wear it. After wearing Aquamarine for some time, you will become more comfortable with your increased awareness, and resistance will ease.

How Aquamarine Works in the Body

When you first wear Aquamarine, its energy focuses on your physical body and quickly brings energetic liquidity to the healthiest areas of your physical form. When an area becomes energetically liquid, it is more fluid, adaptable, and open to the free flow of life energy. Gradually, this liquidity spreads to less healthy areas, starting with those of higher vibration and continuing, though more slowly, into

"I have always been a creative person, yet wearing therapeutic Aquamarine has enhanced my ability to see solutions, create new alternatives for myself, and to use my creative imagination at a new and greatly heightened level. I no longer dread certain aspects of creative tasks and have broken life-long limiting patterns. I experience much greater success from my creative endeavors and feel a greater impulse to create."

C.J.
Boston, Massachusetts

areas of increasingly lower vibrations. When your body has achieved a certain degree of liquidity, the Aquamarine will begin to work on your body's energy currents, one at a time. Usually, it works on the energy current that is most directly involved with the area being highlighted by the Aquamarine. The Aquamarine's focus remains on your physical body, sometimes for weeks or months, before expanding to your emotional and causal aspects.

How Aquamarine Works with Emotions

In your emotional body, Aquamarine works on the concentrations of emotional energy that are eventually passed through the chakras to the physical body to be expressed and felt as emotions. Sometimes, for a variety of reasons, you may not wish to feel or express a particular emotion. When this happens, the energy of the emotion can build and concentrate in your emotional body until you can no longer hold it in. Then the emotion bursts through for expression, often in uncomfortable or inappropriate ways. Aquamarine improves the relationship between your physical and emotional bodies and softens any concentrations of pent-up emotional energy. This allows you to express all your emotions more smoothly and comfortably. Thus, Aquamarine is particularly helpful for people who often experience strong or uncontrollable outbursts.

How Aquamarine Works with the Mind

Your mind, which profoundly influences every aspect of your health, has energetic ties to every part of your being, including your physical body. These energetic ties resemble threads of light. As the stresses of living accumulate, these threads can become darkened with disharmonious energy, causing the threads to tighten their grip in an unhealthy way. When Aquamarine starts working on your physical cells, its light and liquidity touch these threads and begin to infiltrate your mind. This is especially true of Aquamarine in which the color blue dominates. Blue Aquamarine has an affinity with the aspect of your mind that is present in every physical cell, every wave of emotion, and every

"Therapeutic Aquamarine has been an invaluable tool in my practice as a physician and in my personal life. I've found that wearing an Aquamarine necklace heightens my awareness and helps me diagnose my patients' complaints more accurately."

*Patrick Weber, M.D.
Pine Ridge, South Dakota*

memory stored in your causal body. Aquamarine restores light to these energetic threads and relaxes their grip. This allows your physical, emotional, and causal bodies to exercise their own intelligence more fully and to better focus on restoring and maintaining your health.

Aquamarine as a Spiritual Tool

Aquamarine is most beneficial to those who are on a path of spiritual awakening. It helps those who want to know more about themselves, their destiny, and their potential. It is especially helpful for those who have reached apparent plateaus in their spiritual unfoldment, for it can help awaken them to new vistas and help them grow to ever-higher levels.

Soothing Grief and Trauma

Aquamarine can ease any overwhelming physical, mental, or emotional pain, especially the pain of grief. This is, in part, a result of Aquamarine's brightening of the aura. Because you view the world through your aura, when it is made brighter, your outlook is brightened as well. Aquamarine's liquidity effect can also loosen the bonds of traumatic and painful memories. This effect will probably occur only after you have worn Aquamarine for several months.

Prenatal Awareness Technique

A pregnant woman may place Aquamarine over the uppermost portion of her uterus to help her become more aware of and possibly even come into conscious contact with her soon-to-be-born child. If she sleeps with the Aquamarine over her uterus, she may even dream of previous lifetimes they have shared.

Easing the Transition to Life's End

It is Aquamarine's mission to help people evolve and unfold. In the physical world, this sometimes means helping someone complete certain cycles within a physical body. This does not mean that Aquamarine hastens physical death. Yet, when death comes near, Aquamarine can lighten the load, shine the way, and make the experience calmer and

"My first experience wearing Aquamarine was incredible. Within a day, I determined that its energy was worthy of great respect. In the first several hours, I experienced a deep relaxation and fluidity within my body. Later that evening, while chatting with a dear friend, our conversation turned to deep truths, and my whole body felt as if it held a great energy. Tears of beauty, truth, and elation welled up in my eyes. I was and continue to be astounded!"

K.D.
Portland, Oregon

less fearful. Therefore, one of the greatest gifts you can give to a dying person is an Aquamarine necklace. It will help ease the transition.

Aquamarine Rounded Chips vs. Spheres

The most effective and economical way to use therapeutic Aquamarine is in the form of rounded chips rather than spheres. Quality and mass being equal, Aquamarine rounded chips and spheres radiate energies of equal intensity, but chips project their energy more actively and initiate change more forcefully. The effect of Aquamarine chips is similar to that of rough ocean waves pounding a cliff: the waves gradually wear the cliff away. In comparison, Aquamarine spheres act like gentle rain; eventually the rain erodes the rock but not nearly as quickly as the rough waves do.

Therapeutic-Quality Aquamarine

The characteristics of therapeutic Aquamarine vary more than those of most other gemstones. Even the finest Aquamarine necklaces vary in mass, clarity, hue, and depth of color.

Aquamarine naturally occurs in a wide range of color from green to blue, and nearly all Aquamarine is a mixture of both colors. All characteristics being equal, the green aspect focuses primarily on the physical body, while the blue aspect works on both the physical and subtle bodies. The more that blue dominates in the blue-green mix, the more the Aquamarine will focus on the mind. Because the mind has such a powerful influence on the body, the deeper the blue of the Aquamarine, the more effective the Aquamarine will be. Aquamarine color also ranges in intensity from deep and rich to colorless. The depth of Aquamarine's color determines how deeply its energy can penetrate and affect the aura and body.

Aquamarine clarity spans a continuum from opaque to flawless, with all degrees of cloudiness and flaws in between. Opaque and even moderately cloudy Aquamarine are not therapeutic. Slightly cloudy Aquamarine can be therapeutic if it displays a radiant brightness and good color. Although slightly cloudy Aquamarine takes much longer to

Mineral Composition
$Be_3Al_2(SiO_3)_6 + Fe$

A gem variety of beryl, Aquamarine is tinted blue-green by light interacting with traces of iron. Aquamarine is found in Africa, Brazil, Russia, and Colorado.

produce effects than clear Aquamarine, it may be preferable for people who need a more moderate pace of change. The energy of clear or nearly flawless Aquamarine moves rapidly into the aura and body, where it quickly begins to open awareness and reveal truths.

Each therapeutic Aquamarine necklace should have a consistent degree of clarity throughout the necklace and a uniform, clearly definable color. It might seem that by stringing together blue, blue-green, and green Aquamarine, one could enjoy the benefits of all three. On the contrary, such a combination would confuse the body. Each shade of Aquamarine color has a particular energetic character, or personality. The more uniform the color and clarity of an Aquamarine necklace, the more clearly defined its personality and the more focused and strong its therapeutic effects will be.

Aquamarine's color is often enhanced through heat or dye. Although heat treatment does not inhibit Aquamarine's energy, it also doesn't strengthen it. Despite its improved appearance, the heated Aquamarine will continue to project its original, probably rather low quality of energy.

Dye, on the other hand, renders Aquamarine therapeutically useless. Low-quality Aquamarine chips, in particular, are often dyed blue. The dye artificially deepens the gemstones' color but blocks the Aquamarine from radiating any healing energy into the aura and body.

Irradiation of Aquamarine results in the death of the crystal. It destroys the life energy of the gemstone and replaces it with an extremely disharmonious energy. If irradiated Aquamarine is worn, this disharmony will be projected into the aura. The destructive emanations of irradiated Aquamarine will first affect the mind, disrupting mental processes, distorting one's view of reality, and gradually wreaking havoc on one's mental harmony. Eventually, irradiated Aquamarine will distort the emotions as well.

Aquamarine Water: Fountain of Youthful Vitality

Through the use of a special technique, drinking water can be infused with the vitalizing energy of an Aquamarine necklace. The resulting *Aquamarine Water* helps reverse the aging process and treats any ailment associated with hardening, crystallization, or inflammation.

Modern physics teaches us that atomic particles switch constantly between states of matter and energy. When the atomic particles that comprise your body are in an energy state, your body is able to accept and use more life energy. This energy nourishes and invigorates your cells, allowing your body to maintain, evolve, and repair itself. Yet, as the body ages, its atoms naturally spend more and more time in the matter state. In the matter state, cells gradually deteriorate and age. Therefore, one secret to restoring a youthful body is keeping your atoms in an energy state more often than a matter state.

Drinking Aquamarine Water encourages your atoms, and thus your cells, to enter and remain in the energy state. In this state, a cell more easily perceives its "blueprint," or energetic picture of its ideal condition. As a result, the cells permeated by Aquamarine Water naturally let go of the elements that contribute to aging and poor health. The Aquamarine energy also rejuvenates these cells as it dissolves the harmful crystals associated with hardening and inflammation. As the water in your body is gradually replaced with Aquamarine Water, Aquamarine's energy revitalizes and renews your entire body.*

"I have been drinking Aquamarine Water for a month now. At first, I felt almost giddy. This feeling has been replaced by a heightened mental awareness, coupled with a pleasant liquid feeling in my body. I drink it every day I'm in the office. Every sip represents a welcome break from normal business matters as it reminds me of my inner life."

P.v.G.
Wiesbaden, Germany

"Since I've been drinking Aquamarine Water, my TMJ joint pain has gone away."

Paulette Stuurmans, L.M.T.
Orono, Minnesota

---

* *For more information about Aquamarine Water, including instructions on how to make it, see the book,* Aquamarine Water: Fountain of Youthful Vitality, *by Michael Katz.*

Aquamarine Therapy
Discovering the Cause of Illness

An Aquamarine necklace is placed on the body overnight to discover the karmic causes of an illness or other physical condition. Dreams and insights are recorded in the morning and throughout the day.

Therapy Tools

- One or two therapeutic Aquamarine necklaces, preferably of rounded chips
- Non-plastic first aid tape
- Small piece of lightweight cotton cloth

Indication

When you wish to understand the causes of an unwanted physical condition

Effects

When someone has a physical condition, it may seem that the life force is being only physically obstructed, when in fact the obstructions that cause most physical diseases usually occur on inner levels of being, within the subtle bodies. Indeed, nearly every physical condition is the result of inner conditions, blockages, or patterns. Therefore, to experience a more complete physical healing, the inner causes must be addressed and resolved. This Aquamarine technique can help you discover the inner causes of a condition and thus resolve them more successfully.

People often blame their conditions on something in the environment or on something that someone else did. It is easy, for example, for people to blame an illness on a certain disease-causing agent, such as a toxic chemical. Yet it is also true that, without your own karmic patterns and state of consciousness, you would not have developed your condition. On both inner and outer levels, you have set up the circumstances that have brought about your condition. You have done this because the experience of having your condition can help you grow and master the lessons associated with it. This Aquamarine technique can help you become aware of how your past experiences are affecting your condition today and thus help you gain relief by resolving those conditions more swiftly.

This technique is performed at night during sleep, because your resistance to truth is lowered at that time, and you can more easily gain the answers you desire through the dream state. Nonetheless, because your conscious awareness may resist the knowledge you gained during your dreams, your Aquamarine-inspired dreams may be harder than usual to remember. Therefore, recording your dreams and insights is an important part of this procedure.

This Aquamarine technique does not remove physical symptoms or heal your physical body directly. However, once you acknowledge, understand, and accept the reasons for your condition, you will be halfway to a cure.

Procedure

1. Place a notepad and pen by your bedside.
2. Prepare to go to sleep for the night, and get in bed with your Aquamarine necklace.
3. Hold the Aquamarine necklace in your hand, and gaze into the gemstones. Think about your condition, bringing it fully to your mind. As you do, let your eyes drink in the liquid blue-green color of the gems, and relax into the energy of the Aquamarine. Perform this step for 2 to 3 minutes.
4. Place the Aquamarine necklace in a neat pile over the area of your body most affected by your condition (see Fig. AQU-1). Place the gemstones directly on your skin and then place a light cotton cloth over the gems. To secure the gems to your body, tape the cloth to your skin with non-plastic first aid tape. Avoid letting the glue from the tape touch the gems.

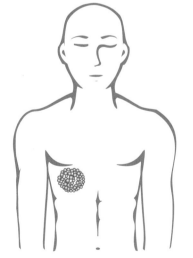

Fig. AQU-1

5. If you have a second Aquamarine necklace, place it around your neck.

6. As you fall asleep, continue to contemplate your condition for as long as is comfortable.

7. Record all your dreams and insights, and interpret them as best you can. Use your own meanings for dream symbols.

   • If you wake up during the night, record your dreams on the notepad.

   • Otherwise, record your dreams in the morning, including any additional ones you may not have recorded during the night.

   • During the day, write down any intuitive insights or unique daydreams you experience.

8. Repeat Steps 1–7 for three consecutive nights.

9. Continue to record and pay attention to your dreams for at least a week after treatment ends.

Post-Treatment Cleansing of Gems

Immediately after completing a treatment, it is important to cleanse the gems of any disharmonious energies released by the body in the course of treatment. See Appendix A: "Care and Cleansing of Therapeutic Gems," on page 397, for cleansing instructions.

Lavender

Awakening to Soul

The gemstone Lavender awakens you to your true spiritual essence. It gradually aligns and integrates all of your physical and subtle aspects. With improved alignment, energetic blockages are released, life energy moves more freely, and every part of your being becomes more receptive to the influence of spirit. As energy flows are corrected, old issues rise to the surface for resolution, and confusing symptoms often disappear. Lavender fosters awareness of your inner aspects as it helps you become a greater vessel for Spirit.

Indications *for Wearing a Therapeutic*
Lavender Necklace

WHEN ONE OR MORE OF THE FOLLOWING APPLY—

YOU ARE EXPERIENCING—

A sense of disconnection from your true purpose in life

Sluggish energy

Problems with the alignment of your spine or joints that result in headaches, neck or back pain, other joint pain, or arthritis

Multiple conditions affecting several areas of your health

Physical illness characterized by confusing or contradictory symptoms

YOU WANT TO—

Improve health on all levels: physical, emotional, mental, and spiritual

Develop greater awareness of your spiritual nature

Align and balance all your chakras

Enhance the effects of another therapeutic gemstone

Increase your receptivity to another life-giving therapy

Find a higher viewpoint in a situation, such as when you are facing a challenging life circumstance or negotiation

Prepare for surgery or a detoxification program

Alleviate pain caused by misaligned bones in the skull, vertebrae, or sacrum

Note: Although it is often referred to as Lavender Quartz or Cape Amethyst, the gemstone Lavender produces its own unique energy and therapeutic benefits.

Benefits of *Wearing a Therapeutic*
Lavender Necklace

Lavender awakens you to your true spiritual essence. It helps you embrace your spiritual birthright and make it a reality. To do this, it aligns and integrates all your bodies—physical, emotional, mental, causal, and intuitive. As your physical and subtle bodies move toward alignment and greater cooperation, they become more aware of each other. This increased awareness further improves alignment and enhances the flow of life energy throughout your entire being.

The physical body has seven major chakras through which life energy flows. These chakras are also reflected in each of the subtle bodies. These subtle-body reflections are some of the primary channels through which life force flows from its infinite source through the subtle bodies to the physical body. When all the chakras in all the bodies are perfectly aligned, life force flows freely to enliven and nourish one's entire being. Yet this is rarely the case; in response to the various stresses of life, any or all of our subtle- and physical-body chakras may have shifted out of their ideal positions. As a result, the natural flow of life energy throughout our being becomes impeded, and a host of ailments can arise.

When you wear a necklace of therapeutic Lavender spheres, their energy radiates into your entire aura. There, the Lavender energy begins to abolish the negative energies that weigh you down and prevent your physical and subtle bodies from aligning themselves. The Lavender also strongly encourages all your chakras in all your bodies to move into better alignment with each other. It does this by awakening each of your bodies to become aware of its relationship with the next highest body. This inspires all your bodies and all your chakras to align and cooperate with each other.

With each step toward better alignment, old issues come to the surface for resolution, and old blockages are released. Energies that have been stuck begin to flow freely, relieving you of long-time burdens. As all the chakras in all your bodies become more aligned with each other, more life force can flow through them to nourish and balance you on every level. As a result, you become stronger, more creative, and more loving.

Although its action remains the same for whoever wears it, Lavender's effects may vary greatly from one individual to the next. Because of this, it is difficult to describe exactly what kinds of effects you might expect from wearing Lavender. What one person may experience, another may not. It is also difficult to isolate Lavender's effects on the physical, emotional, causal, or mental body, since it works with each body to an equal degree and on each person as a whole being. Among therapeutic gemstones, this property is unique to Lavender.

Lavender helps you master yourself on all levels by increasing your awareness of your inner aspects, of your own spiritual essence, and of your connection with spirit. When all aspects of your being become aligned, an unobstructed channel is opened through which the life force can flow to the physical plane. When this occurs, your attention is automatically turned toward the source of this life force. The natural result is an expansion of consciousness and a spiritual awakening.

Enhancing Other Gemstones' Effects

Lavender can improve the effectiveness of any type of energy medicine therapy, including gemstone therapy. It does this by dissolving the negative energies that inhibit healing energies from entering your aura, thus enhancing your receptivity to all healing energies.

Some gemstones can abolish certain negative energies in one particular body more rapidly, completely, and forcibly than Lavender. But no other gemstone can simultaneously address the negative energies in all the subtle bodies with the same strength and the same high level of efficiency. For this reason, wearing a necklace of Lavender spheres is an ideal way to enhance the effects of any other therapeutic gemstone necklace.

Support for Cleansing Programs

As part of people's desire for spiritual advancement, many are striving to perfect the health of their physical bodies. This striving is expressed to some extent in the currently popular practice of cleansing toxins from the physical body. However, those who put attention only on the physical body and think that, by cleansing it, they can become more spiritual have it backwards. If you wish to perfect the physical body, you must first work to align your physical and subtle bodies. Then life force can flow more easily through them, helping you to become cleansed, balanced, and healed on all levels.

Clarifying Symptoms

When people with illnesses that are difficult to diagnose or that don't fit textbook descriptions wear a necklace of Lavender spheres, unclear and confusing symptoms often disappear or are resolved. Also, conditions whose causes and symptoms are lodged very deeply often come to the surface and are more easily diagnosed. This occurs because of the improved alignment of the person's physical and subtle bodies and the resulting increase in the flow of life force. People with these kinds of symptoms can benefit from wearing Lavender for at least one to two weeks before seeing a physician.

Finding a Higher Viewpoint

One of the greatest gifts you can give someone with whom you are experiencing disharmony is a Lavender necklace—and hope that the person will wear it. You should also consider wearing Lavender yourself. Because Lavender expands awareness, it can help both of you see your conflict from a broader viewpoint.

If you are planning an important negotiation, you might consider giving Lavender to the person with whom you are negotiating. If you both wear Lavender during your meetings, the resulting expansion of awareness will help each of you see the other's position in a new way. This may even include the intertwining connections between everyone

"I use a Lavender necklace in almost every treatment with my clients. I have the client wear it beforehand to prepare the body and afterward to make sure the treatment's effects are carried into the person's energetic fabric."

Kathy Miller, R.N.
Oak View, California

involved in the situation. If you wear Lavender while you are sleeping the night before negotiations, you may have dreams of the karma, or cycles of cause and effect, between the negotiating parties, and your understanding of the entire situation may deepen.

Supporting Lavender's Work with Quartz

Although Lavender's balancing force is not as strong as that of Quartz, its ability to open the physical body to the life force is much greater. The unique strengths of these two gemstones can be combined to create an effective therapy. For example, an individual can wear a Quartz necklace during any therapy in which Lavender is being placed on a specific area.[13] This will help the physical body to accept in a more balanced way the changes that will occur when greater life force is called to the area.

Therapeutic-Quality Lavender

The Lavender gemstone is a derivative of colorless Quartz. Yet, unlike Quartz, the finest therapeutic Lavender is not optical in quality. Rather, it contains three elements, all of which are present in the same sphere: *lavender color*, *translucency*, and *patches of cloudy white or light lavender color*. Each therapeutic Lavender sphere exhibits a unique combination of the three essential elements. They work together to fulfill Lavender's mission and produce its effects.

Lavender Color

The lavender color defines the Lavender gemstone's mission. The energy of the color lavender has an affinity with the higher levels of our mental, emotional, and even physical bodies. When each of these bodies is stimulated with the energy of lavender, the body awakens to its relationship with the next highest body, inspiring alignment and cooperation among them all.

Mineral Composition
SiO_2 + Mn + Fe

Lavender, also known as Lavender Quartz or Cape Amethyst, is silicon dioxide colored lavender by the presence of manganese and iron in specific quantities. Lavender is found in South Africa, other African countries, and Brazil.

---

13 *For an example of a Lavender therapy, see page 236.*

Translucency

The translucency in the gemstone clears the path for Lavender's energy to do its work. Without translucency, Lavender's work slows down drastically. Although non-translucent Lavender can generate the necessary changes, its path through the physical and subtle bodies is greatly hindered.

Cloudy Patches

The patches of cloudy white or light lavender color act as regulatory components by encouraging alignment to unfold in a balanced way. Without these patches, Lavender promotes alignment without attending to the need for change to occur in a balanced, gradual fashion. The cloudy aspect also helps the physical body to regain its balance more swiftly after taking a step toward greater alignment.

Optical-quality Lavender, which is completely translucent and contains no cloudy white or light lavender patches, will bring about alignment at the greatest possible speed. In the hands of an experienced gem therapist who knows how and when to use such a strong force, it is an invaluable tool. However, to prevent the physical body from reacting negatively to such a forced alignment, optical Lavender should be worn only for very short periods.

The finest quality Lavender is free of contaminants. Black flecks, a brown or green tinge, or any foreign matter that muddies the lavender color lowers the quality of Lavender's energy and diminishes its therapeutic effects. The energy of such Lavender cannot reach into the higher vibratory levels of the wearer's being.

Lavender Therapy
Pain Relief and Realignment Technique

Lavender is placed on a painful, tight, or misaligned area to soothe pain and strongly promote healing. Its energy opens a passageway from your subtle bodies to your physical body, allowing more life force to flow to the distressed area. This therapy is particularly helpful for painful joints; it encourages their realignment as it eases pain.

Therapy Tools

One or two therapeutic necklaces of Lavender spheres (8 mm, 10 mm, or 12 mm)

Indications

When you are experiencing any of the following in a localized area of your body—

- Pain
- Injury
- Tightness or muscle strain
- Structural misalignment
- Joint pain caused by arthritis, injury, or some other condition

Effects

When you place Lavender spheres on a painful, injured, or tight area, the Lavender's energy opens a passageway from your inner dimensions, or subtle bodies, to your physical body, allowing more life force to flow to the ailing area. As it opens this pathway, the Lavender also awakens each body to the next subtler body. This inspires all bodies—physical, emotional, causal, mental, and intuitive—to align with each other and improve their cooperation.

As the ailing area is flooded with life force, it is encouraged to open, relax, and accept this healing energy. Pain is soothed. If the area is suffering from any kind of misalignment, such as a structural or skeletal misalignment, the Lavender's aligning influence encourages the area to realign itself.

This therapy is particularly effective for soothing painful joints, such as those in the hands, feet, and spine. In arthritic joints, the influx of life force can help ease inflammation and thus relieve pain.

Procedure

1. Place one or two Lavender necklaces on the area you wish to treat, preferably directly on your skin. If you have enough Lavender, layer it.
   - If you are treating your spine, lay the Lavender lengthwise along your spine. Center the necklace(s) over the most distressed area (see Fig. LAV-1).
   - If you are treating joints other than those in your spine, wrap the Lavender around the painful joints (see Fig. LAV-2).
   - If you are treating an organ or muscle, place the Lavender in a neat pile directly on the area (see Fig. LAV-3).
2. If you wish to secure the Lavender to your body for some time, place the gemstones on your skin and then place a light cotton cloth over the gems. To secure the gems to your body, tape the cloth to your skin with non-plastic first aid tape. Avoid letting the glue from the tape touch the gems.

Time Guidelines

Keep the Lavender on the treatment area for as long as you wish— indeed, the longer, the better. If you sleep with the Lavender in place, your condition may be significantly improved by morning.

Post-Treatment Cleansing of Gems

Immediately after completing a treatment, it is important to cleanse the gems of any disharmonious energies released by the body in the course of treatment. See Appendix A: "Care and Cleansing of Therapeutic Gems," on page 397, for cleansing instructions.

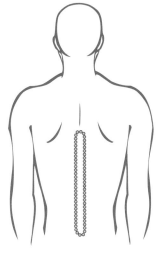

Fig. LAV-1

Fig. LAV-2

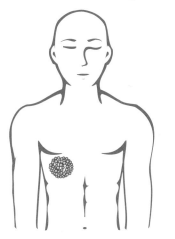

Fig. LAV-3

Indigo

Developing Intuition

Indigo helps develop the intuition. It carries the indigo ray throughout your being, absorbing the limiting mental energies that obstruct the intuition and cloud the mind. Through its profound resonance with the intuitive body, Indigo builds bridges between your intuition and your conscious awareness. It teaches you to distinguish between mental concepts and direct perception so that you may better hear the whisperings of soul.

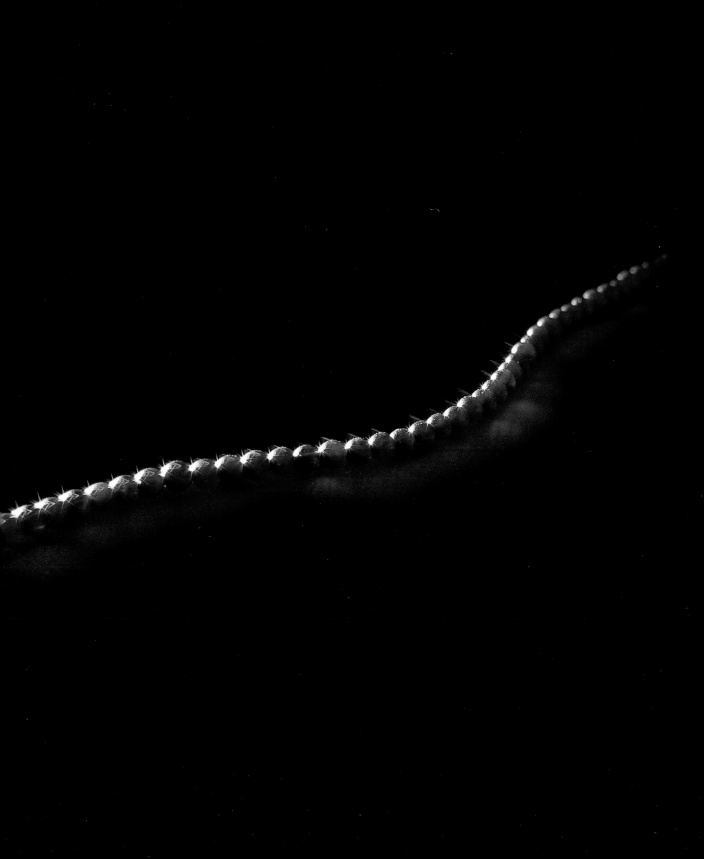

Indications *for Wearing a Therapeutic*
Indigo Necklace

YOU ARE EXPERIENCING—

Difficulty hearing your own, true inner voice

Lack of trust in your intuition

Mental cloudiness

Any unwanted condition of the skeletal system, including the bones, ligaments, joints, or cartilage

YOU WANT TO—

Develop and clarify your intuition

Gain clarity about your true nature or life purpose

Clear your aura and body of negative mental energies, both your own and those of others

Foster a broader, more spiritual viewpoint

Improve your recollection of dreams

Benefits of *Wearing a Therapeutic Indigo Necklace*

Indigo helps develop your intuition. It is the gemstone bearer of the indigo ray.[14] When you wear a necklace of Indigo spheres, the indigo ray is radiated throughout your being, absorbing the limiting mental energies that obstruct the intuition and cloud the mind. The ability of both Indigo and Sodalight to absorb mental energies is no coincidence: Indigo is the crystalline form of Sodalight.

Self-realization is the recognition of oneself as soul. A crucial step toward this goal is to listen to the whisperings of the true self in day-to-day situations. Some people call these inner nudges "intuition." To help you better hear these whisperings, Indigo energy constructs bridges between your intuition and your conscious awareness. As impulses of truth arise from the highest self, the intuitive body is the first to hear them. The mind then receives these whisperings, filtering and distorting them according to its own conditioning and agenda. Often they are heard incorrectly, translated into dream-like symbols, or not detected at all. By constructing energetic bridges, Indigo allows intuitive data to bypass the mind and seep directly into your conscious awareness.

When the mind is bypassed, the intuition becomes a source of information separate from the mind. The bridge provided by Indigo allows mind-thoughts to come through one set of channels, while intuitive information travels another. Thus, the two types of information become more separate and identifiable. This makes it easier to determine whether the information originated in the mind or in soul. However, Indigo can help only to a certain degree. To develop your intuitive sense fully, you must exercise your intuition and practice trusting it.

---

14 *See page 40 for more information on the vital role of color rays in restoring and maintaining health.*

"When I treat my chiropractic patients, wearing Indigo enhances my intuition. I get to the bottom of their issues with greater clarity and a little more quickly than I otherwise might. I notice that, when wearing Indigo, I'm more focused, and my interpretation of my patients' problems is sharper."

Dr. Anna Just-Buddy
Chiropractic Physician
Conyers, Georgia

Mineral Composition
$Na_4Al_3(SiO_4)_3Cl$

Indigo is the translucent or transparent form of Sodalight. It is found in the Ural Mountains of Russia and Mt. Vesuvius in Italy, and in Norway, Germany, Africa, Brazil, Bolivia, Canada, Maine, and Montana.

When life brings the inevitable changes required for spiritual growth, Indigo helps keep the mind from overreacting. The indigo ray steps quietly through the mind, suggesting that something greater lies beyond it. It whispers that your highest self, your spiritual essence and the mind's governor, orchestrates your life's experiences for your spiritual unfoldment. Thus, the indigo ray quietly lays a foundation in the mind and helps it to maintain a more refined balance.

The Indigo gemstone fosters a conscious connection with your intuition and helps you envision your true dreams and aspirations. It shows you your potential to attain your dreams, and it helps you see how to achieve them. Indigo expands your consciousness and opens the door to higher levels of knowingness, while teaching you to shine with your own inner light.

Indigo and the Bones and Joints

Each of the seven color rays of the life force is particularly healing and nourishing to certain aspects of the physical body. The indigo ray nourishes and supports the skeletal system, including the bones, ligaments, joints, and cartilage. Consequently, wearing Indigo can help strengthen these parts of the body and resolve certain conditions associated with them.

Therapeutic-Quality Indigo

To accurately determine its quality, Indigo must be observed with a light source behind it. A light source reveals therapeutic Indigo's true indigo-blue color and translucency. Without it, the Indigo's color appears much darker, and its translucency disappears.

As the crystalline form of Sodalight, Indigo shares Sodalight's tendency to contain white streaks or clouds. The finest quality Indigo is neon-like cobalt blue, translucent, and free from white clouds. As spheres move away from this finest quality, they contain more white and are less translucent. Spheres that are nearly opaque are of low therapeutic value. Spheres in which the white overtakes the indigo hue are non-therapeutic.

Like Sodalight, Indigo can become whiter as it absorbs negative energies from the environment and from your aura. This cloudiness may take as long as years or as little as weeks to develop. The Indigo remains effective, however, until the cloudiness overwhelms the indigo color of the spheres.

Indigo Therapy
Removing Mental Blocks to Healing

An Indigo necklace is placed on a localized area of the body to remove mental energies that have accumulated there and that are disrupting the area's health and inhibiting its recovery.

Therapy Tools

One therapeutic necklace of Indigo spheres (4 mm or 6 mm)

Indications

- When you suspect that the healing of a localized area is inhibited by certain mental energies, attitudes, or recurring thoughts, especially those regarding the area's condition
- When an ailment in a localized area is associated with weakened structural components, such as bones, joints, ligaments, muscles, or fascia

Effects

When you place Indigo on a localized area of your body, the Indigo helps remove the disharmonious mental energies embedded in the area's cells. These energies of mental origin clutter the area, disrupting its health and inhibiting its recovery. They include negative thoughts, attitudes, and concepts specific to the area that may have been generated by you or by others in your environment. They also include random mental energies that you have picked up from the atmosphere.

Every cell in your body has its own "blueprint." This blueprint is an energetic picture of the cell's optimal state of health. Illness occurs when the cell's structure or functioning strays from this ideal. The blueprints themselves are never altered or distorted by disease. No matter how sick your cells may be, each of them retains its blueprint for optimal health.

The Indigo placed on your body sets up a cyclical flow of its own energy through all your inner dimensions, or subtle bodies, to the highest level of your mind. As the Indigo energy cycles back to the gems, it collects thought-forms from throughout your being that are impinging on the ailing area. In this way, it frees the area from the disrupting influence of mental clutter. Perhaps even more important, the Indigo energy also collects and exchanges blueprint information with all the cells it touches. This sparks all the cells to take action to move toward a more optimal state of health.

Procedure

Arrange an Indigo necklace into a neat pile, and place it directly on your skin on the area you wish to treat. Hold the Indigo in place with your right hand (see Fig. IND-1).

If you wish to keep the Indigo in place for a long period, instead of holding it, secure the gems to your body. To do this, place the gemstones on your skin and then place a light cotton cloth over the gems. Then, tape the cloth to your skin with non-plastic first aid tape. Avoid letting the glue from the tape touch the gems.

Time Guidelines

Keep the Indigo in place for at least 10 minutes and for as long as you wish thereafter. The longer you keep the Indigo in place, the more deeply and thoroughly it will work.

Post-Treatment Cleansing of Gems

Immediately after completing a treatment, it is important to cleanse the gems of any disharmonious energies released by the body in the course of treatment. See Appendix A: "Care and Cleansing of Therapeutic Gems," on page 397, for cleansing instructions.

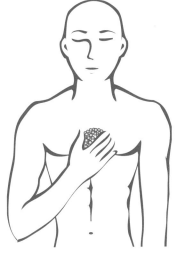

Fig. IND-1

Amethyst

Attaining Wisdom

Amethyst helps you attain wisdom by reminding every aspect of your being of its inherent spiritual nature. Amethyst and the purple ray it carries draw your attention beyond the mind to the realm of pure spiritual knowledge and then bring this wisdom back into clear, conscious thought. Amethyst helps you let go of all that is old and all that holds you back so that you may fully embrace your spiritual destiny.

Indications *for Wearing a Therapeutic*
Amethyst Necklace

YOU ARE EXPERIENCING—

A disconnection from your own inner source of wisdom

Inability to let go of a situation that is holding you back

Being easily thrown off balance emotionally by interactions with others

Frequent emotional extremes

Any unwanted condition of the nervous system

YOU WANT TO—

Become more attuned to your own inner source of wisdom

Release yourself from certain attachments

Let go of a past situation

Develop your intuition or inner knowing

Improve your ability to focus

Express yourself with more confidence

Speak or sing with greater ease

Benefits *of Wearing a Therapeutic Amethyst Necklace*

Amethyst helps you attain wisdom by reminding every aspect of your being of its inherent spiritual nature. Amethyst is the gemstone bearer of the purple ray.[15] It can help you let go of all that is old and all that holds you back—on every level and in every aspect of life—so that you may fully embrace your spiritual destiny.

When you wear a necklace of Amethyst spheres, it forms a column of energy that extends from your physical body through all your inner bodies to Soul itself. This column allows Amethyst energy to rise upward from your heart to your head and beyond, into the innermost, spiritual aspect of your being, bringing your attention with it. In the process, Amethyst draws your attention through your inner bodies, increasing your awareness and knowledge of them. Then, Amethyst and the purple ray bring this wisdom back into clear, conscious thought. The longer you wear Amethyst, the stronger and wider this column of energy becomes.

Amethyst's purple ray reflects the highest aspect of the mind, which is also known as the intuition. It stirs the intuition. This stirring helps your mind become aware of its own intuitive aspect and, ideally, of that which lies just beyond it—soul itself. When your mind becomes aware of its highest aspect, the energy that the mind once fed its undesirable tendencies is redirected. If Amethyst is worn long enough, these undesirable tendencies will begin to dissolve.

Amethyst can also help you understand and let go of anything that keeps you attached to a condition. When worn as a necklace of spheres, Amethyst affects all your subtle bodies, bringing the perspective needed to let go of attachments.

---

15 *See page 40 for more information on the vital role of color rays in restoring and maintaining health.*

"Since wearing my Amethyst necklace, I've found that my sleep is much more relaxed and restful. Even my dreams have changed for the better. I've also noticed that things I used to worry and fret about don't seem to faze me as much. My conversations with people are more straightforward, too—I feel more confident to say what I really feel."

E.B.
Dallas, Texas

Amethyst promotes both inner and outer focus. By focusing your attention on a higher, more spiritual state, Amethyst keeps you from falling prey to the many distractions that impede spiritual growth. As it helps dissolve the duality between inner and outer experience, Amethyst helps you see that all of life is spiritual.

Amethyst urges you on all levels to look beyond yourself to the level of pure spirit and the true self. Within Amethyst's blueprint is a memory of pure spirit, where matter, energy, space, and time do not exist, and where there is no duality. This memory also lies in your cells' blueprints. When you wear Amethyst, its blueprint resonates with those of your cells. The memory of your cells' optimal state is awakened, and the call of soul to return to this higher awareness is rekindled.

When you wear Amethyst in a necklace that lies near your heart chakra, its energy first connects with your emotions. It stimulates the area where emotions are born and uplifts the area's consciousness. This upliftment fosters a higher perspective on your emotions and helps reduce or balance emotional extremes. The balancing effect on the emotions is cumulative. Therefore, if you are easily imbalanced by others, you should wear Amethyst continually to cultivate this balance and allow it to grow.

When an Amethyst necklace falls near the throat, the purple ray tends to flow directly to the head and mind, bypassing the emotions and increasing the amount of energy flowing in through the throat chakra. This gives energy to the voice. Therefore, if you must address a group but are afraid to speak, you will benefit from wearing Amethyst around your neck near your throat. Wearing such a necklace will also benefit those who lack the self-confidence to express themselves or who speak too quietly or with uncertainty.

Amethyst should never be worn in a necklace that reaches much below the heart chakra. Necklaces of Amethyst that are too long will start to draw energy from the rest of the body to the stomach area, thus diffusing the necklace's focus and creating confusion.

Amethyst and the Nervous System

Each of the seven color rays of the life force is particularly healing and nourishing to certain aspects of the physical body. The purple ray nourishes and supports the body's communication system, including the nerve cells and brain. Consequently, wearing Amethyst can help strengthen these parts of the body and resolve certain conditions associated with them.

Amethyst and Gold

Those who love to wear gold can wear it freely with Amethyst. Not only will the two look beautiful together, but the Amethyst will provide an understanding and supportive influence by helping lovers of gold understand why they may cling to certain attitudes, feelings, or conditions. This understanding is important, because it will form the basis for lovers of gold to take further steps in their evolution.

Therapeutic-Quality Amethyst

Amethyst color occurs naturally in a wide range from light to dark purple. Therapeutic Amethyst falls somewhere in the middle of this range and resembles the vibrant purple seen in a rainbow. As Amethyst moves away from this optimal color and becomes darker or lighter, its therapeutic value diminishes. The lightest purple is not the gemstone known as Lavender but only a washed-out Amethyst.

Clarity also plays a key role in Amethyst quality. Flaws and inclusions, or foreign matter, detract from its ability to radiate its healing energy. A tiny amount of flaws in a sphere is acceptable. However, when evaluating Amethyst, be aware that flaws disrupt or block the sphere's ability to radiate its energy in direct proportion to the flaws' size. The exceptions are minor flaws that have a prismatic effect. When a sphere with these flaws is moved in natural light, the Amethyst displays a rainbow or partial rainbow of colors. This property is an asset. All other flaws and inclusions—especially cloudiness, dark flecks, internal fractures, or pieces of the rock matrix in which the Amethyst grew—inhibit the

Mineral Composition
SiO_2 + Mn + Fe

Amethyst is a gem form of silicon dioxide, or Quartz, and derives its purple color from the presence of manganese and iron. Some of the many places in which Amethyst is found include Brazil, Uruguay, the Ural Mountains of Russia, and New Jersey.

Amethyst's energy and should be avoided. Poor drill holes or any damage to the sphere's surface, such as scratches, gouges, or chipped areas, also render Amethyst non-therapeutic.

To judge Amethyst quality accurately requires experience and the opportunity to compare many Amethyst specimens of different grades and colors. Amethyst of ideal color with no inclusions is extremely rare.

Amethyst Therapy

Chakra Therapies

An Amethyst necklace can be placed on any of six major chakras to treat a variety of conditions or to promote awareness. Amethyst energy affects each chakra differently. The following therapies and techniques offer seven ways to derive benefits from Amethyst chakra treatments. (See Fig. AME-1 for an illustration of chakra locations.)

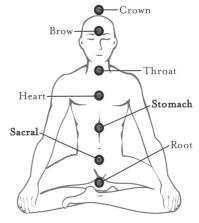

Fig. AME-1

Therapy Tool

One therapeutic necklace of Amethyst spheres (6 mm, 8 mm, or 10 mm)

Sacral Chakra—Prenatal Upliftment

Indication

When you are pregnant and wish to enhance the vitality of your unborn child

Effects

This technique uplifts the unborn child. It helps forge a stronger connection between the fetus' body and consciousness. When the baby is born, this enhanced connection will help the baby begin life with greater vitality.

Procedure

Lie on your back, and place the Amethyst necklace in a neat pile or spiral on your belly at its highest point (see Fig. AME-2). Leave the necklace in place for 20 to 30 minutes. You may perform this technique a maximum of three times a week.

Fig. AME-2

Stomach Chakra—Stomachache Therapy

Indications

- Stomachache, especially in children
- Weakened stomach

Effects

When Amethyst is placed on the stomach chakra, it draws to the stomach healing energies from other, stronger areas of the body. This therapy is very helpful for soothing stomachaches, especially in children.

Procedure

- For an acute stomachache, hold or otherwise secure an Amethyst necklace on your stomach chakra until the pain eases or disappears.
- For chronic stomachache, place the Amethyst on your stomach chakra for 30 to 60 minutes daily.
- If you wish to secure the Amethyst to your body for some time, place the gemstones on your skin and then place a light cotton cloth over the gems. To secure the gems to your body, tape the cloth to your skin with non-plastic first aid tape. Avoid letting the glue from the tape touch the gems.

Heart Chakra—Insight into Attachments

Indication

When you wish to understand why you feel attached to a certain situation

Effects

This technique can bring insight and enhance your understanding of the reasons you may be attached to certain conditions or situations in your life.

Procedure

1. Lie down on your back in a quiet place, and make yourself comfortable.
2. Think about the situation or issue you wish to address. Feel any attachment to it.
3. Place the Amethyst necklace on your heart chakra, and keep it there for 15 to 30 minutes.
4. Be open to any insights or intuitive feelings about the reasons for the attachment.

Throat Chakra—Public Speaking and Other Speech Support

Indications

- When you must address a group but are afraid to speak
- When you desire more confidence about expressing yourself
- When you speak too quietly or with uncertainty
- When you wish to strengthen your voice
- When you are preparing to sing or otherwise perform with your voice

Effects

The Amethyst energy flowing through your throat chakra opens passageways for more life energy to enter your throat. This strengthens your throat chakra and makes additional energy available to your voice.

Procedure

Do one of the following:

- Lie on your back and place an Amethyst necklace in a neat pile on your throat chakra for about an hour.
- Wear a short Amethyst necklace that lies close to your throat chakra for as long as you wish.

Brow Chakra—Spiritual Development Technique

Indications

- When you wish to encourage your spiritual growth
- When you wish to become more aware of your inner dimensions, or subtle bodies

Effects

This technique opens your brow chakra and strengthens the circuit of energy that continually flows in through the throat and out through the brow. When this flow is strengthened, you become more aware of your subtle bodies, which in turn spurs your spiritual unfoldment.

Procedure

1. Bunch an Amethyst necklace in your hand and hold the Amethyst on the top of your head for 30 to 60 seconds. This prepares you for the Amethyst's action by opening your brow chakra.

2. Lie on your back and place the Amethyst in a neat pile or spiral on your brow chakra for 30 to 60 minutes.

Brow and Crown Chakras—Headache Therapy

Indication

Headache

Effects

If your headache is caused by a build-up of excess energy in your head, this therapy will open your brow and crown chakras and allow your head to discharge its excess energy.

Procedure

1. Do either of the following:
   - Sit up and place an Amethyst necklace in a neat pile or spiral on your crown chakra.
   - Lie on your back and place an Amethyst necklace in a pile on your crown chakra, gently securing it there with a natural-fiber pillow.

2. If you don't feel significant relief after 15 minutes, lie on your back and allow the Amethyst simply to rest on your forehead.

Crown Chakra—Mental Imbalance Therapy

Indications

- When you wish to resolve mental imbalances caused by stagnant mental energy
- When you desire support for cranio-sacral therapy

Effects

Stagnant mental energy is a common cause of mental imbalances. This therapy helps release stagnant mental energies by opening the brow chakra and encouraging a flow of energy in through the throat and out through the brow. As long as the brow remains open, energy will not be able to collect in the mind and stagnate there.

Procedure

1. Do either of the following for 20 to 30 minutes once a day:
   - Sit up and place an Amethyst necklace in a neat pile or spiral on your crown chakra.
   - Lie on your back and place an Amethyst necklace in a pile on your crown chakra, gently securing it there with a natural-fiber pillow.
2. Between treatments, wear a short Amethyst necklace around your neck to support the flow of energy into your throat and out through your brow.

Time Guidelines

Unless otherwise indicated, any of these Amethyst treatments can be performed for approximately 15 to 60 minutes every day. Let your intuition guide you in determining exactly how long to perform a particular treatment.

Post-Treatment Cleansing of Gems

Immediately after completing a treatment, it is important to cleanse the gems of any disharmonious energies released by the body in the course of treatment. See Appendix A: "Care and Cleansing of Therapeutic Gems," on page 397, for cleansing instructions.

Purple Rainbow Fluorite

Expanding Consciousness

Purple Rainbow Fluorite breaks up the patterns, congestion, and blockages that limit the natural tendency of one's consciousness to expand. It initiates profound changes in the way the body accepts the life force, especially the purple and indigo color rays. This gemstone's powerful ability to abolish impediments helps stubborn conditions progress in their healing. Purple Rainbow Fluorite heightens spiritual experiences during dreams and meditations and in daily life.

Purple Rainbow Fluorite cylinders combined with
Amethyst and Lavender spheres

Indications for *Wearing a Therapeutic*
Purple Rainbow Fluorite Necklace

WHEN ONE OR MORE OF THE FOLLOWING APPLY—

YOU ARE EXPERIENCING—

Blocks to the expansion and development of your consciousness

Any condition that is resisting the positive effects of other treatments

Any unwanted condition of the nervous system

Any unwanted condition of the skeletal system, including the bones, ligaments, joints, or cartilage

YOU WANT TO—

Expand and develop your consciousness

Heighten your spiritual experiences during dreams, meditation, or in daily life

Free yourself of a pattern of ill health

Free yourself of a pattern of unhealthy behavior

Enhance the color-ray benefits of wearing a therapeutic Amethyst or Indigo necklace

Benefits *of Wearing a Therapeutic*
Purple Rainbow Fluorite Necklace

Purple Rainbow Fluorite breaks up the patterns, congestion, and blockages that limit the natural tendency of one's consciousness to expand. It initiates profound changes in the way the body accepts the life force, especially the purple and indigo rays.

Purple Rainbow Fluorite has a two-fold mission. One aspect of its mission is to enable the physical body to accept greater amounts of the indigo and purple color rays. The second is to help people let go of old patterns and to create newer, less limited patterns. To accomplish the second aspect of its mission, Purple Rainbow Fluorite abolishes impediments in the body, emotions, and mind. Because of this ability, Purple Rainbow Fluorite can help stubborn conditions progress in their healing.

In a healthy body, energy naturally flows in through the throat chakra and out through the brow chakra. Purple Rainbow Fluorite strengthens this flow and enables the throat chakra to accept higher energies. As a result, energies leaving the brow chakra will also be higher. This flow of higher energies will enhance experiences related to the brow chakra, either in daily life or during dreams, meditations, and spiritual exercises. These heightened spiritual experiences will lead to greater understanding, knowledge, and wisdom on all levels. This is a fundamental effect of Purple Rainbow Fluorite.

By enabling your physical body to accept a greater flow of indigo ray, Purple Rainbow Fluorite also prepares your body to accept the indigo ray's influence. The indigo ray fosters a more holistic, spiritual viewpoint.

Purple Rainbow Fluorite also prepares you to accept a greater amount of purple ray, which can lead to greater wisdom and spiritual inspiration. The purple ray opens your awareness to the worlds within you, helping you reach higher states of consciousness.

Purple Rainbow Fluorite is for those brave and adventurous individuals who possess the strength and stamina to make fundamental changes—for Purple Rainbow Fluorite strongly initiates change.

Ensuring Balanced Change— Purple Rainbow Fluorite Combinations

Making the profound changes needed for the growth of consciousness demands careful maintenance of one's own balance. Wearing a solid necklace of Purple Rainbow Fluorite can cause serious imbalances by unleashing too many changes too quickly. Therefore, Purple Rainbow Fluorite should always be combined with other balancing and uplifting gemstones in a necklace. When you wear Purple Rainbow Fluorite in a properly designed combination necklace, the desired effects will occur in balance.

Handling with Care

Because Purple Rainbow Fluorite is physically very soft, it can scratch and break easily. To avoid damaging it, Purple Rainbow Fluorite should always be handled as carefully as possible and stored separately from other gemstones. Because breaks and heavy scratches inhibit Fluorite's work, heavily scratched Fluorite should be re-polished, and any broken Fluorites in a necklace should be replaced.

Therapeutic-Quality Purple Rainbow Fluorite

Therapeutic Purple Rainbow Fluorite displays bands of dark purple and indigo within a base of colorless or light- to medium-purple Fluorite. When examining a Purple Rainbow Fluorite sphere or cylinder for therapeutic value, from one direction it should appear completely dark purple; when turned 90 degrees, it should display the dark purple bands. Spheres should be cut so that the bands lie perpendicular to the drill hole. Therapeutic Purple Rainbow Fluorite has no hint of green.

Purple Rainbow Fluorite can be divided into six grades of therapeutic quality: Exquisite-Plus, Exquisite, Very Fine, Fine, Fair, and Acceptable.

Mineral Composition
CaF_2 + Y + Ce

Purple Rainbow Fluorite is calcium fluoride colored by traces of yttrium and cerium. It is formed from magmatic solutions in veins near ores of silver and zinc. Purple Rainbow Fluorite occurs in England, China, Switzerland, Norway, Africa, Australia, New York, Illinois, and Kentucky.

As Fluorite quality moves away from the highest level, all elements in the sphere or cylinder get progressively fuzzier, and fewer bands appear.

Exquisite-Plus

In Exquisite-Plus Fluorite, the purple bands are crisp and well-defined in a colorless or nearly colorless Fluorite base, and each sphere contains at least five or six bands.

Exquisite

In Exquisite Fluorite, the dark purple bands are slightly less distinct, and the base is nearly colorless.

Very Fine

In Very Fine, the bands appear to be bleeding slightly into the base, and the base has a little more color than Exquisite.

Fine

In Fine, the bands are fuzzier than Very Fine but still recognizable.

Fair and Acceptable

In Fair and Acceptable therapeutic quality, the bands appear to have bled somewhat into the surrounding Fluorite, with no clear separation between them and the Fluorite base; these two grades have little therapeutic value. Although qualities lower than Fair and Acceptable are the most plentiful, they are not therapeutic.

The therapeutic effectiveness of Purple Rainbow Fluorite increases exponentially from one level of quality to the next higher level. For example, Very Fine is ten times more potent than Fine, Exquisite is 100 times more potent than Fine, and Exquisite-Plus is 1,000 times more potent than Fine.

When making a necklace with Purple Rainbow Fluorite, the most important consideration after quality is that the Fluorites are energetically compatible with each other. Selecting spheres that are similar in vibration and appearance enhances the overall harmony, and therefore effectiveness, of a necklace. Collections of compatible Fluorites are called "families."

"Wearing Purple Rainbow Fluorite has both a soothing and an uplifting effect on me. There is a distinct pleasure in wearing it, reminiscent of the bliss one can feel in meditation. Since wearing it, my awareness and perception have become keener."
D.C.
Newfoundland, Canada

Citrine

Fulfilling Your Potential

Citrine and the yellow ray loosen your hold on all that no longer serves you, so that you may progress to the next higher state of being. Citrine unwinds tension and increases flexibility in the cells, organs, and body as a whole, thereby encouraging your body to relax and move into greater alignment. Citrine gradually opens inner hearing. It helps you fulfill your spiritual potential by encouraging you to embrace ever-higher states of consciousness.

Indications *for Wearing a Therapeutic*
Citrine Necklace

WHEN ONE OR MORE OF THE FOLLOWING APPLY—

YOU ARE EXPERIENCING—

Difficulty perceiving your higher purpose

Difficulty letting go of bothersome thoughts, feelings, or situations

Inflexibility anywhere in the body, mind, or emotions

Spinal misalignment

Any kind of stomach distress or dysfunction

Any unwanted condition of the organs of elimination (skin, kidneys, intestines, bladder, urinary tract, and certain aspects of the liver)

YOU WANT TO—

Release what no longer serves you—physically, mentally or emotionally

Increase your flexibility on all levels

Release tension in your body, emotions, or mind

Develop your ability to hear the subtle, nonphysical sounds of nature

Benefits *of Wearing a Therapeutic*
Citrine Necklace

Citrine prepares your body, emotions, and mind to accept a greater flow of the yellow color ray. The yellow ray is the aspect of the life force that helps us release what no longer serves us and to accept what we need in order to move to the next higher state.[16] This aspect of Citrine also has a greater overall purpose—to help you fulfill your spiritual potential by encouraging you to embrace ever-higher states of consciousness.

Citrine works to loosen blockages and increase flexibility through the wave-like motion characteristic of the yellow ray. Citrine works gradually, one step at a time, to increase flexibility on a cellular level. This flexibility enhances the ability of the substances within a cell to move around as required—either within the cell or through the cell membrane. These substances can include the cell's organelles and fluids. Any intracellular processes that require movement are also enhanced and made more efficient.

If enough Citrine is worn over an adequate length of time, this flexibility will begin to extend beyond the cellular level to the organs and organ systems to which the cells belong. Most obvious will be Citrine's effect on the muscular system. After wearing a Citrine necklace for a while, you may find that you can stretch a little farther.

As a living organism, the body wants all its components to be in proper alignment. When any component is out of alignment, the flow of life force that keeps the body alive and gives it spiritual sustenance diminishes. As the body ages, it grows more and more out of alignment. Citrine can help the body—at any age—relax to the point where the life force can rush in, take hold, and move the physical body into a healthier state of alignment.

---

16 *See page 40 for more information on the vital role of color rays in restoring and maintaining health.*

Citrine's ability to loosen blockages and increase flexibility can be felt as a stirring or unwinding effect. This unwinding supports Citrine's ability to move the body into greater alignment. When worn as a necklace, Citrine unwinds the entire body, especially the stomach chakra. If the stomach chakra is stuck or tightly shut, the Citrine will gently massage it and encourage it to open.

In someone with a yellow-ray deficiency, emotions are often out of balance. By providing yellow-ray nourishment, Citrine fosters awareness of one's emotional center. Thus, Citrine can greatly benefit those who react in emotional extremes or whose emotional nature lacks balance.

The Sound of Citrine

"I have found that, on some of my clients, Citrine helps their bodies unwind and relax so rapidly that they rebuild good health more quickly."

Kathy Miller, R.N.
Oak View, California

Sound is just as integral a part of the life force as light. Thus, each color ray of the life force expresses a unique sound as well as a unique color. Citrine's crystalline matrix amplifies the sound of the yellow ray. Subtle sounds such as this are often difficult to hear amid the noises of daily living. If you wear Citrine continually, these sounds will become more audible. The more you listen to the sound of Citrine, the more your ears will be cleansed and the more clearly you will hear the subtle sounds of the universe.

This cleansing of your inner hearing may allow your ears to open to the different sounds of all the gemstones. Each gemstone carries its own music, a unique and enchantingly beautiful sound. If you can hear the sound of a gemstone, you will become more attuned to its energy, and its powers will increase many fold. Citrine's sound is heard more easily than the sounds carried by the other color-ray gemstones. Thus, by opening your inner ears, Citrine can also prepare you to accept the greatest benefits that any gemstone can give.

Citrine and the Eliminatory System

Each of the seven color rays of the life force is particularly healing and nourishing to certain aspects of the physical body. The yellow ray nourishes and supports the organs of elimination, including the skin, bladder, urinary tract, kidneys, intestines, and eliminative aspects of the liver. Consequently, wearing Citrine can help strengthen these parts of the body and resolve certain conditions associated with them.

Increasing Citrine's Effectiveness

In most cases, one necklace of Citrine works exclusively on a cellular level unless its effects are magnified in some way. The best way to magnify Citrine's effects is to wear a necklace of very high quality Citrine or to wear additional Citrine—either by wearing a necklace with larger beads or by wearing a second or third necklace.

Citrine Rounded Chips vs. Spheres

Citrine breaks up hardened energies and fixed states of consciousness. Although Citrine in spherical form produces this effect, rounded chips enhance it. A gemstone's energy radiates from a sphere in a perfectly regular fashion, while it escapes from a rounded chip in an irregular one. In the case of Citrine, this irregularity helps break up old states of consciousness, thus helping Citrine deliver its benefits more easily.

Therapeutic-Quality Citrine

Only pure-yellow Citrine can draw the yellow ray to the body. The color of therapeutic Citrine ranges from light to deep yellow and sometimes possesses a golden glow. Very pale Citrine does not manifest yellow-ray energy strongly enough to produce therapeutic effects. Dark-amber or brownish Citrine can actually be detrimental, because it muddies the energy flow to the atoms, molecules, cells, and organs that are dependent on the yellow ray for life. Indeed, any degree of black or brown within Citrine is a toxic contaminant.

Internal flaws dull Citrine's appearance and diminish its ability to express the yellow ray. Slight surface flaws are acceptable, as are a very small number of internal cracks, but only if they occur in Citrine that is pure, bright yellow.

Ideal Citrine is flawless and the true yellow of the rainbow. Citrine that displays the special optical property known as gem candescence radiates a greatly enhanced flow of Citrine energy.

"Citrine is great for releasing tension in my neck, back, and solar plexus. I get results in less than an hour after putting on the necklace."

Judith Greenwood, L.M.T.
Richardson, Texas

Mineral Composition
SiO_2 + Fe

Natural Citrine, a yellow variety of Quartz, is rare. It forms most often when Amethyst formations lie near natural heat sources in the Earth's crust. Its yellow color comes from the presence of iron in the crystal. Citrine is found in Brazil and Madagascar.

Citrine Therapy
Tension Release

Holding Citrine on the crown chakra while performing a movement exercise helps unwind tense muscles, thus allowing the bones and joints, particularly in the neck, back, jaw and shoulders, to move into greater alignment.

Therapy Tools
One or two therapeutic necklaces of Citrine rounded chips

Indications
- When you are experiencing any of the following in your head, neck, jaw, shoulders, back, or hips:
  - Tightness or pain caused by strain or injury
  - Stress-related tightness and structural misalignment
- When you want to supplement other spinal-alignment therapies, such as chiropractic and cranio-sacral treatments

Effects
In this technique, Citrine and yellow ray energy, in combination with physical movement, help you relieve muscular tightness and achieve better head, neck, and spinal alignment. Tightness and misalignment are often indications of a blockage in the flow of yellow ray. When you hold Citrine on your crown chakra, the Citrine's yellow-ray energy flows down the center of your spine and then back up its sides to collect in your neck and head. When enough energy has gathered there, it begins to encourage your head, neck, shoulders, and back to move. As you move and these areas receive an influx of yellow ray, the areas begin to unwind and release the blockages to the yellow ray that have contributed to their misalignment.

After you have held Citrine on your head for a while, you may notice that your head feels heavier when you remove the Citrine, even though the gemstones' weight is gone. Then, when you replace the Citrine, your head may feel lighter again. Citrine's energy and the effect of the yellow ray on the crown chakra create this effect.

The greater your deficiency or blockages in the flow of yellow ray, the longer it will take for you to achieve better alignment.

Procedure

Fig. CIT-1

1. Ideally, wear a therapeutic Citrine necklace around your neck for several days. This technique works more quickly and effectively when you perform Step 1 before going on to Step 2. However, if you are very flexible or especially sensitive to gemstone energy, you may be able to skip this step and still derive the full benefits of the treatment.

2. Stand up in an area where you can move the upper part of your body without bumping into anything. Close your eyes, if you wish.

3. Remove the Citrine necklace from around your neck.

4. Bunch the necklace in your right hand, and hold it on your crown chakra for a minute or two (see Fig. CIT-1).

5. While continuing to hold the Citrine on your crown, gently move your head back and forth or in a circular motion. Let your mind relax, and let go of thoughts. Perform this step for a minute or so.

6. Allow Citrine's energy to guide the movements of other parts of your body. Let your head, neck, shoulders and back move, stretch, and twist in whatever directions feel most comfortable.

   • If you wish to decrease the intensity of the treatment, switch hands and place your left hand over the Citrine. This will slow down the rate and intensity of change in your spine.

   • If you wish to increase the intensity of the treatment, add another necklace to your crown. Do this only after you have first tried using a single necklace.

7. When you feel that your body has completed a cycle of unwinding, remove the Citrine from your head.

8. To maintain the treatment's benefits, wear the Citrine around your neck between treatment sessions. This will counteract your body's tendency to tighten up and become misaligned again.

Time Guidelines

The first time you perform this technique, practice it for 10 to 15 minutes. You may gradually increase the time with subsequent sessions. You can perform this technique daily.

If you have chronic structural imbalances of the neck or head, it may be helpful to keep the Citrine on the top of your head for several hours a day between treatments. This will encourage further unwinding but at a much slower and gentler rate. You may wear the Citrine under a natural-fiber hat or fastened around a bun of hair, using a natural-fiber tie. If you start to feel uncomfortable or spaced out, remove the Citrine from your head and wear it around your neck. Wait a day or two, and then try placing it on your head again.

Post-Treatment Cleansing of Gems

Immediately after completing a treatment, it is important to cleanse the gems of any disharmonious energies released by the body in the course of treatment. See Appendix A: "Care and Cleansing of Therapeutic Gems," on page 397, for cleansing instructions.

Masculine and Feminine
Healing and Empowerment

Green Tourmaline

Pink Tourmaline

Green Tourmaline

Empowering the Masculine

Green Tourmaline balances the masculine and feminine aspects within a man, empowering him to realize his full potential. It carries the masculine ray, which vitalizes the masculine aspect in all living beings. Green Tourmaline strengthens every molecule in a man's body, tones his reproductive system, and reverses any disharmonious tendencies in his body, emotions, and mind. Green Tourmaline broadens a man's awareness as it maximizes the flow of his life force, granting him courage, vigor, and vitality.

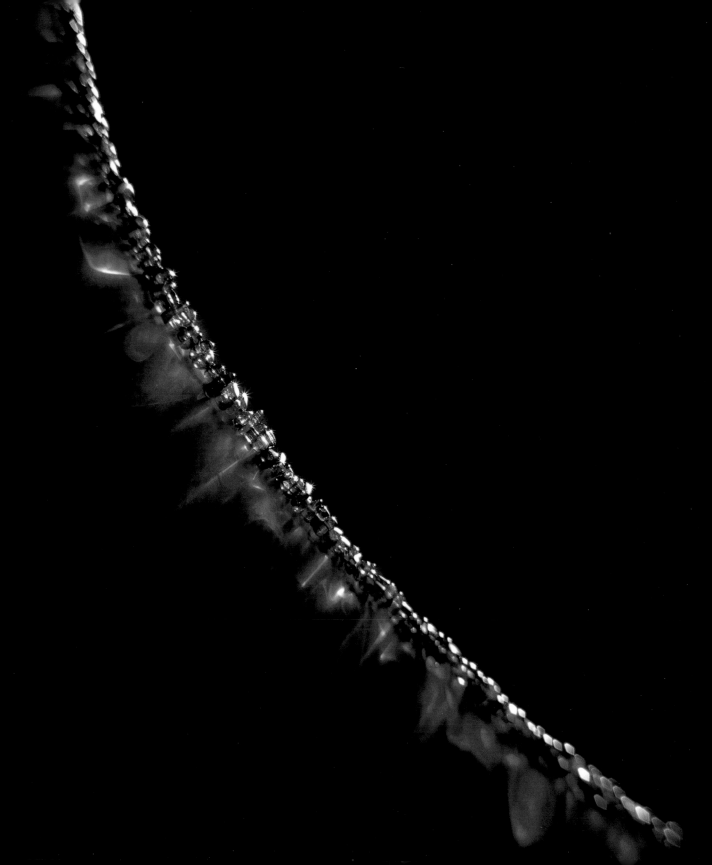

Indications *for Wearing a Therapeutic*
Green Tourmaline Necklace

For men

YOU ARE EXPERIENCING—

Diminished physical strength or prowess

Any kind of physical distress or disease

An endocrine imbalance

An unwanted condition in your reproductive system

YOU WANT TO—

Empower your masculine nature

Experience more courage, vigor, and vitality

Improve physical endurance

Enhance athletic performance

Increase sexual prowess

Strengthen and tone your reproductive system

Harmonize and balance your masculine and feminine aspects

For women

You want to enhance athletic performance (*to be worn only during workouts and competitive events*)

When you sense that your masculine aspect is weakened, suppressed, or undeveloped

When you sense that your feminine aspect is overwhelming your healthy expression of masculine energy

Benefits of *Wearing a Therapeutic*
Green Tourmaline Necklace

Green Tourmaline balances and empowers men by harmonizing the masculine and feminine aspects within them. It carries the masculine ray, which vitalizes the masculine aspect in all living beings. Green Tourmaline gives a man the strength, courage, and self-confidence he needs to realize his full potential. It broadens a man's awareness as it strengthens every molecule in his body.

Masculine and feminine energies are fundamental components of life, and both must be present for life to exist. Like the color rays, masculine and feminine energies have gemstone carriers: Green Tourmaline carries the male energy, and Pink Tourmaline carries the female energy. These gemstones act as energy sources to keep each gender independent and strong.

Fundamental to an understanding of Green Tourmaline is that all men and women have and express both male and female energies. No man expresses 100 percent masculine energy; nor does a woman express solely feminine energy. For a man to be healthy and strong, he needs to have and express an appropriate balance of masculine and feminine energies. Any degree of gender imbalance can diminish his strength and energy. Green Tourmaline can help men resolve gender imbalances.

The way energies flow in a man's body differs in many respects from the way energies flow in a woman's. Green Tourmaline resonates with the way energies flow in a male body, and it strengthens and uplifts the male flow. When a man wears Green Tourmaline, it maximizes the life force flowing through him.

Green Tourmaline also enhances the chakras' abilities to receive and release energies, thereby making all energies required by the body, including color rays, more available to the body. Green Tourmaline helps strengthen and heal a man's endocrine and reproductive systems. Because the endocrine system regulates so many vital functions, his whole body naturally becomes stronger and more energetic.

Green Tourmaline promotes balance in the physical, emotional, and mental bodies. It does this by strengthening the weakest link in the chain. First, its energy fills a man's aura and gathers information about all his bodies. Then it identifies and focuses its energy on the weakest area of his physical body. When the physical body has achieved a certain degree of balance, the Tourmaline's energy moves to the weakest area of his emotional body and works there. Finally, it moves to the weakest part of his mental body. When the mental body has been brought to a certain degree of balance, the Tourmaline's energy returns its focus to the physical body and starts the cycle again.

Each time the Green Tourmaline cycles through a man's body, emotions, and mind, it takes each of them to a higher level of strength and healing. This process continues for as long as the Tourmaline is worn. Even after wearing Green Tourmaline for only a day, a man often feels physically stronger. If he continues to wear it, he will find himself becoming emotionally stronger and then mentally stronger.

Before the weakest link can be strengthened, it must be recognized. It takes courage to recognize one's weaknesses and to face them. Therefore, when a man first puts on Green Tourmaline, the Tourmaline's initial response is to give a feeling of strength, courage, and self-confidence. This occurs as soon as Green Tourmaline touches a masculine aura.

Any man, even the healthiest on Earth, can benefit from wearing Green Tourmaline—because, as far as health is concerned, there is always another step to take. As a man attains greater health, his attention often turns away from his physical problems to encompass a greater understanding and awareness of himself and of life. This eventually leads to self-mastery. Before one can become a master of spirit, one must first master one's physical body, emotions, memory, mind, and intuition. Green Tourmaline helps a man achieve this mastery.

"After three weeks of wearing Green Tourmaline, I started noticing positive changes in my person—not just physical, but mental changes too. When I wear it, I recover much faster after competitive events and workouts. This lets me shorten my breaks and get in more training time. I've started wearing Green Tourmaline 24 hours a day. My experiences tell me that anyone can benefit from the Green Tourmaline necklace—not just athletes."

Mark Foster
British Olympic Swimmer
Winner of six Gold Medals at the
2002/2003 FINA World Cup while
wearing Green Tourmaline

Time Guidelines and Amount to Wear

Because of the intensity of Green Tourmaline's effects, men should wear only one necklace of Green Tourmaline at a time. Some men may even find it uncomfortable to wear one necklace 24 hours a day. Some may want to wear it only during the day and not at night; for some, even this may be too much. If a man wears Green Tourmaline too long, he may experience a headache or some irritability. If this occurs, he should remove the Tourmaline as soon as he feels any discomfort. The next day, he should put the necklace back on for a short period, and then ease into wearing it regularly by gradually increasing the time he wears it each day.

No matter how many hours a day that a man wears Green Tourmaline, he must wear it every day. Only then will he experience Green Tourmaline's greatest healing effects. After wearing a necklace of rounded Green Tourmaline daily for a month, the effects will be unmistakable.

Green Tourmaline and Aventurine

Although Green Tourmaline and Dark Green Aventurine both initiate physical healing, they are two different tools with two different actions. Some people's conditions require force and power to be healed; others call for a gentler approach; and still others require a combination of the two. Green Tourmaline works with force and power. Compared to the power of Tourmaline, Aventurine's work is quite gentle.

Too much healing force and power can make some people virtually explode, especially if someone is already a pent-up dynamo of stress and tension. Such an individual would do better to wear Aventurine for several weeks before wearing Green Tourmaline. The Aventurine will help his cells begin the process of opening up and releasing their disharmonies.

However, if the pent-up person is also very weak, he can wear a short, lightweight necklace of Green Tourmaline, a longer necklace of Quartz, and an even longer necklace of Dark Green Aventurine. In someone who is both very weak and very tight, the forces of the two green gemstones will be balanced by the presence of the Quartz. The

"Since I began wearing Green Tourmaline, I have broken nine World Masters Records and won three World Championship titles. I believe I would not have broken these world records without the Green Tourmaline necklace. It gives me a lot of strength, and I recover faster from hard workouts. Curiously, it also gives me more sexual interest and power."

Glen Christiansen
Swedish Olympic Medalist

Aventurine will make the physical-healing changes while the Green Tourmaline gives the body strength.

Green Tourmaline and Women

In general, women should not wear Green Tourmaline, except for short periods. If a woman wore a necklace of Green Tourmaline for an extended period, her masculine nature would eventually overwhelm her feminine nature. One imbalance after another would manifest. Her emotional strength would be crushed, and eventually she would suffer from hormone imbalances. Therefore, it's best for women to wear Green Tourmaline no more than several days a month.

However, at times it can be beneficial for a woman to bolster her masculine energy—for example, if she is experiencing a deficiency of such energy. Symptoms of a such a deficiency can include difficulty asserting herself in the world; a sense that she is continually being put down, abused, or manipulated; or a perceived lack of feminine identity. Wearing a therapeutic Green Tourmaline necklace for a short period may help correct these imbalances.

Another example of a situation in which a woman can benefit from wearing Green Tourmaline is when she is training for or competing in an athletic event. The Green Tourmaline can help improve endurance and strength.

Creating Harmony Between Mates

See "Creating Harmony Between Mates," on page 290, for a technique that uses both Green and Pink Tourmalines to help resolve disharmonies between mates.

Therapeutic-Quality Green Tourmaline

Green Tourmaline's natural color varies from olive- to emerald-green, in shades that range from light to medium-dark. Green Tourmaline that is dull, cloudy, or not true in color is non-therapeutic. Therapeutic-quality Green Tourmaline is relatively free of inclusions and is radiant in appearance.

Mineral Composition

$Na(Mg,Fe)_3Al_6(BO_3)_3(Si_6O_{18})(OH,F)_4$

Green Tourmaline is a boron-aluminum silicate with elements of sodium, lithium, and/or potassium. Tourmalines were originally called *ash drawers* because of their ability to strongly repel or attract lightweight substances, such as ashes, in sunlight. Tourmalines are found in Africa, Brazil, Madagascar, Ceylon, Burma, Russia, California, and Maine.

Green Tourmaline Therapy
Hydrotherapy for Men

This therapy for men combines the energy of Green Tourmaline with water to strengthen and energize all the cells in a man's body. A man submerges himself in bathwater that has been suffused with Green Tourmaline energy and thereby infuses his individual cells with this energy.

Therapy Tools

- One therapeutic necklace of Green Tourmaline rounded chips
- Bathtub with faucet
- One cup of non-iodized sea salt

Indications

- When a man is experiencing physical disharmony that affects his entire body, such as fatigue, a cold or flu, or a more serious systemic disease
- When a man has been wearing Green Tourmaline without feeling improvement in his health, possibly indicating a need to focus the gemstones' energy at the cellular level
- When a man desires an extra infusion of Green Tourmaline energy

Contraindications

Green Tourmaline Hydrotherapy is not recommended for women. A woman who feels the need for Green Tourmaline's energy should wear a Green Tourmaline necklace around her neck for a short period.

Effects

This therapy produces a relatively mild infusion of Green Tourmaline energy in bathwater. It acts like a tonic for individual cells throughout a man's entire body, especially the cells of his skin, soft tissue, muscles, and organs. Because the infusion is mild, the Green Tourmaline energy does not penetrate the body deeply; therefore, its effects on the bones, tendons, and ligaments are less significant.

Green Tourmaline's energy cannot be directly imparted to calm water. Some kind of movement is required to carry the Tourmaline's energy into the water molecules. The action of water streaming down a strand of Green Tourmaline chips creates enough molecular friction to infuse the Green Tourmaline energy into the water.

Procedure

Caution: Do not skip Step 1 below. An uncleansed necklace can release disharmonious energies into the bathwater.

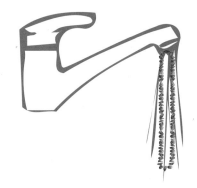

Fig. GTR-1

1. Thoroughly cleanse the Green Tourmaline necklace you will be using for the treatment—
   • Hold the necklace under alternating hot and cold running water for one or two minutes. If you are cleansing the necklace in a bathtub, allow this water to run down the drain; do not use this water for your treatment.
   • If possible, then place the necklace in direct sunlight for 15 to 30 minutes.

2. Start running water into a clean bathtub. Make sure the water is a comfortable temperature.

3. Pour one cup of non-iodized sea salt into the bathtub while the water is running.

4. Hold the Green Tourmaline necklace under the running water, so that the necklace hangs in the middle of the stream (see Fig. GTR-1).
   • If the necklace has a clasp, fasten it. Then hold the necklace by its clasp so that the length of the double strand you've created hangs in the middle of the stream.
   • If the necklace is longer than 24 inches, hold the necklace by its middle so that you create a quadruple strand in the middle of the streaming water.

5. When the water is three to four inches deep, enter the tub. Continue holding the Green Tourmaline under the running water until the tub is full enough to submerge as much of your body as possible.

6. Turn off the water, and leave the Green Tourmaline necklace in the tub.

7. Relax and soak in the bathtub for about 15 minutes.

8. When you have finished soaking in the water—
   - Cleanse the Green Tourmaline necklace (see Step 1 for instructions).
   - Put the necklace around your neck.
   - Drain and wash the tub.

Time Guidelines

About 15 minutes after the water has been turned off, the concentration of Green Tourmaline energy in the water starts to decline rapidly. After about 30 minutes, its effects are negligible, perhaps only five to 10 percent of what they were during the first 15 minutes.

Post-Treatment Cleansing of Gems

Immediately after completing a treatment, it is important to cleanse the gems of any disharmonious energies released by the body in the course of treatment. See Appendix A: "Care and Cleansing of Therapeutic Gems," on page 397, for cleansing instructions.

Pink Tourmaline

Empowering the Feminine

Pink Tourmaline balances the feminine and masculine aspects within a woman, empowering her to reach her full potential. It carries the feminine ray, which vitalizes the feminine aspect in all living beings. The powerful light that Pink Tourmaline draws to the body dissolves both the symptoms and causes of physical conditions, especially those of the female reproductive organs. Pink Tourmaline helps a woman understand and come to peace with her feminine and masculine selves as it fosters the inner harmony and strength she needs to develop her true feminine power.

Pink Tourmaline chips combined with
Biwa Pearls and 14K gold beads

Indications *for Wearing a Therapeutic*
Pink Tourmaline Necklace

WHEN ONE OR MORE OF THE FOLLOWING APPLY—

For women

YOU ARE EXPERIENCING—

A sense of disempowerment

An endocrine imbalance

An unwanted condition in your reproductive system

Any kind of physical distress or disease

YOU WANT TO—

Empower your feminine nature

Experience more self-confidence and vitality

Strengthen and tone your reproductive system

Ease menstrual cramps or other irregularities associated with your reproductive organs

For both women and men

YOU WANT TO—

Protect yourself from other people's negative thoughts and feelings

Protect yourself from negative influences in an environment that is potentially hostile or full of negative mental or emotional energies

Avoid the draining effects of a job involving intense public interaction, such as healthcare, retail work, or public speaking

Shield yourself from the harmful effects of electromagnetic radiation

Maintain your vitality when you are traveling or work in an airport

Benefits of *Wearing a Therapeutic*
Pink Tourmaline Necklace

Pink Tourmaline balances and empowers women by harmonizing the feminine and masculine aspects within them. It carries the feminine ray, which vitalizes the feminine aspect in all living beings. Pink Tourmaline gives women the power, understanding, and awareness to realize their full potential. It helps them realize how their feminine and masculine natures coexist and interact, and it encourages these aspects to achieve greater harmony.

Feminine and masculine energies are fundamental components of life, and both must be present for life to exist. Like the color rays, feminine and masculine energies have gemstone carriers: Pink Tourmaline carries the female energy, and Green Tourmaline carries the male energy. These gemstones act as energy sources to keep each gender independent and strong.

Pink Tourmaline also has a secondary mission. This is to protect its wearer from harmful external energies, such as electromagnetic radiation, microwaves, and the negative thoughts and emotions of others. It does this by forming a protective shield in the aura of any woman or man who wears it. This protective function is essential to Pink Tourmaline's ability to carry out its primary mission. Pink Tourmaline helps protect a woman from the energies of other people's concepts and attitudes while she is reevaluating herself, contemplating the changes she wants to make, and taking the steps to make those changes.

Centuries of oppression have led many women to believe that their masculine aspect is wrong; or it has taught them to believe that males in general are wrong, egocentric, and not as strong as they think they are. Yet women consist of both masculine and feminine energies. Therefore, until a woman releases her negative concepts about male energy, she will not be in harmony with herself. Pink Tourmaline helps a woman understand both her male and female aspects and improves communication between them, thereby creating inner and outer harmony.

Pink Tourmaline helps a woman understand and come to peace with her feminine and masculine aspects as it fosters the inner harmony and strength she needs to develop her true feminine power. The feminine energy is creative, visionary, and intuitive. Masculine energy fuels achievement. When these two aspects of a woman's inner being are enhanced, the creative visionary meets the conquering hero. Pink Tourmaline helps a woman blossom into her true potential—with the power to get it done.

Pink Tourmaline's energy dissolves disharmonious energies on all levels of being, in both the physical and subtle bodies. Therefore, its energy dissolves both the causes and effects of disharmonious conditions. Because of its mission regarding women, Pink Tourmaline has particularly strong and beneficial effects on a woman's reproductive system. It offers many effective treatments for ailments associated with women's reproduction, such as uterine cramps and infertility. It can also be used to improve the overall tone of a woman's reproductive organs.

The shield formed by Pink Tourmaline helps protect its wearers from external disharmonious energies. It does not protect them from their own inner disharmonies. If someone already experiences or expresses a certain disharmonious energy, it is difficult to protect that person from external forces of the same disharmony. For example, if you have greed within you, Pink Tourmaline cannot protect you from greed. It can protect you from disharmonies that are foreign to you. When people are protected, they have the freedom to be braver and more adventurous than they would otherwise be. They also have the freedom to think new thoughts and feel new emotions.

When a woman masters both her masculine and feminine aspects, there is nothing she cannot do. She will be limited only by how far she wishes to go. Pink Tourmaline can help women reach this state of strength, confidence, and balance.

A Specialized Tool

Unlike most of the other gemstones described in this book, Pink Tourmaline should not be worn as a solid necklace on a daily basis or even for more than a day at a time, because doing so can interfere with one's essential energy flows. Pink Tourmaline is a highly specialized tool. When used properly and with focus, it can yield profound therapeutic benefits. However, to be worn as a necklace for an extended period, Pink Tourmaline must be harmoniously combined with other gemstones.

When you wear a solid necklace of Pink Tourmaline around your neck, the Tourmaline forms a nearly impenetrable energetic shield. At first, the shield deflects only negative, foreign, or unwanted energies. However, the longer you wear the Pink Tourmaline, the stronger the shield grows. The energetic shield created by a solid necklace is so impenetrable that it disallows any feedback that would regulate its strength. If the Pink Tourmaline is worn long enough, all energies are deflected except those essential to life, and even these are negatively affected.

Wearing a solid Pink Tourmaline necklace can cause other problems, as well. Pink Tourmaline's energy enters the body through the lower four chakras and sometimes through the throat chakra. It exits only in a gentle flow through the brow chakra. Wearing even one solid necklace can bring more Pink Tourmaline energy into the body than the body can express through the brow chakra. Therefore, if you wear a necklace made entirely of Pink Tourmaline, the pressure of its energy will soon build in your head. Consequently, a headache or pressure in your brow is a sure sign that you have been wearing too much for too long. For this reason, a solid Pink Tourmaline necklace can distort your balance of mental energy and accentuate negative thought patterns. If you continue to wear this much Pink Tourmaline, your emotions will soon exhibit the same imbalances.

Therefore, you should not wear Pink Tourmaline as a solid necklace unless you are performing a specific therapy, doing something potentially

"Being mindful of the strong effects of Pink Tourmaline, I wore it only while I slept every few nights. After each use, I noticed slight changes in the muscular-skeletal structure of my back, shoulders, and neck. After six weeks, my posture had undergone a major change. I was standing more erect, my shoulders had dropped, and I had released stiffness in my lower back, while also eliminating occasional headaches associated with tension in my shoulders."

M.H.
Scottsdale, Arizona

dangerous, or entering a very disharmonious environment. Then, a solid necklace will allow you to focus more of your strength on the task at hand and less on self-protection. Wear the solid necklace around your neck for a maximum of 24 hours. Then, if you still require protection, place the solid necklace in a pocket.

For everyday use and protection—and to experience all its other benefits—Pink Tourmaline should be combined with other gemstones in a necklace. However, one must be sure that these other gemstones do not impede, confuse, interfere with, or cancel out its work. For example, Green Tourmaline should not be combined with Pink Tourmaline, because it will negatively affect the Pink Tourmaline's work.

Creating Harmony Between Mates

"Since I began wearing Pink Tourmaline and my husband began wearing Green Tourmaline, it's fair to say that individually and as a couple, we've been catapulted to a new level of awareness and harmony."

Susan Gold
Holistic Health Counselor
Bonita, California

Disharmonies often arise in relationships between mates. Whatever the cause, a wonderful therapy for ailing relationships is for the man to wear Green Tourmaline and the woman to wear Pink Tourmaline in a properly designed necklace.

Green Tourmaline gives a man strength and teaches him to balance his masculine and feminine natures. Because Green Tourmaline's energy will fill the atmosphere in the house, it will also affect the woman's aura and nourish her masculine aspect in a gentle, harmonious way. Using Pink Tourmaline nourishes a woman's feminine nature and teaches her how to balance her feminine and masculine aspects. The Pink Tourmaline's energy will touch and affect her mate's aura, too. Pink Tourmaline is a strong protector for both genders. When the man begins to feel this protection, consciously or not, he will feel safe and thus more comfortable to work on balancing his own feminine and masculine natures.

Pink Tourmaline opens lines of communication between masculine and feminine, thereby fostering balance. When a man and woman each wear the appropriate Tourmaline, the Tourmalines do not cancel each other out, as happens when the same person wears both Tourmalines together. Instead, each person benefits from the other's Tourmaline. The result is an opening of communication between the man and the woman and an increase in balance between the masculine and feminine energies within each of them.

If a man and woman wish to resolve problems in their relationship, they should try wearing Green and Pink Tourmaline. If they are not having problems, it will strengthen and vitalize their relationship. If, on the other hand, the individuals want to separate and end their relationship, the woman should wear Green Tourmaline, and the man should wear Pink Tourmaline. If they do this, the relationship will probably end within weeks—the man and woman will not be able to live with each other.

Pink Tourmaline and Men

Pink Tourmaline does not imbalance men the way Green Tourmaline can imbalance women. When a used by a man, Pink Tourmaline will provide the same energetic protection it does for a woman. A man can also use Pink Tourmaline to heal, strengthen, and better understand his own feminine aspect. Wearing a properly designed Pink Tourmaline necklace will encourage a man, consciously or unconsciously, to recognize and become more in tune with his feminine nature.

Often, when this happens, a man won't like what he sees or won't be able to accept it—especially if his feminine nature needs attention and healing. Therefore, one of the greatest gifts a man can give himself is to give Pink Tourmaline to the woman with whom he is sharing his life. As Pink Tourmaline energy fills the woman's aura, it will also affect his aura. Because the Pink Tourmaline's influence won't be as strong as if he wore it himself, this may help him balance and heal his feminine qualities more easily. Also, the aura of protection created by the Pink Tourmaline around the couple will enable the man to feel safe enough to begin balancing his own masculine and feminine energies.

Pink Tourmaline for Healthcare Practitioners

During a therapy session, health practitioners such as physicians, counselors, and bodyworkers must often divide their attention between their work with the client and the need to protect themselves

"As a therapist I find that, while working, I cannot be without Pink Tourmaline. The energetic protection it offers allows me to be open and receptive to my clients in situations where I would otherwise feel a need to protect myself. I'm able to work very deeply and give my full attention to holding a deep therapeutic intention."

Paulette Stuurmans, L.M.T.
Orono, Minnesota

from the energy surrounding or being released by the client. Wearing a Pink Tourmaline necklace protects a practitioner from these released energies, thus freeing him or her to focus fully on the client. The practitioner should wear a solid Pink Tourmaline necklace around the neck only for the duration of the treatment session and not continually. Alternately, the practitioner can keep a solid Pink Tourmaline necklace in his or her pocket all day.

Protection During Healing

Pink Tourmaline's protective properties can have an additional, indirect healing effect on the body. When outside influences bombard a particular part of the body, they often prevent or inhibit it from healing. These influences may include the energies of the thoughts, feelings, attitudes, concepts, and prayers that friends and family may be directing toward an ailing person or the ailing part of that person's body. Not only must the body focus on healing, but it must also contend with these outside influences. Despite good intentions, these influences may or may not be in the body's best interest. If the person wears a properly designed Pink Tourmaline necklace, the affected organ or area will be able to relax its defense mechanisms. It will be able to place its full attention and energy on healing, cleansing, or rejuvenating itself.

Protection During Travel

Wearing a solid necklace of Pink Tourmaline may be warranted when you are in an airport. Airports have a plethora of scattered and disharmonious energies. They are filled with electromagnetic radiation, loud noises, stale air, anxious and negative thoughts caused by plane delays, and emotional clouds from numerous sad partings. Once you are on the plane, however, a solid necklace is no longer appropriate, particularly if you will be flying for a long period.

Wearing a properly designed Pink Tourmaline necklace or keeping a solid Pink Tourmaline necklace in your pocket will also protect you from the stresses of travel. No matter where you are—in a foreign country or a foreign part of your own country—you will be protected

"I've worn a combination Pink Tourmaline necklace often for three years and have noticed subtle but distinct changes in myself. I used to be overly sensitive to other people's moods and had a hard time in social settings. Now I feel more powerful, confident, and protected. My appearance has become more feminine, and I take better care of myself. I believe that wearing Pink Tourmaline has also improved my communication with my fiancé."

Alison Stewart, L.M.T.
Chapel Hill, North Carolina

from the energies and influences that are alien, disharmonious, and potentially harmful to your body.

Therapeutic-Quality Pink Tourmaline

Pink Tourmaline occurs in a variety of colors, ranging from light pink to dark pink to deep purple-pink. Pink Tourmaline with an orange or brown cast is less therapeutic than its pinker cousins. The strongest and highest quality Pink Tourmaline, known as Rubellite, appears bright and clear and contains few inclusions or flaws. Its color is a deep, purplish pink. The closer Pink Tourmaline is to this color, the more therapeutically effective it will be.

Mineral Composition
$Na(Mg,Fe)_3Al_6(BO_3)_3(Si_6O_{18})(OH,F)_4$

Tourmalines are among the most complex minerals on Earth. Tourmalines are boron-aluminum silicates that can also contain sodium, lithium, and/or potassium. Pink Tourmaline is rich in lithium. Tourmalines are found in Africa, Brazil, Madagascar, Ceylon, Burma, Russia, California, and Maine.

Pink Tourmaline Therapy
Gynecological Health and Fertility Therapy

This therapy helps tone and heal a woman's reproductive organs by infusing them with Pink Tourmaline energy, feminine energy,[17] and several color rays.[18] At the same time, it helps resolve the inner causes of physical disharmony in the reproductive system. This therapy can assist women who are having difficulty conceiving.

Therapy Tools

- One therapeutic necklace of Pink Tourmaline rounded chips
- Alternately, a properly designed combination necklace containing Pink Tourmaline

Indications

- When a woman is experiencing any disharmony associated with her reproductive organs, such as painful or irregular periods, uterine fibroids, ovarian cysts, absence of menses, or problems in menopause
- When a woman wishes to improve her fertility and has no structural defects in her reproductive organs

Effects

Because of Pink Tourmaline's mission regarding women and its ability to radiate the feminine ray, Pink Tourmaline has particularly strong effects on a woman's reproductive organs. This therapy tones a woman's entire reproductive system and helps heal problems associated with it. Pink Tourmaline's energy affects both physical and inner disharmony and thereby addresses both the causes and effects of ailments associated

---

17 *See page 287 for more information on the feminine and masculine energies.*

18 *See page 40 for more information on the vital role of color rays in restoring and maintaining health.*

with the reproductive system, such as uterine cramps or fibroids, ovarian cysts, irregular periods, and problems in menopause.

This Pink Tourmaline therapy can also greatly assist women who are having difficulty conceiving. The fundamental causes of infertility are often mental and emotional as well as physical. This Pink Tourmaline therapy unwinds the tensions and stresses contributing to infertility on a physical level; at the same time, it addresses the deeper, nonphysical causes of infertility. Thus, it can help women who are infertile for unknown or apparently inexplicable reasons.

Pink Tourmaline strongly draws the feminine ray and several color rays, including the white ray, to the body. These rays are pulled toward Pink Tourmaline with such force that they, along with the energy of Pink Tourmaline itself, quickly form a protective shield around the placement area. At the same time, the energy and light drawn to the area begin to unwind the tension and stress contributing to the area's physical disharmonies and start dissolving them.

As Pink Tourmaline pulls the light from its ultimate source to your body, the light moves through the mental and emotional areas of your aura that correspond to the physical placement area. In the process, the color rays and Pink Tourmaline energy dissolve the negative mental and emotional energies associated with the area's condition. This is significant, because physical disharmonies are usually caused by disharmonies on inner levels. Pink Tourmaline's light dissolves both the causes and effects of an unwanted condition. For this reason, this Pink Tourmaline therapy can offer true and lasting changes after you have completed only a few treatments.

When a physical area is painful, injured, or weakened, its energy becomes increasingly disharmonious, and a vortex of negative energy is generated in the area. This vortex spirals in an unhealthy direction. When you place Pink Tourmaline on such an area, layer after layer of the area's cells switch the direction in which their vortices are spinning, and their energies become harmonious again.

I had good success performing a Pink Tourmaline therapy on a woman trying in vitro fertilization. She had not previously been ovulating from her left ovary. After I performed the Pink Tourmaline therapy on the ovary, it produced several very vital eggs.

Jacqline Tice, C.M.T.
Center Valley, Pennsylvania

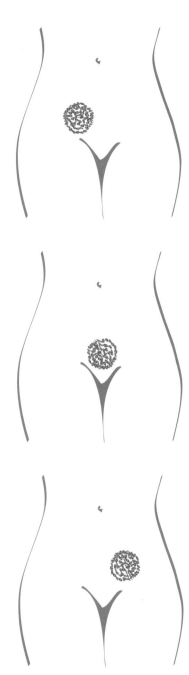

Fig. PTR-1

Procedure

1. Determine the following, if necessary, by consulting your physician:
   - The part of your reproductive system that is the focal point of the condition you wish to treat
   - The exact location of your uterus and ovaries
2. Mentally divide your reproductive system into three sections:
   - Left (left fallopian tube and ovary)
   - Middle (uterus)
   - Right (right fallopian tube and ovary)

   These are the three areas on which you will be placing the Pink Tourmaline in the steps below (see Fig. PTR-1).
3. Lie down on your back. Ideally, position yourself so that your abdomen is exposed to direct sunlight, even if it is just the sunlight coming through an open window. Otherwise, lie down wherever you are most comfortable. If sunlight is not available, the effects of the treatment will be similar but not as strong.
4. Place the Pink Tourmaline necklace in a neat pile on your skin on the section that contains the focal point of the problem. Perform this step on three consecutive days, and then go to Step 5.
5. On the fourth day, place the Pink Tourmaline on a second section of your choosing.
6. On the fifth day, place the Pink Tourmaline on the third section.
7. Repeat Steps 3–6 twice. This will take a total of ten more days.
   Example: If you have identified the left ovary as the focal point, place the Pink Tourmaline on the left section for treatments on three consecutive days. On the fourth day, place the Tourmaline over the middle section, and on the fifth day place it over the right section. Then repeat the entire sequence two more times over the next ten days.
8. Repeat Steps 3–6 twice again, but now divide the number of treatments on each section more evenly: give three treatments to the focal-point section and two treatments to each of the other sections.

Time Guidelines

This protocol takes a total of 29 days: Steps 3–7 take 15 days to complete, and Step 8 takes 14 days to complete.

When performing this treatment in sunlight, keep the Pink Tourmaline in place for 20 to 30 minutes per treatment. When performing it without sunlight or on cloudy days, keep it in place for about 60 minutes per treatment. Pink Tourmaline's energy is very strong. The higher its quality, the stronger it is. Therefore, if you are using Exquisite-quality Pink Tourmaline, cut all treatment times in half.

If, at any time, you experience additional pain or discomfort, immediately remove the Pink Tourmaline. Then reapply it the next day, perhaps for a shorter period.

Alternative: Equal Time

If you do not know which area of your reproductive system is the focal point, or if all three sections are equally distressed, place the Pink Tourmaline over each section for the same number of treatments. For example, first place it over the left section for one treatment, then the middle section for one treatment, and then over the right section for one treatment. Repeat this sequence every three days. Perform this alternative version for 28 consecutive days.

Attempting Pregnancy

You can start trying to become pregnant anytime after beginning to practice this therapy. Be aware that waiting for at least one treatment cycle will provide time for physical changes to start taking place. Continue repeating the entire therapy until you become pregnant.

Post-Treatment Cleansing of Gems

Immediately after completing a treatment, it is important to cleanse the gems of any disharmonious energies released by the body in the course of treatment. See Appendix A: "Care and Cleansing of Therapeutic Gems," on page 397, for cleansing instructions.

Healing and Nourishing with Earth Energies

Agate

Leopardskin Jasper

Poppy Jasper

Quartzite

Riverstone

Onyx

Agate

Nature's Nourishing Energies

Agate deeply nourishes your physical body with earthtone color rays while fostering cooperation among all of your body's parts. By opening lines of communication within your body, Agate's earthtones help coordinate your body's myriad functions. Agate also alerts your body's innate intelligence to your current state of health so that your body can rally its own resources to resolve any disharmonies. By flooding you with life-giving earthtones, Agate helps you forge a stronger connection with the Earth and feel more grounded and comfortable living in the physical world.

Indications for *Wearing a Therapeutic Agate Necklace*

YOU ARE EXPERIENCING—

Jet lag

Spaciness or not feeling grounded

Disconnection from nature caused by living or working in an urban or industrial setting

Living or working away from land, such as at sea or in airplanes

Living in a tall building

Travel by sea, air, rail, or automobile

Difficulty adapting to a recent move to a new environment

Working under artificial lights

A longstanding physical condition that has not responded well to other treatments

YOU WANT TO—

Prevent jet lag

Connect more deeply with nature and the Earth

Enhance physical healing by coordinating your body's resources

Support the work of certain other gemstones

Benefits of *Wearing a Therapeutic Agate Necklace*

Agate deeply nourishes your physical body with earthtone color rays while fostering cooperation among all of your body's parts. By forming lines of communication within your body, Agate's earthtone energies help coordinate your body's myriad functions. The improved cooperation among your body's parts alerts your body's innate intelligence to your state of health, so that your body can call on its own resources to resolve any disharmonies.

The earthtone color rays carried by Agate hold the key to its effects. Earthtones are combinations of color rays and subtle sounds whose vibrations are compatible with physical matter. Earthtones are different from the color rays seen in a rainbow, which are pure divisions of white light. In contrast, earthtones represent a broad array of earthy, muted colors, shades, and color combinations. Agate naturally occurs in all varieties of earthtones.

The seven color rays of the rainbow nourish your physical body indirectly by feeding its subtle, nonphysical counterparts. Yet your body also needs direct color-ray support. This support must come from vibrations that are compatible with physical matter—namely, the earthtones. Not surprisingly, the earthtone vibrations in our environment come from matter itself—from the trees, plants, minerals, rocks, and even manmade objects around us. The earthtone colors in our environment emit vibrations that make a physical connection with the body. Agate's earthtones express frequencies that are easily accepted by the physical matter of our bodies. Agate provides the colors that deeply and directly nourish the physical body.

When you first wear a necklace of Agate spheres, its earthtones flood your neck, head, shoulders, and chest with earthtone color rays. If you continue to wear the necklace for several days, Agate will fill your entire body with its energy and establish lines of communication among your organs, glands, joints, bones, muscles, and nerves. These communication lines naturally improve coordination and cooperation among all these parts of your body. The longer you wear Agate, the deeper its energy and thus these lines of communication penetrate your body.

This improved coordination among your body's components naturally draws the attention of your brain and the innate centers of intelligence in your other organs. In response, your brain and organs direct your body's own resources—including nutrients and biochemicals—toward any areas of disharmony, distress, or imbalance.

If your body does not have the resources to repair a particular imbalance, the distressed area will find a way to alert you and thus encourage you to bring the required resources into your life. You might experience this as the appearance or intensification of symptoms. This will be your body's way of communicating a need for some kind of action on your part. In this case, you will be wise to take further action—such as by consulting a physician, taking the proper medicine, or taking some other measure to help heal the area.

Agate helps address imbalances in two ways: first, by directing some of your body's energies and physical resources, such as white blood cells, to the distressed area; and, second, by nourishing the area with earthtone color rays. This doesn't mean that the area will automatically heal. It simply means that you will now have additional resources to help effect a positive change in the area.

Nature's Nourishment in a Necklace

Agate is a symbol of the Earth and of nature. The earthtone colors it expresses are those expressed by trees and plants, minerals and rocks, clouds and sky, and the planet itself. Earthtones are in harmony with nature; they also nourish and support nature. Consequently, by wearing Agate, you can forge a stronger connection with the Earth and be nourished by the very energies that nourish the planet.

The earthtone color rays are vital to the life of the body. This is one reason that a walk in nature can feel so healing. If your work or lifestyle keeps you out of natural settings, you are most likely suffering from an earthtone deficiency. This deficiency can be met by wearing an Agate necklace. Agate is a rich and abundant source of the same vital earthtones emanated by plants, water, soil, and sky. When you wear an Agate necklace, you are nourished by a continual flow of nature's earthtone color rays. Thus, it is particularly helpful for people who love nature and the outdoors or who have a special affinity with the Earth but who must work inside a building or live for long periods at sea.

Adapting to a New Environment

Whether you live in the forest, seaside, or city, your world is filled with earthtone color rays. While earthtones emanating from living things, and even the sky and soil, are more vital and nourishing than those of artwork, furniture, or painted interior walls, the colors in your home and other manmade environments also provide some color ray support.

Your body naturally becomes accustomed to the earthtone spectrum provided by its environment. The longer you and your ancestors have lived in a particular kind of environment, the more ingrained in your cells that environment's earthtone spectrum will have become. For this reason, some people find it hard to change environments—for example, to leave behind the earthtone spectrum of the countryside and start a new life in the city, or vice versa.

If soon after you move to any new environment, you experience unusual fatigue or symptoms that cannot be corrected with better diet, reduced stress, or more sleep, it might mean that your body is having difficulty adjusting to the new earthtone spectrum around you. Simply wearing an Agate necklace can help. It is best to wear Agate as much as possible—ideally, constantly for several weeks. A therapeutic Agate necklace offers a balance of earthtone color rays that allows your body to pick and choose the colors it needs to correct any earthtone deficiencies. It helps you to live more comfortably in any environment you choose.

"I was so grateful to have my Agate necklace for my flight back to Norway. Usually I feel drained—you know, the pale grayish been-on-the-plane-for-eight-hours feeling you have by the time you reach the airport. But both during and after the flight, I felt rejuvenated and relaxed."

E.H.
Sofiemyr, Norway

Adjusting to Travel

Agate's ability to provide the body with earthtone color rays on demand makes it an invaluable tool when you are traveling. By having a constant and abundant source of earthtone color rays, your body won't be limited by the different earthtone spectrums in your new environment, and your trip will likely go more smoothly and comfortably.

Agate is particularly helpful if you are leaving land to take an airplane flight or ocean voyage. It will help you maintain a better connection with the Earth's vibrations, making you feel more centered and balanced, thus allowing you to think more clearly and function at your best when you arrive.

Supporting Other Gemstones' Work

If you wear Agate along with another therapeutic gem necklace that highlights a particular area of distress, Agate's energies and earthtones will be drawn to the highlighted area and concentrate there. For example, if you wear Agate with Dark Green Aventurine, which highlights your weakest organ, Agate's energies will collect in the organ. The highlighted organ or area will quickly identify which earthtones it needs and which it does not. Unneeded earthtones will exit the area. Those left behind— usually a spectrum of three or four earthtones—will be the ones needed most by the area.

Therapeutic-Quality Agate

A therapeutic-quality Agate necklace has a good balance of many different earthtone colors. Agate expresses the earthtone version of the rainbow colors. Thus, a therapeutic necklace has spheres of pink, teal, blue-gray, yellow-green, red-green, red-lavender, lavender, or other colors, shades, and color combinations. These variations of color in an Agate necklace offer a broader and richer experience of Agate's benefits. Each person's body is unique and comprised of unique vibrations. A therapeutic Agate necklace contains spheres that can fill all types of vibrational deficiencies in the person who wears it.

Mineral Composition
SiO_2 + Al + Fe

Agate is banded chalcedony composed of layers of crypto-crystalline Quartz in which differently colored layers alternate, usually in concentric forms. Agate's other components vary greatly but usually include aluminum and iron oxide. Agate is found in Germany, India, Brazil, Egypt, Mexico, and many areas in the U.S.

Agate's colors should be strong, distinct, and clear. Pale, pastel-colored Agate does not emanate its vibrations strongly enough to affect most people. Agate with strong colors provides the body with stronger and clearer earthtone support. This is particularly crucial today, when the physical body must contend with so many physical stimuli. The noise of modern life overwhelms the body's ability to hear the subtle sounds of nature. In order for nature to speak to the human body, it must do so loudly and clearly.

Therapeutic-quality Agate occurs in a range of clarity, from opaque to various grades of translucency. The spheres in an Agate necklace should contain a consistent degree of clarity.

Agate Therapy

Improving Communication Within the Body

Agate is placed on an ailing area of the body to flood the area with Agate's nourishing earthtone color rays and to foster communication and cooperation between the area and other related parts of the body. This improved communication eases unhealthy compensations among these parts and encourages the body to heal any associated condition.

Therapy Tool

One therapeutic necklace of Agate spheres (8 mm or 10 mm)

Indications

When any organ or localized area of your body is experiencing any of the following—

- Illness
- Injury
- Pain
- Stiffness
- Weakness

Effects

This Agate therapy forms energetic connections among different parts of your body so that they can help each other overcome their imbalances and achieve greater health. When Agate is placed on an ailing area of the body, the Agate floods the area with nourishing earthtone color rays. These color rays concentrate in the area and open lines of communication between it and other, related parts of the body. Thus, it encourages these parts to cooperate with each other.

Cooperation among the body's organs, glands, joints, muscles, and other components is vital to their healthy functioning. Because all parts of the body are so interrelated, a problem in one part is often caused or exacerbated by problems in another part. For example, an ailment in the wrist and elbow can be caused or aggravated by problems in the shoulder. Furthermore, ailments can arise when part of the body starts to compensate for problems in another part. For instance, a knee can compensate for a weak ankle and, in doing so, start to malfunction because of the added stress and strain.

Placing Agate on a troubled area of the body allows all the components related to that area to work together better. Inappropriate compensations start to ease and relax. For example, if you place Agate on a troubled wrist, all parts of your arm will begin to cooperate, and compensations in the muscles surrounding the wrist and in the forearm, upper arm, and shoulder will relax.

You might find it easier to perceive the release of muscular compensation than other kinds of compensation, because muscle relaxation is more easily seen and felt.

Procedure

1. Arrange an Agate necklace in a flat circle or spiral on the area you wish to treat, preferably directly on your skin (see Fig. AGA-1).
2. Keep the Agate in place for at least three to five minutes.
3. Move the Agate to another location that is logically related to the original treatment area. For example, if you originally placed the Agate on your wrist, place it on your elbow or shoulder. Keep the Agate in place for at least three to five minutes.
4. Repeat Step 3 until you have treated all the areas you think might be involved in the distress of the original treatment area.
5. For ongoing support, wear the Agate necklace around your neck between treatment sessions.

Time Guidelines

The instruction in Step 2 to keep the Agate on each treatment area for three to five minutes is a minimum time. For a deeper and more thorough treatment, you can keep the Agate in place for several hours while engaging in quiet activity—for example, while you are reading

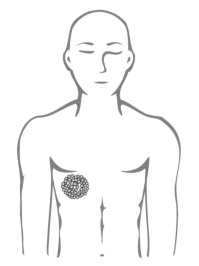

Fig. AGA-1

or watching TV. If you perform longer treatments, treat only one area per day.

In general, Agate therapy takes time to achieve its full effects. It also takes time for Agate's effects to be noticed. The benefits of this therapy may not be felt until hours after you have completed it, when you may suddenly realize that a change has occurred in the treatment area.

Post-Treatment Cleansing of Gems

Immediately after completing a treatment, it is important to cleanse the gems of any disharmonious energies released by the body in the course of treatment. See Appendix A: "Care and Cleansing of Therapeutic Gems," on page 397, for cleansing instructions.

Leopardskin Jasper

Attracting Beneficial Influences

Leopardskin Jasper helps draw into your life whatever you need for physical healing. By energetically charging the areas of your aura that reflect your true needs, Leopardskin Jasper helps you attract whatever is required to fulfill them. If worn long enough, Leopardskin Jasper will strengthen and fine-tune your body's overall regulatory mechanism, increasing your personal magnetism and individuality. Leopardskin Jasper also assists people who constantly invite disharmony into their lives by helping them to attract forces of harmony and to repel forces of disharmony.

Indications *for Wearing a Therapeutic*
Leopardskin Jasper Necklace

YOU ARE EXPERIENCING—

Any unwanted physical condition

Any kind of condition related to regulatory function, such as that
of the heart, brain or endocrine system

Regular attraction of disharmony into your life

YOU WANT TO—

Repel unhealthy influences

Attract into your life whatever your body needs to improve
physical health

Strengthen your individuality and personal magnetism

Benefits *of Wearing a Therapeutic*
Leopardskin Jasper Necklace

Leopardskin Jasper helps draw into your life whatever you need for physical healing. When Leopardskin Jasper spheres encircle your neck, the spheres' energy flows into your aura, where it captures information about you. This information then rides on the return flow of Leopardskin Jasper energy back to the spheres around your neck. In this way, the Leopardskin Jasper learns your needs.

Once Leopardskin Jasper has learned your requirements for physical healing, it charges the areas in your aura that reflect these needs. This charge helps attract whatever is needed to fulfill those needs. Do not be surprised at what Leopardskin Jasper might help draw to you. It might be a physician, certain foods or medicines, or a book on a new healing method. All these things are patterns of energetic frequencies. Medicines, herbs, fresh mountain air, and a trip to the beach are also distinct frequency patterns. Leopardskin Jasper does not distinguish between energies and the physical forms they take.

However, Leopardskin Jasper does discriminate between true and artificial needs. An example of an artificial need is a child's "need" to have ice cream for dessert, while his true need might be for an apple. Leopardskin Jasper helps attract whatever will satisfy one's true needs, which are not necessarily the same as desires or wishes.

To sustain life, all living things must be regulated with extreme precision. Every part of a living organism depends on every other part. If one part suffers an imbalance, other parts will be affected. When Leopardskin Jasper is cut into spherical form, circular patterns appear on the spheres. The Leopardskin's energy emanates from these circles, which act somewhat like control knobs to help regulate the body's energies. When you wear Leopardskin Jasper around your neck, it brings greater balance and regulation to your physical body as a whole.

If you wear Leopardskin Jasper spheres long enough, your overall regulatory mechanism will improve and become more defined. As a result, your personal magnetism and individuality will increase. The definition of who you are will become more specific. As you become more self-defined, you will naturally repel individuals with dishonorable intentions. Just as Leopardskin Jasper can attract harmonious influences, it can also repel disharmonious ones. The longer Leopardskin Jasper is worn, the stronger the repelling force will be. It may take many months of continually wearing Leopardskin Jasper before this force becomes strong enough to repel people who don't have your best interests at heart.

Because of this effect, Leopardskin Jasper can assist people who constantly attract disharmony into their lives by helping them to attract sources of greater harmony and to repel the negative influences that create disharmony. Leopardskin Jasper will continue to work until the positive influences succeed in reversing this disharmonious tendency.

Directing Leopardskin Jasper's Work

Left to its own devices, Leopardskin Jasper focuses on the area of your body with the most rapidly declining health. If you wish, however, you can focus the Leopardskin Jasper's effects on a different issue of your own choosing. To do this, you can use your mental intention to direct the Leopardskin Jasper to the issue. You can also initiate other healing forces to direct the Leopardskin's focus there. For example, if you wear Leopardskin Jasper along with another therapeutic gemstone necklace, the Leopardskin will attract what the body needs to support the work of the other gemstone; or, if you take a remedy to address a particular issue, the Leopardskin Jasper will support the remedy's work.

How to Wear Leopardskin Jasper

It is particularly beneficial to wear a Leopardskin Jasper necklace so that it touches your skin, rather than over clothing.

"Wearing Leopardskin Jasper brought me the awareness of what I needed in order to heal a lifelong emotional issue that was affecting my physical well-being. Now, that issue no longer has any pull on me. Leopardskin Jasper drew to me a way to be free."

Judith Greenwood, L.M.T.
Richardson, Texas

Animals

Animals may experience even greater effects than human beings when they wear Leopardskin Jasper, because their minds won't interfere with its work. The minds of animals don't tell them that they need ice cream instead of apples.

Therapeutic-Quality Leopardskin Jasper

In the highest quality therapeutic Leopardskin Jasper, a necklace's spheres display many black and gray circles on a rich golden background. These circles are well defined and contrast sharply with the background color. This golden background can have a range of other tones, including tan, yellow, orange, red, and brown. In low-quality Leopardskin Jasper, fewer circles are apparent; also, the background color lacks a golden quality and looks dull and washed out.

Nearly all the Leopardskin Jasper spheres available today are cut and drilled using petrochemicals, the residue of which can be often detected by a kerosene-like odor. Such Leopardskin Jasper is not therapeutic. When it is worn, the body braces itself against the energy of the chemicals and, in doing so, resists the energy of the Leopardskin Jasper itself. To be therapeutic, Leopardskin Jasper must be cut and shaped using only water.

Mineral Composition
$SiO_2 + FeO_2$

Leopardskin Jasper is a granular form of chalcedony, or cryptocrystalline Quartz, that is colored tan, brown, yellow, orange, and red by iron oxides. It is formed in deposits relatively close to the Earth's surface in flows of magma. Leopardskin Jasper is found in Mexico, India, Siberia, Australia, Scotland, Brazil, California, Arkansas, and Texas.

Leopardskin Jasper Therapy
Regulation Therapy

Leopardskin Jasper is used to treat an organ or gland that is experiencing a regulatory dysfunction. Placing Leopardskin Jasper on the ailing area improves either its self-regulation or its regulatory capacity within the body. This therapy is particularly useful for organs and glands that perform regulatory functions, such as the brain, heart, and certain glands.

Therapy Tools
One therapeutic necklace of Leopardskin Jasper spheres (8 mm or 10 mm)

Indications
- When one of your organs or glands is experiencing any of the following dysfunctions:
  - Improper self-regulation
  - Metabolic dysfunction
  - Lack of synchrony within itself or with the rest of the body
  - Improper responses to messages from other parts of the body
- When any of your organs or glands that perform regulatory functions—such as the brain or heart or the pituitary, pineal, or hypothalamus glands—are weak or malfunctioning in some way

Effects
When Leopardskin Jasper spheres are placed on an organ or gland that is experiencing some kind of regulatory dysfunction, the Leopardskin Jasper helps regulate its functioning. The Leopardskin improves both the input and output capacities of the organ or gland. It helps call to the area the physical resources needed by the organ or gland to function in harmony with the rest of the body—for example, minerals, enzymes, vitamins, and other nutrients. At the same time, the Leopardskin enhances the ability of the organ or gland to excrete hormones or other substances and to expel wastes.

Leopardskin's work is most effective on organs and glands with regulatory functions, such as the brain, heart, and pituitary gland. The thicker the pile of Leopardskin Jasper placed on the area, the more deeply its energy can penetrate the area's cells.

Procedure

1. Place a Leopardskin Jasper necklace in a neat pile on the area you wish to treat (see Fig. LSJ-1).

   If you are treating your brain, cover as much of your skull as possible with the Leopardskin Jasper. This may require two or more Leopardskin Jasper necklaces. Do your best to hold them in place with a natural-fiber bandana or scarf.

2. Between treatments, wear a Leopardskin Jasper necklace around your neck. This will help your body maintain its improved functioning.

Using Your Intuition

While it is true that the thicker the pile of Leopardskin Jasper, the more deeply it can penetrate an organ, it is important to use your intuition when applying Leopardskin. Your body may need only one or two necklaces of Leopardskin Jasper over an organ, when you think it needs five. If you apply too much Leopardskin Jasper, the organ may overcompensate. Then it may seem like the Leopardskin is making the condition worse, when in fact you are either applying too much at one time or your treatments are too frequent or too long. If your condition appears to worsen, cut back. Use your discretion and intuition to find a balance.

Time Guidelines

When performing this therapy, keep the treatments short, regular, and periodic. For the first two weeks you are performing it, place the Leopardskin Jasper on the treatment area for five minutes, three or four times a day. Wear the Leopardskin around your neck between treatments.

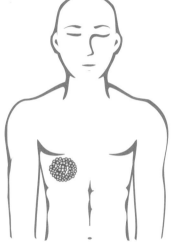

Fig. LSJ-1

After the initial two-week period, you may very gradually increase the treatment time: add two minutes to your treatments each week until you reach a maximum of ten minutes per treatment. Continue performing treatments three or four times a day and wearing the Leopardskin Jasper around your neck until your condition is resolved.

Post-Treatment Cleansing of Gems

Immediately after completing a treatment, it is important to cleanse the gems of any disharmonious energies released by the body in the course of treatment. See Appendix A: "Care and Cleansing of Therapeutic Gems," on page 397, for cleansing instructions.

Addressing Nonphysical Factors

Leopardskin Jasper's focus is on the physical reconditioning of an organ or gland that is not regulating itself properly. Many influences affect the life of a human body. Therefore, when treating a physical problem, it is recommended that you work with other gemstones or therapies that can address the underlying emotional, karmic, or mental issues that may be contributing to the physical condition.

Poppy Jasper

Enlivening Your Body

Poppy Jasper enlivens your physical body by throwing vortices of uplifting energy toward areas where energy flow is blocked. These vortices break up physical impediments, energetic blockages, and encrusted patterns so that your body can accept more life-giving energy. Poppy Jasper acts somewhat like adrenaline, waking up and energizing areas of the body that appear to be sleeping. Wearing Poppy Jasper encourages a deeper recognition of your connection with the life of the Earth. It inspires a positive, joyful attitude and gives you the motivation and energy to take creative action.

Indications for Wearing a Therapeutic
Poppy Jasper Necklace

YOU ARE EXPERIENCING—

Mild depression

General sluggishness or low energy

Sluggish functioning of an organ, gland, or other area of the body

Low energy caused by caffeine withdrawal

YOU WANT TO—

Feel more energetic, positive, or joyful

Have more energy and motivation to perform a certain task

Brighten your outlook

Replace caffeine

Have more energy during the pushing phase of childbirth

Benefits of *Wearing a Therapeutic*
Poppy Jasper Necklace

Poppy Jasper enlivens your body by throwing vortices of uplifting energy toward areas where energy flow is blocked. These vortices help to break up the physical impediments, encrusted patterns, and energetic blockages that prevent life force from entering certain parts of your body. Poppy Jasper's energy is positive, happy, and joyful. It inspires, invigorates, and energizes your entire being.

Poppy Jasper's energy acts somewhat like adrenaline. When your adrenaline flows, you work harder and faster, and you feel a joy that keeps you going. Like adrenaline, Poppy Jasper gives you the motivation, inspiration, and energy to act. Therefore, you should not expect to wear Poppy Jasper and sit still for long. You will want to move, do something, and change. Poppy Jasper can give you the extra energy you may need in order to get through challenging situations.

When Poppy Jasper is worn around the neck, its adrenaline-like energy wakes up and enlivens areas of the body that appear to be sleeping. It also initiates movement in areas of the physical body where energy flows are stuck or blocked. These blockages do not always manifest in specific pockets or areas. Cells throughout the body often have a blocked or tight quality, thus preventing energy from flowing through the cells properly. When Poppy Jasper is worn, these blockages are released. These releases may be felt as spontaneous muscle twitches and stretches, sometimes referred to as unwinding movements.

When your physical body becomes freer of these impediments, it is able to accept more energy, and this allows it to do things it previously could not do. More energy also makes you feel good. When you wear Poppy Jasper, your outlook is brightened and becomes more cheerful— you feel happy to be alive. You may also attain a deeper recognition of your connection with the life of the Earth, and this too will invigorate

"One weekend morning, I was sitting in my big comfy chair not wanting to do anything. I knew I had tons to do, and I thought of Poppy Jasper. As I got up to put it on, I told my husband, 'If I put this on, I'll be up and moving in 20 minutes.' Well, I put on the necklace and settled down in my chair again. Pretty soon I had the urge to get up and get going, so I started my morning chores. A few minutes later my husband's watch alarm went off. When I asked him what it was set for, he said he had timed me. We looked at each other and laughed. The Poppy Jasper had gotten me up and moving even faster than I had predicted!"

C.J.
Portland, Oregon

you. The more you wear Poppy Jasper, the more you will experience all these effects.

Support in Childbirth

Poppy Jasper can provide a woman with extra energy during the pushing phase of childbirth. Wearing a Poppy Jasper necklace will give the mother additional channels within her body from which she can access more energy, specifically for pushing. She should put on the Poppy Jasper only after the transition phase of labor is completed and pushing has begun.

Caffeine Replacement

Because of its energizing effects, Poppy Jasper can be used as a coffee or caffeine replacement or as an aid in withdrawing from coffee or caffeine.

Therapeutic-Quality Poppy Jasper

Therapeutic Poppy Jasper is predominantly brick-red, with areas of gray-black and occasional patches or specks of white. The red areas appear like opaque landmasses floating in crystalline gray-black oceans. The white areas can look like patches of ice on the land or water. In therapeutic Poppy Jasper, the gray-black areas cover between 20 and 70 percent of each sphere, and the white areas occur only in several spheres in a necklace. A Poppy Jasper necklace that contains no white and displays only very small gray-black areas in most spheres is not therapeutic.

Mineral Composition
SiO_2 + FeO_2

Poppy Jasper is a semi-opaque to opaque form of chalcedony, or cryptocrystalline Quartz, that is colored red by large amounts of iron oxides. It is found in Germany, Scotland, Sicily, Siberia, California, Oregon, Idaho, Texas, and Montana.

Poppy Jasper Therapy
Enlivening Localized Areas

This Poppy Jasper therapy awakens and enlivens any area of the body whose energy flows are stuck, blocked, or "asleep." Certain blockages are released, and a greater flow of energy to the area is initiated.

Therapy Tool

One therapeutic necklace of Poppy Jasper spheres (8 mm or 10 mm)

Indications

When an organ, gland, or other area of your body seems sluggish, blocked, or "asleep"

Effects

When you place Poppy Jasper on an organ, gland, or other area that is sluggish or appears to be sleeping, the gemstones' energy enlivens and awakens the area. Poppy Jasper works to remove obstacles to the area's healthy flow of energies by breaking up physical impediments, undesirable energetic patterns, and other blockages. The dissolution of these blockages allows the ailing area to accept a greater influx of life force, which encourages healing in the area.

Procedure

Place a Poppy Jasper necklace in a neat pile or flat spiral on the area you wish to treat (see Fig. POP-1). Place the necklace either directly on your skin or over a light layer of natural-fiber clothing.

If you wish to secure the Poppy Jasper to your body for some time, place the gemstones on your skin and then place a light cotton cloth over the gems. To secure the gems to your body, tape the cloth to your skin with non-plastic first aid tape. Avoid letting the glue from the tape touch the gems.

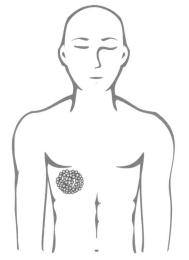

Fig. POP-1

Time Guidelines

Perform your first treatment for approximately 15 to 20 minutes. You may gradually increase this time, with subsequent treatments lasting up to 60 minutes per day.

Post-Treatment Cleansing of Gems

Immediately after completing a treatment, it is important to cleanse the gems of any disharmonious energies released by the body in the course of treatment. See Appendix A: "Care and Cleansing of Therapeutic Gems," on page 397, for cleansing instructions.

Quartzite

Anchoring Positive Change

Quartzite stabilizes positive changes by anchoring them in the fabric of your physical and subtle bodies. It helps prevent you from slipping back to your old state after you undergo any uplifting change, such as a healing or spiritual experience. Quartzite helps the body establish a new state of balance that includes the beneficial change. When you are experiencing rapid changes, Quartzite also helps you maintain your perspective and overall balance by regulating your rate of change.

Indications *for Wearing a Therapeutic*
Quartzite Necklace

WHEN ONE OR MORE OF THE FOLLOWING APPLY—

YOU ARE EXPERIENCING—

A tendency to slip back to an old state following any
uplifting change

Feeling overwhelmed by many rapid changes

Hyperactivity

Overactive mind

YOU WANT TO—

Stabilize the effects of a life-supporting therapy

Anchor the effects of an uplifting experience

Temporarily slow down the rapid pace of inner changes

CONTRAINDICATIONS

Pregnancy

Benefits of *Wearing a Therapeutic*
Quartzite Necklace

Quartzite stabilizes positive changes by anchoring them in the fabric of your physical and subtle bodies. It helps prevent you from slipping back to your old state after you undergo any uplifting change, such as a healing therapy or spiritual experience. Quartzite also ensures that changes do not occur so rapidly that your overall balance is upset; it holds the reins and prevents changes from occurring too swiftly.

Because a human being consists of so many dimensions, Quartzite cannot anchor every change in every dimension at once. However, people's changes usually have focal points, and this is where Quartzite does its work. It focuses on the area of your life that is experiencing the most change, activity, and growth. This area is usually reflected as the most highly charged part of your aura. Quartzite throws an energetic anchor on this area. It produces a still point, in which the Quartzite essentially asks the body to stop these changes for a while, reevaluate itself, and make any necessary corrections.

Often when we place a great deal of attention on one area of our lives, we neglect other areas. Attention carries life force. Therefore, if you focus most of your attention on the area that is changing most and withdraw your attention from other areas, these other areas will suffer from a lack of life energy. Quartzite energy puts changes in the area receiving the most attention "on hold." While these changes are on hold, you can more easily turn your attention to the other, neglected areas. If these areas need to release something, they will be able to release it; if they need to relax, they will be able to relax, and so on. With these needs taken care of, when the Quartzite is removed, you will be in a better position to handle all your changes.

Because inner changes and growth are regarded as a barometer of personal progress, people often perceive change as a good thing. Yet sometimes a person may not feel completely ready for certain changes or may feel overwhelmed by change and lose perspective. When changes seem overwhelming to you, it is probably because they are happening too rapidly and your other aspects are calling for attention and nourishment.

This is when it is wise to wear Quartzite. When you wear Quartzite, the primary focus of your changes is put on hold, and your other aspects are given the chance to be nourished and provided for. This temporary hold will also give you the chance to gain some perspective and readjust your life accordingly. When you remove the Quartzite, its anchoring effect will dissipate, so that you can resume your changes at their previous rate and give them your full attention once again. Hopefully, you will be able to continue in a more balanced way.

Quartzite can also be used to anchor a specific positive change. Often, when we've had an uplifting experience, we want to hold on longer to its beneficial effects. Such an experience might include reading an inspiring book, receiving a healing therapy, attending an illuminating seminar, or being blessed with a spiritual experience. When you have experienced a beneficial change, a healing, or some degree of progress, Quartzite helps stabilize that progress. Wearing Quartzite for several hours after such an experience helps stabilize your uplifted state, thereby helping you to integrate it more profoundly into your being. At the same time, this stabilization helps establish a new state of balance that includes this change. Then, when you remove the Quartzite, you will be more inclined to take the next step forward than to slip back to your previous state.

Quartzite's ability to produce a still point can be helpful for people whose minds are overactive or who are hyperactive in general. As the Quartzite stabilizes the person's brain waves, his or her thought processes slow down. Also, people who suffer from mental illnesses caused by erratic brain-wave activity may experience some symptom relief when wearing Quartzite.

When you wear Quartzite, it encourages your physical body to slow down—not metabolically, but in its movements. The Quartzite doesn't discourage you from moving or moving quickly. Instead it promotes efficiency in your physical movements. As you go about your activity, you may notice that your physical body is moving with more grace. Interestingly, you may not notice this effect until after you have removed the Quartzite.

Contraindication in Pregnancy

A pregnant woman should not wear Quartzite around her neck or place it on her spine. Doing so could obstruct the vortex of life force centered on the fetus. Until her child is born, a pregnant woman should use Quartzite only on her extremities—such as her knees, feet, elbows, or hands—and only for very short periods.

A One-Person Gemstone

Because Quartzite stores records about the person who wears it, ideally a Quartzite necklace should become the personal tool of only one person. However, it can also serve as a wonderful tool for a physician or therapist to use on multiple patients.

Wearing Quartzite by Itself

Quartzite is the only gemstone described in this book that must be worn alone. If it is used with another therapeutic gemstone necklace, the Quartzite's effects will be canceled out. This property is unique to Quartzite.

Amount to Wear

Quartzite has profound effects when used appropriately and sparingly. No one should wear more than one Quartzite necklace at a time. A necklace that falls just above or slightly below the heart will work best. When the necklace falls directly to the heart, its effects emphasize the energies of the heart chakra. Ideally, Quartzite's energy should affect your entire being and all your aspects equally.

A child should use one short necklace that, when worn around the neck, falls significantly above the stomach area.

"Before a group therapy session, the facilitator asked each of us what we wanted from the session. I said I wanted clarity, inspiration, and to hold on to what I received and take it back into my life. After the session, someone handed me a Quartzite necklace, and I wore it for 20 minutes. I had an immediate feeling of stabilizing the therapy experience, and I kept something of it over the next six months. I now use Quartzite when I have a breakthrough and I want to sustain my progress."

Peter Borten, L.Ac.
Licensed Acupuncturist
Portland, Oregon

Time Guidelines

In general, it is best to wear Quartzite for no more than two hours at a time. Never wear it constantly for more than one week at a time. If you wear it for a week, wait several weeks before considering whether you need to wear it again. When you remove the Quartzite, your attention will return to the original focus of your changes. By wearing the Quartzite for only short periods, your body will not be shocked by the effects of rapid change returning to your life.

Because children are growing and changing much more rapidly than adults, they should wear Quartzite infrequently and never more than an hour at a time.

Therapeutic-Quality Quartzite

Therapeutic-quality Quartzite occurs in a range of clarity, from opaque to various grades of translucency. It has a rich, pure white color. To be therapeutic, Quartzite must have no impurities or other colors, specks, or spots within it.

Quartzite that is opaque can be used to anchor purely physical changes or to help the body catch up to some of the inner changes resulting from other gemstone therapies. However, for general therapeutic use, Quartzite with some degree of translucency is preferred over opaque. The spheres within a given Quartzite necklace should have a consistent degree of translucency. Spheres that display some opalescence possess an added therapeutic value. When some people wear Quartzite, their natural body oils can make the Quartzite appear more translucent. This does not affect the Quartzite's therapeutic effectiveness.

The energy of transparent, clear Quartzite falls outside the frequency picture of therapeutic Quartzite and is more akin to the energy of Quartz.

Mineral Composition
SiO$_2$

Quartzite is composed of tightly interlocking grains of metamorphosed Quartz in which small amounts of feldspar or mica may also be evident.

Quartzite Therapy
Stabilizing Positive Changes

Quartzite is placed on a localized area of the body or worn around the neck to anchor and stabilize the positive changes resulting from another life-promoting therapy that has either a physical or inner focus.

Therapy Tools

One or two therapeutic necklaces of Quartzite spheres (8 mm or 10 mm)

Indications

- When you wish to stabilize and anchor the positive changes resulting from a life-promoting therapy that treats any of the following:
  - A localized area of your body
  - Your body as a whole
  - Your emotions
  - Your mind
  - Your entire being
- When you tend to slip back to your previous state after receiving any kind of uplifting, life-giving treatment

Effects

When used as a post-treatment following any kind therapy that is life giving and healing, this Quartzite therapy helps stabilize the new, more positive state that resulted from the therapy. The Quartzite helps anchor the energies of your new state. At the same time, it helps make your whole being more receptive to and comfortable with these new, higher vibrations. Thus, it allows your physical and subtle bodies to begin living from the new, improved state, rather than treating these higher vibrations as somewhat foreign.

For example, if you place Quartzite over a knee where physical therapy has just been performed, the Quartzite helps the benefits of the therapy remain with the knee. It stabilizes the effects of the therapy while the rest of your body is given a chance to accept and adapt itself to the knee's new situation. Afterward, when you remove the Quartzite, the knee will tend to maintain the therapy's healing and uplifting effects.

Procedure

Immediately following a treatment that has initiated a positive change somewhere in your physical or inner being, do one of the following—

- If the treatment had a physical focus, place the Quartzite on the area of your body that was the focus of the treatment (see Fig. QUT-1). For example, after you have received a chiropractic adjustment, place one or two Quartzite necklaces over the length of your spine (see Fig. QUT-2).
- If the treatment had an inner focus (emotional, mental, or spiritual), place a Quartzite necklace around your neck.

Time Guidelines

For treatments with a physical focus

When following up a treatment on a localized physical area, if you are relatively healthy, keep the Quartzite in place for five to 15 minutes.

If the change made was very great, or if you are in a very weakened condition, keep the Quartzite in place for 20 to 30 minutes. Then place one Quartzite necklace around your neck for about an hour.

For treatments with an inner focus

The stabilization of new inner states requires longer Quartzite applications than the stabilization of physical changes. When following up a treatment with an inner focus, wear the Quartzite around your neck for at least one hour and no more than 12 hours. Tune in to your body's signals, paying attention to any urges you may have to remove the Quartzite before this maximum time has elapsed.

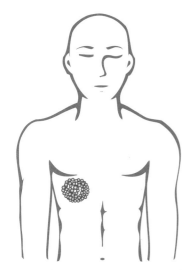

Fig. QUT-1

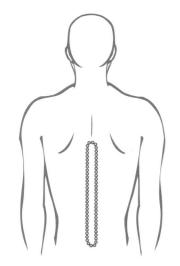

Fig. QUT-2

Post-Treatment Cleansing of Gems

Immediately after completing a treatment, it is important to cleanse the gems of any disharmonious energies released by the body in the course of treatment. See Appendix A: "Care and Cleansing of Therapeutic Gems," on page 397, for cleansing instructions.

Amount to Use

For this or any other Quartzite therapy, do not place more than two Quartzite necklaces at a time anywhere on your body. Using more than that will inhibit your body's adaptation to the positive changes initiated in the treatment area.

Riverstone

Accelerating Change

Riverstone's energy accelerates change. It energizes your aura, speeding the resolution of any process you are experiencing. Riverstone helps you move more swiftly through the changes associated with a particular process, such as a therapy or cleansing. Because Riverstone will lend its unbridled energy to any activity, positive or negative, you must provide a focus for its work—for example, through mental intention or by wearing another therapeutic gemstone. When used as an adjunct to meditation, Riverstone energizes your whole being and helps you make the changes that lead to deeper spiritual experiences.

Indications *for Wearing a Therapeutic Riverstone Necklace*

YOU ARE EXPERIENCING—

Frustration with your progress in making changes in yourself, your health, or your life

Feeling stalled in your spiritual practice

YOU WANT TO—

Accelerate certain positive changes in your body or your life

Heighten experiences in meditation or other spiritual practice

Break out of a rut

Intensify or accelerate the effects of another life-promoting therapy or therapeutic gemstone

Accelerate the process of labor and transition during childbirth

Benefits of *Wearing a Therapeutic*
Riverstone Necklace

Riverstone's energy accelerates change. It energizes your entire aura, speeding the resolution of any physical or inner process you are experiencing. Riverstone helps you move more swiftly through the changes associated with a particular process. For example, if your body is in a cleansing mode, the cleansing is sped up; if your body is in a specific healing mode, the healing is accelerated.

Riverstone attracts and absorbs a type of energy released by moving water. This energy enlivens the Riverstone, increasing the velocity, strength, and power of the Riverstone's energy. Like wild, unbridled horses, Riverstone's energy races in every direction. Because human beings are made mostly of water, when a human being wears Riverstone, the Riverstone has a vast source of potential energy to tap into and transform.

How quickly Riverstone accelerates a change depends on how long you wear it—for as soon as you remove the Riverstone, the accelerating force behind the change stops. How quickly it works also depends on how disciplined you are in focusing on the change you desire. The results of wearing Riverstone with a focus are quite different from those of wearing it without one.

Wearing Riverstone without a focus means wearing it with no specific goal in mind or without another gemstone or healing influence to give the Riverstone direction. If you wear Riverstone without a focus, undirected changes will occur and confusion will result. These undirected changes might be in your outlook, attitudes, feelings, or physical circumstances or in the way you react to certain stimuli. When using Riverstone, you must have a clear intention, along with the motivation and desire to change. If even one of these factors is missing, wearing Riverstone can lead to imbalances and be quite detrimental. For example, without a clearly defined goal, the Riverstone energy might attach itself to the energy of a disease and accelerate its development.

Before putting the Riverstone around your neck, you must spend three to five minutes strongly focusing on and thinking about your reason for wearing it. This short contemplation period will focus mental energy on the situation you wish to address. This mental energy acts like a beacon, guiding the Riverstone energy toward the situation of choice. When the energies of the Riverstone and the situation become linked, the situation's energy enters a swiftly-moving current of Riverstone energy. The Riverstone cannot take the situation's energy and run with it in any direction; it must follow the projected course of your intention.

To focus Riverstone's work, you can also wear or use it with another therapeutic gemstone. Riverstone can serve as a powerful element in a gemstone energy medicine protocol, helping you to move more swiftly through the changes characteristic of the other gem. For example, if the gemstone has a certain healing effect, this effect is accelerated; if it has a balancing effect, the movement toward balance is hastened. Be aware, however, that as things speed up, your life might seem to go further out of balance. Yet you will simply be letting go of the things creating the imbalance at a much faster rate.

Enhancing Spiritual Practice

If you enjoy meditation or spiritual contemplation, you can wear Riverstone around your neck either during your quiet time or just beforehand. During spiritual practice, you focus on the spirituality within you, and this is indeed a strong focus. When Riverstone is used as an adjunct to meditation or contemplation, your whole being becomes energized. It helps you make the changes that will lead to heightened spiritual experiences.

Accelerating Other Therapies' Effects

Riverstone also can be used to accelerate the effects of other energy medicine protocols, such as herbal therapies. Again, the Riverstone must be applied for short periods and with the clear intention of supporting the other therapy.

Facilitating Emotionally-Focused Gemstones

Compared to the physical body and its processes, emotions are highly volatile. Because of this, directing Riverstone's raw element of change at the emotions could destabilize them and create havoc. Therefore, one must use extreme caution when wearing Riverstone with an emotional focus or applying it with an emotionally focused gemstone, such as Ruby or Roselle. The Riverstone applications can be frequent, but they must always be brief. For example, you can wear the Riverstone necklace several times a day but only for a few minutes each time; or you can wear the Riverstone several times a week for 15 minutes to an hour each time.

Knotted vs. Unknotted Riverstone Necklaces

A Riverstone necklace is most powerful when no knots are tied between its spheres. However, even in a knotted necklace, the energetic attraction from one sphere to the next is strong enough for the Riverstone energy to pass through the space between them. Although its effects are not as strong, a knotted necklace might be preferable for most people, because it is less likely to compromise the wearer's balance.

Support in Childbirth

There is no activity in human experience more focused than the birth and delivery of a child. During labor, every cell in the mother's body is concentrated on this one goal. If a woman wishes to employ Riverstone during childbirth, it is best to place it around her neck after labor is well under way. If labor is progressing slowly or has become stalled, Riverstone will help speed up the process. It will help the mother dilate and move through transition.

After transition and during the pushing stage, Poppy Jasper is the gemstone of choice. It will give the mother access to more energy for pushing.

"With Riverstone, things accelerate for me and flow faster. When I was in school as an adult, wearing Riverstone helped me complete projects for my computer class more quickly. Even just getting to school happened faster with Riverstone. When I find myself in the fast lane and want to keep up, Riverstone helps me get a lot done in a short time."

Audelia McCrowell, L.M.T.
Rainier, Washington

Time Guidelines

Riverstone should be worn for only one or two hours at a time.

Therapeutic-Quality Riverstone

Therapeutic-quality Riverstone is creamy tan with patches and veins of white or light brownish-white. Riverstone is a soft gem and must be shaped into spheres carefully. Beware of Riverstone spheres that have a shiny quality. This indicates that the stones have been sprayed with a clear coating to keep the stones from deteriorating. This coating renders the Riverstone non-therapeutic. Only untreated, therapeutic-quality Riverstone should be worn or used therapeutically.

Mineral Composition
CaCO$_3$

Riverstone is a form of limestone, a sedimentary rock composed primarily of calcium carbonate minerals.

Riverstone Therapy
Enhancing Another Therapy

Riverstone is placed on a localized area of the body to prepare it to receive a life-promoting therapy, such as another gemstone therapy. The Riverstone enlivens the area's cells and makes them more receptive to the effects of other healing energies.

Therapy Tool
One therapeutic necklace of Riverstone spheres (8 mm or 10 mm)

Indications
- When you wish to accelerate the effects of another therapy
- When an ailing area has been resistant to treatment

Effects
Riverstone can accelerate the effects of nearly any life-promoting treatment performed on a localized area of your body. The Riverstone not only helps your body become more open and receptive to the effects of another treatment; it also enhances the healing energies derived from that treatment. In this Riverstone pre-treatment, you place Riverstone on an ailing area to prepare it for a primary therapy. The Riverstone's energy concentrates in the placement area, enlivening the area's cells and loosening their undesirable energies.

When you place the Riverstone directly on your skin, the Riverstone may begin to feel warm. This warmth is the awakening of the Riverstone's energy by your aura and your body's life force. The onset of this warmth occurs usually within 15 to 30 minutes and indicates that the Riverstone's excitation of your cells' vitality has begun. You may also perceive that the treatment area starts to feel energetically slippery. This is because the Riverstone, in effect, lubricates the area's energy to make it more adaptable to change.

The Riverstone energies and the enlivened vitality of the cells remain undirected until you perform the primary therapy, which then provides them with a particular healing focus. This is why it is important to perform the primary therapy as soon as Riverstone has prepared the area.

Procedure

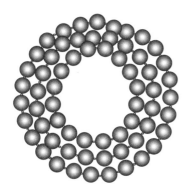

Fig. RIV-1

1. Fold over a Riverstone necklace to form a neat circle consisting of two or three rings of Riverstone (see Fig. RIV-1).
2. Place the Riverstone circle directly on your skin over the organ, area, or chakra you wish to treat. Center the circle around the epicenter of the distressed area.
   - If you are treating a small area, fold over the necklace again to create a smaller circle consisting of three or four rings.
   - If you are treating a larger area, such as a shoulder or hip, unfold the necklace and drape it around the area.
3. Keep the Riverstone in place for 15 to 30 minutes.
4. Immediately perform the primary therapy—
   - If the primary therapy involves a gemstone placement, lay the other gemstone directly on the skin inside the Riverstone circle.
   - If the primary therapy involves a different type of energy medicine, if possible, perform the treatment inside the Riverstone circle. Adjust the size and shape of the circle to accommodate this treatment. For example, if you are applying an herbal poultice, adjust its size and shape to fit inside the Riverstone circle.
5. Remove the Riverstone necklace five to ten minutes before you finish the primary therapy.

Time Guidelines

Place the Riverstone on the treatment area for 15 to 30 minutes before performing the primary therapy. You can adapt this time according to the density of the area you are treating. For example, the cells in a bone take about 30 minutes to achieve readiness, whereas the soft tissue of an organ or muscle takes about 15 minutes.

Enlivening Riverstone with Cold Water

Because Riverstone picks up energy from moving water, you can greatly enliven it by holding the Riverstone under cold water running from a faucet. Cold water is more effective than hot water for this purpose.

Because holding the Riverstone under running water strongly intensifies its effects, it is best to try performing the Riverstone treatment once or twice without enlivening the gems with running water. You may find that you don't feel a need to intensify the treatment any further.

If and when you decide to enliven the Riverstone, hold it in the running water for 15 to 30 seconds, and then immediately place the Riverstone on your body. If you feel that you can handle even more intense effects, the next time you perform this treatment, keep the Riverstone under the running faucet for a full minute before applying it to your body.

The Riverstone's enlivement will reach its peak 10 seconds after you remove the necklace from the running water. Thereafter, the Riverstone's energies will retain this extra charge for about 15 minutes, after which the excitation will start to dissipate noticeably.

Post-Treatment Cleansing of Gems

Immediately after completing a treatment, it is important to cleanse the gems of any disharmonious energies released by the body in the course of treatment. See Appendix A: "Care and Cleansing of Therapeutic Gems," on page 397, for cleansing instructions.

Onyx

Becoming Grounded

Onyx stabilizes, heals, and strengthens your root chakra so you may become more grounded and productive in the physical world. Onyx absorbs all seven color rays, then brings them into your body through the root chakra. As Onyx's energy rises to your brow, it releases to each chakra the color rays needed by the chakra. This energetic support helps your chakras become more adaptable, enabling you to perform multiple tasks with greater ease and thus to manifest your creative vision in the world.

Indications for *Wearing a Therapeutic Onyx Necklace*

WHEN ONE OR MORE OF THE FOLLOWING APPLY—

YOU ARE EXPERIENCING—

Feeling spaced out or scattered

Feeling overwhelmed by the need to perform multiple tasks

Difficulty concentrating or focusing

Difficulty manifesting your intentions and goals in the world

YOU WANT TO—

Feel more grounded

Perform multiple tasks with more ease and focus

Become more productive

Break an undesirable habit

Benefits of Wearing a Therapeutic
Onyx Necklace

Onyx stabilizes, heals, and strengthens your root chakra so that you may become more grounded and productive in the physical world. Onyx brings the seven color rays to all your chakras, except the crown chakra. In this way, Onyx strengthens your chakras at the deepest level so that they may function properly. It also promotes a healthy relationship among all your chakras, particularly between the root and sacral chakras, whose work is closely interwoven.

Some people have negative attitudes about the root chakra or consider it less important than the other chakras. If the root chakra were unnecessary, it would not be part of the human form. When your root chakra is balanced and functioning properly, you have the strength to perform and thrive in the physical world and to develop the higher chakras. Indeed, a strong and stable root chakra is needed to help you withstand the changes that will come into your life as you develop the higher chakras.

It is the nature of Onyx's energy and its black color to absorb the seven color rays and bring them into the body. Its energy enters your root chakra. Then it rises up through your body, giving each chakra the message that it is all right for it to open up and accept color rays and other beneficial energies as your body needs them.

Onyx also acts like a lubricant for your chakras. In the course of a busy day, when you are faced with many decisions and must move from activity to activity, it is essential to have well-lubricated chakras that can respond to life's shifting requirements. If your chakras are stuck and unresponsive, you may feel as though you just can't seem to manifest your goals, dreams, and intentions. For example, you may want to finish a particular project; you have the intention and desire to do it, but things just get in the way, and you can't seem to follow through.

By lubricating your chakras and bringing them the color-ray nourishment they need, Onyx helps your chakras become more adaptable, thus enabling you to perform multiple tasks with greater ease and to manifest your creative vision in the world.

Releasing Bad Habits

Onyx can help you break undesirable patterns or habits. These habits may be physical, emotional, or mental. An undesirable habit is a form of disharmony, and where all colors of the rainbow exist in balance, there can be no disharmony. Onyx helps your body become strong enough to accept an optimal and balanced amount of color rays on its own. When this happens, the overall quality of your energy rises, making it easier for you to recognize your limiting patterns and habits.

To help you let go of a particular habit, first Onyx encourages you to become aware of that habit. It does this by intensifying your attachment to the habit—but only to the point where you recognize that the attachment exists. In this way, Onyx helps you see that what is destructive is not so much the habitual behavior itself, but your attachment to it. For example, many people who drink too much or smoke don't believe they have a problem. When Onyx is worn by a person who has, for example, a habit of smoking, he will find his attachment to smoking intensifying. This doesn't mean that he will smoke more cigarettes or that the habit will get worse. Instead, the intensification will encourage him to recognize his attachment to smoking. With this recognition will come the realization that he is out of control and that the habit is controlling him.

As your attachment to a habit intensifies, Onyx also gives you strength. This strength is important, because it will prevent you from losing balance when the realization dawns that you are out of control. Instead, you will have the strength to let go of the attachment and recognize that it no longer controls you. If you continue to wear Onyx, you will also gain the strength to break the karmic ties with the habit, so that it is less likely to return.

If you want to focus Onyx's effects on a particular habit, you can simply decide to put your attention on that habit. If you don't choose a particular habit, Onyx will first address your attachment to your most destructive habit. If you choose a habit that is really a manifestation of a deeper attachment, Onyx will work on the underlying attachment first. For example, if you choose to release a habit concerning food, when the underlying attachment really concerns your concept of giving and receiving love, Onyx will focus on the underlying attachment.

Breaking and letting go of habits causes a change in one's overall balance. Although this can be uncomfortable, Onyx will not create more imbalances or initiate more changes than you can handle. Because it helps the chakras accept the proper balance of color rays, Onyx will improve your overall balance. Consequently, you won't be overwhelmed by the changes that come with the breaking of habits. Indeed, you will have the strength to make the changes required.

Becoming Grounded

To live fuller lives, many people must become more secure and grounded in their physical bodies. Because of its effects on the root chakra, Onyx helps its wearer become more grounded. Therefore, people who tend to feel spacey, disoriented, or detached will particularly benefit from Onyx. So will people who have difficulty concentrating on important tasks or who tend to live almost exclusively on the emotional or mental level. Often, such people struggle to maintain adequate awareness of what is occurring around them in the physical world. Onyx can be a helpful tool for these individuals, especially when they must drive, use potentially dangerous power equipment, or perform some other task requiring intense concentration for safety reasons. At such times, these individuals should place Onyx on whatever part of the body is safest and most comfortable for them. The Onyx could be worn around the neck, placed in a pocket, or laid in the lap.

Therapeutic-Quality Onyx

Therapeutic Onyx spheres are a deep, consistent black, and their shape and drill holes are precise and even. Unlike most other gems, Onyx's therapeutic power is enhanced by dye. Indeed, black Onyx is derived by dyeing gray Onyx black.

"I am not a very grounded person. I walk on my toes and am pretty clumsy. I'm also a multi-tasker, and I get overwhelmed by all the projects I have going. When I wear Onyx, I feel so efficient as I work, I can't believe how much I get done. I also feel very balanced and strong in my feet. As a massage therapist, my worst quality is time management. When I wear Onyx, my sessions are much more organized, timely, and productive."

Alison Stewart, L.M.T.
Chapel Hill, North Carolina

Mineral Composition
SiO$_2$

Onyx is a variety of chalcedony, or cryptocrystalline Quartz. It occurs naturally in parallel bands of black and white or gray and white color. Onyx is found in Uruguay, Brazil, Germany, and Madagascar.

Onyx Therapy
Grounding Technique

Placing Onyx on the front and back "doors" of the root chakra improves the chakra's functioning, so that you feel more grounded, can adapt to challenges more fluidly, and can perform multiple tasks with greater ease.

Therapy Tool

One therapeutic necklace of Onyx spheres (8 mm or 10 mm)

Indications

When you are experiencing any of the following—

- Insecurity, instability, or feeling ungrounded on a physical, emotional, mental, or energetic level
- A sense of being ineffective, overwhelmed, or unable to connect with your inherent strength and energy
- A tendency to feel spaced out, disoriented, or detached from yourself or society
- Trouble maintaining your focus when you are driving, using potentially dangerous power equipment, or performing other tasks that require intense concentration for safety reasons
- An occupation or lifestyle that requires you to solve a variety of problems or perform multiple tasks continually, such as those faced by a busy manager, homemaker, physician, teacher, etc.

Effects

Each of your seven major chakras has two openings, or "doors." A chakra's "front door" is its manifestation on the front of your body, and its "back door" is its counterpart on the back of your body. One of the back door's functions is to act as an escape valve: when too much energy collects in a chakra, some of the pressure can be released through its back door.

The two doors also act like opposite poles of a magnet. Optimal health requires that the chakra poles are flexible. To accommodate daily challenges to your body, mind, and emotions, each pole's magnetism must be able to reverse itself. In other words, the south pole must be able to take on a north polarity, and vice versa. This ability to shift chakra poles maximizes your access to your inner resources and contributes to a sense of confidence and strength.

Sometimes, however, life's demands can overwhelm your chakra poles' ability to switch polarities as needed. The poles can become sluggish or even stuck in an old state, or position, that no longer serves you. When this happens, your ability to respond with fluidity and flexibility to various situations in your life can suffer. If your chakra poles are stuck, you may feel ungrounded, overwhelmed, ineffective, or unable to connect with your inherent strength and energy.

This Onyx therapy lubricates your root chakra and restores the ability of its poles to switch their polarities as situations require. This improved flexibility enhances the functioning of your root chakra, so that you feel more grounded, can adapt to life's challenges more fluidly, and perform multiple tasks with greater ease.

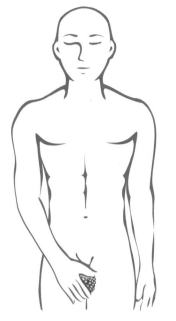

Fig. ONX-1

Procedure

1. Standing up, hold an Onyx necklace with your right hand on the front door of your root chakra (see Fig. ONX-1). Hold it there for 10 to 20 seconds.

   Continue to hold the Onyx with your right hand as you perform all the steps below.

2. Quickly move the Onyx to the back door of your root chakra (see Fig. ONX-2). Hold it there for 10 to 20 seconds.

3. Quickly return the Onyx to the front door of your root chakra. Hold it there until you feel an intuitive urge to move it to the back door. If, after 30 seconds, you don't feel this urge, go to Step 4.

4. Quickly move the Onyx to the back door of your root chakra. Hold it there until you feel an intuitive urge to move it to the front door. If, after 30 seconds, you don't feel this urge, go to Step 5.

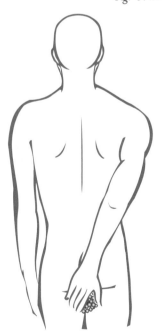

Fig. ONX-2

5. Quickly move the Onyx to the front door of your root chakra. Hold it there for a maximum of 30 seconds:
   - If, within 30 seconds, you feel an intuitive urge to move it to the back door, return to Step 4.
   - If, within 30 seconds, you don't feel an intuitive urge to move it to the back door, remove the Onyx and end the treatment.

Time Guidelines

To establish greater flexibility in your root chakra, perform this technique once a day for a week. Thereafter, to maintain the chakra's flexibility, you can perform this technique once every other week.

Post-Treatment Cleansing of Gems

Immediately after completing a treatment, it is important to cleanse the gems of any disharmonious energies released by the body in the course of treatment. See Appendix A: "Care and Cleansing of Therapeutic Gems," on page 397, for cleansing instructions.

A Vision of Gemstone Energy Medicine

The uses of therapeutic gems described in this book comprise a new form of energy medicine—*gemstone energy medicine*. This exciting new form encompasses a complex energetic model of the human organism and prescriptions for wearing and using therapeutic gems that produce profound, long-lasting, and multidimensional benefits.

This book focuses on the benefits of thirty therapeutic gemstone necklaces. Yet necklaces are simply one tool in the diverse gemstone "toolbox" used in this new field. Indeed, the field of gemstone energy medicine encompasses many kinds of therapy tools and techniques. This chapter briefly introduces the wide variety of therapies and techniques used in gemstone energy medicine and lays out a vision for the wider use of these extraordinary tools for healing and transformation.

Introducing Other Therapy Tools and Techniques

In previous chapters, we've learned that wearing gemstone-sphere necklaces around the neck allows the gemstones' energy to work in a holistic way on multiple levels of the wearer's being. The necklace's gems radiate their energies into the various layers of the wearer's aura and body that are addressed by that type of gemstone. There, these energies perform their unique healing actions. Therapeutic necklaces can also be applied in other ways to the body and aura that focus the gems' benefits there.

The gemstone tools, therapies, and techniques described below also focus the gemstones' actions in more specific—and yet no less powerful—ways.

Gemstone Energy Medicine Tools

Gemstone energy medicine includes the following therapeutic tools based on the gemstone sphere.

Solid gemstone-sphere necklace

Spherical or other rounded gemstones of one type strung into a therapeutic necklace

When worn around the neck, a solid gemstone-sphere necklace works holistically: its energy fills various layers of the aura and employs the gem's particular focus to address the underlying causes of a condition. When a necklace is placed on specific areas of the body or applied in other ways, the gems' healing energy is either directed to the placement area and corresponding areas in the aura or otherwise focused to yield unique effects.

Combination gemstone-sphere necklace

Spherical or other rounded gemstones of several types strung into a therapeutic necklace

Whereas solid necklaces offer the therapeutic benefits of one type of gemstone, combination necklaces combine two or more types of gems in one necklace. These necklaces unite individual gems' effects with the influence of certain numbers and gem sequences to create new healing energies and unique benefits. (See photograph on p. 259.)

Single spheres

Undrilled gemstone spheres not strung into necklaces

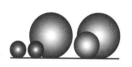

The versatility and focus provided by single gemstone spheres can be employed in a wide variety of therapies and techniques. Leaving the spheres undrilled increases their therapeutic effectiveness.

Gem poultice

A quantity of undrilled gemstone spheres in a small, natural-fiber mesh sack

The concentration of gemstone energy generated by a gem poultice makes it useful for a variety of applications, particularly placements on the major and minor chakras.

Gem therapy disk

Gemstone spheres woven together in rows to form flat disks of varying sizes

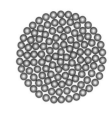

These tools are used in some gemstone placement therapies to provide a concentrated dose of a gemstone's energies to a particular area of the body. For example, a Dark Green Aventurine therapy disk, comprised of gemstone spheres woven together to form a four-inch circular mat, is placed on the chakra located on the sole of each foot to produce specific therapeutic effects.

Gem circle

Gemstone spheres strung into a small, open circle, usually two to three inches in diameter

Gemstone circles are used to concentrate gemstone energy in a small area of the body. Because other gemstones can be placed in the middle of the circle, this tool can be particularly useful for therapy protocols that combine different gems for specific effects.

Color ray wheel

A small circle of beeswax in which various configurations of the color ray gemstones are embedded

Color ray wheels are used to help correct specific deficiencies and/or excesses of color rays in the physical and subtle bodies.

Gemstone/herbal poultice

A combination of a hot herbal infusion and a large quantity of small, single gemstone spheres

The actions of the herbs and gemstones, which are specially selected and customized for a given situation, support each other to create a unique synergistic effect.

Spinal strand or mat

Gemstones spheres strung into single or multiple strands long enough to span the entire length of the spine, plus the neck and head

This tool concentrates gemstone energy in the spine, neck, and head.

Tisrati

A strand of rounded gemstones that snugly encircles the head and lies across the brow chakra and just above the ears

Tisratis are made with a variety of gemstones to perform craniosacral therapy, heighten awareness in focused ways, and help treat conditions associated with the head.

Gem cap

Spherical gemstones tightly woven into a cap and worn on the head

Gemstone caps focus gemstone energy on the brain and skull for a variety of therapeutic purposes.

Gemstone Energy Medicine Techniques

Gemstone energy medicine includes the following therapeutic techniques to address specific conditions in a variety of ways.

Gemstone Necklace Therapy

Gemstone necklaces are worn around the neck, allowing the gems' energies to radiate into the wearer's aura and body to neutralize disharmonies and nourish body, mind, emotions, and spirit. Gemstone necklace therapy is the primary focus of this book.

Window Therapies

Various gemstone energy medicine tools are applied to specific points or areas, called *therapy windows*, located on the body or in corresponding areas of the aura. Therapy windows act as portals to these areas. Placing gemstones on the body's windows allows a gemstone's energy to more easily penetrate the skin and access the area of the body being targeted by the therapy. These areas can include organs, glands, joints, or other parts of the body. Windows can also be opened, either in the aura or on the body, to allow better access to specific illnesses, conditions, life situations, physical traumas, or areas of pain.

Placement Therapies

Infusions

A gemstone necklace, poultice, therapy disk, mat, or single sphere is placed on a specific area of the body—such as an ailing organ, joint, limb or other area of distress—to infuse the gems' energies into the physical area and its counterparts in one or more of the subtle bodies.

Other Placement Therapies

A gemstone necklace, poultice, therapy disk, circle, or single sphere is placed on an area of the body to elicit specific effects not necessarily related to the area. For example, some gemstones can be placed on the soles of the feet to alert the entire body to certain conditions; other gemstones can be placed on the head to release energetic impurities in the spine.

Chakra Therapies

Gemstone necklaces, poultices, therapy disks, or single spheres are placed on major and minor chakras to treat chakra-related conditions or to restore balance and vitality to the chakra system as a whole.

Acupoint Therapy

Single gemstone spheres allow acupuncturists and other therapists who work with acupuncture points to take a quantum leap in their diagnosis, treatment techniques, and results. Single gemstone spheres are used in place of needles to treat acupuncture points by touching and/or taping the gems to the points. In addition, single gemstone spheres are used to treat entire meridian lines as well as the subtle bodies' *acupoints* by accessing these points in the client's energetic field, or aura. Treating subtle-body acupoints can eliminate the underlying causes of recurrent or stubborn conditions.

Color Ray Therapy

The seven color ray gemstones[1] are used to correct deficiencies and excesses of color rays in the physical and subtle bodies. The two primary modes of Color Ray Therapy are (1) wearing one or two necklaces that contain color ray gems and (2) using a simple apparatus called a *color ray wheel* to apply customized configurations of the color ray gems to the body and aura.

Gemstone Hydrotherapy

Gemstone energy is infused into bathing water, in which the entire body or a part of it is either submerged or showered for a variety of therapeutic purposes.

Aquamarine Water Therapy

Through the use of a special technique, drinking water is infused with the energy of the gemstone Aquamarine. The resulting Aquamarine Water helps reverse the aging process and treats any ailment associated with hardening, crystallization, or inflammation.

Contemplative Techniques

Therapeutic gemstone necklaces and single spheres are used to heighten the user's awareness for various purposes, such as to uncover the hidden causes of a condition or to help resolve unwanted emotional, karmic, or mental patterns more swiftly.

Diagnostic Techniques

Gemstones necklaces, single spheres, or *tisratis* are applied to the body or in the aura to ascertain the location of specific anchor points, therapy windows, and other treatment areas.

---

1 See page 40 for more information on the seven color ray gemstones.

The Gifts of Gemstone Energy Medicine

Taken together, the techniques and tools of gemstone energy medicine can offer healing and upliftment for almost any condition of the body, mind, or emotions. Today, we are able to appreciate and utilize gems for their true purpose—not only to open new doors in science and technology but to help us take the next important steps in our health and well-being on every level. Therapeutic gems are uniquely suited to answer the needs and desires of people who are seeking powerful and enduring results from energy medicine. Easy to use and apply, these radiant and abundant gifts of the Earth can help restore the human organism to its natural state of vitality and joy. Therapeutic gems allow us to heal ourselves holistically and deeply, in ways that reveal to us our own infinitely subtle and complex nature. These are the gifts of gemstone energy medicine—medicine for today and the future.

Common Conditions and Therapeutic Gems

Using this Guide

This guide suggests specific gem necklaces and gem therapies to address a variety of common conditions, both chronic and acute. Simply wearing a therapeutic gem necklace can support healing and provide around-the-clock energetic support. The *Necklace to Wear* column alphabetically lists the gem necklaces that can be worn to help resolve a particular condition or issue. The *Therapy to Perform* column lists gem therapies that focus a gem's energies in specific ways to support the resolution of a particular condition.

Remember, like all energy medicine treatments, therapeutic gems address the energetic underpinnings of a condition. Sometimes this results in dramatic relief of acute symptoms. Other times, it may take some time to see symptom relief as the gems' energy works on supporting the resolution of the underlying cause.

The gem necklaces and therapies indicated on the following pages are specifically suggested for the conditions listed here. However, other gems and therapies may also significantly support the resolution of any of these conditions, depending on the condition's underlying cause and other factors. All the therapeutic gemstone necklaces described in this book work holistically and will foster harmony, health, and balance in the person wearing or using them.

Note: The information in this guide should not be considered as a substitute for consultation with a licensed healthcare professional or as a replacement for any medical treatment. This information is for educational purposes only.

CONDITION	NECKLACE TO WEAR	THERAPY TO PERFORM
Abandonment or loss, sense of	MOTHER OF PEARL RHODONITE	
Absorption of nutrients, difficulty with	AGATE BLOODSTONE CITRINE	
Accidents, recurring	LEOPARDSKIN JASPER PURPLE RAINBOW FLUORITE QUARTZ RHODOCHROSITE	
Acid reflux or heartburn, chronic	CITRINE RHODONITE (when aggravated by stress)	AMETHYST: Chakra Therapies (Stomach Chakra) QUARTZ: Life Force Infusion
Acne	BLOODSTONE CARNELIAN CITRINE PINK TOURMALINE (for women)	BLOODSTONE: Strengthening Localized Immune Response (on affected area) CARNELIAN: Revitalizing and Cleansing Infusion (on liver)
Addiction	DARK GREEN AVENTURINE* EMERALD* LIGHT GREEN AVENTURINE* ONYX+ QUARTZ+ RHODOCHROSITE+ *For physical symptoms +For emotional/causal component	LIGHT GREEN AVENTURINE: Organ Tonic* QUARTZ: Life Force Infusion* RHODOCHROSITE: Inner-Conflict Resolution* *On affected area
Aging, negative effects of	AQUAMARINE CITRINE EMERALD LAVENDER MALACHITE POPPY JASPER QUARTZ	AQUAMARINE WATER CITRINE: Tension Release DARK GREEN AVENTURINE: Awakening the Body EMERALD: Green Ray Infusion GREEN TOURMALINE: Hydrotherapy for Men LIGHT GREEN AVENTURINE: Organ Tonic MALACHITE: Dissolving Disharmony POPPY JASPER: Enlivening Localized Areas QUARTZ: Life Force Infusion
AIDS (*See* HIV/AIDS support)		

Condition	Necklace to Wear	Therapy to Perform
Air travel	AGATE PINK TOURMALINE	
Alcoholism (*See* Addiction)		
Allergies	BLOODSTONE CARNELIAN LAVENDER QUARTZ	
Anemia	BLOODSTONE	
Anxiety	CARNELIAN MOTHER OF PEARL ONYX RHODONITE	RHODONITE: Emotional Regulation Therapy
Apathy	CARNELIAN POPPY JASPER RUBY	
Arthritis, rheumatoid	AGATE BLOODSTONE CARNELIAN INDIGO LAVENDER	AGATE: Improving Communication Within the Body AQUAMARINE WATER BLOODSTONE: Strengthening Localized Immune Response LAVENDER: Pain Relief and Realignment Technique MALACHITE: Dissolving Disharmony QUARTZ: Life Force Infusion
Artificial lights, frequent overexposure to	AGATE PINK TOURMALINE	
Asthma	DARK GREEN AVENTURINE EMERALD LIGHT GREEN AVENTURINE QUARTZ	EMERALD: Green Ray Infusion* QUARTZ: Life Force Infusion* *On chest
Athletic performance	GREEN TOURMALINE	
Attention deficit disorder	BLUE SAPPHIRE ONYX POPPY JASPER SODALIGHT	
Autoimmune condition support	BLOODSTONE CARNELIAN	BLOODSTONE: Strengthening Localized Immune Response* *(Continued on next page)*

Condition	Necklace to Wear	Therapy to Perform
Autoimmune condition support (*Continued*)	Quartz	CARNELIAN: Revitalizing and Cleansing Infusion* DARK GREEN AVENTURINE: Awakening the Body EMERALD: Green Ray Infusion* *On organs or glands involved in immune function
Awareness, desire to expand	Amethyst Aquamarine Blue Sapphire Indigo Lapis Lazuli Lavender Purple Rainbow Fluorite	AMETHYST: Chakra Therapies (Brow Chakra) LAPIS LAZULI: Inquiry Technique
Back pain (*See* Joint pain or condition)		
Balance in life, desire for	Quartz Rhodonite	
Behavior patterns, unhealthy or destructive	Purple Rainbow Fluorite Rhodochrosite	
Bladder infection	Bloodstone Carnelian Citrine Dark Green Aventurine Emerald	BLOODSTONE: Strengthening Localized Immune Response CARNELIAN: Revitalizing and Cleansing Infusion EMERALD: Green Ray Infusion QUARTZ: Life Force Infusion
Bone, broken	Indigo Lavender Sodalight	BLOODSTONE: Strengthening Localized Immune Response LAVENDER: Pain Relief and Realignment Technique QUARTZ: Life Force Infusion
Bone condition	Indigo Sodalight	
Brain, any complaint	Amethyst Blue Sapphire Emerald Leopardskin Jasper Purple Rainbow Fluorite	LEOPARDSKIN JASPER: Regulation Therapy

CONDITION	NECKLACE TO WEAR	THERAPY TO PERFORM
Bronchitis	BLOODSTONE CARNELIAN DARK GREEN AVENTURINE EMERALD	BLOODSTONE: Strengthening Localized Immune Response CARNELIAN: Revitalizing and Cleansing Infusion DARK GREEN AVENTURINE: Awakening the Body EMERALD: Green Ray Infusion QUARTZ: Life Force Infusion
Bruise		BLOODSTONE: Strengthening Localized Immune Response LAVENDER: Pain Relief and Realignment Technique QUARTZ: Life Force Infusion
Burdened, sense of being	AQUAMARINE ROSELLE SODALIGHT	ROSELLE: Releasing Stress in the Heart SODALIGHT: Emotional Pain Resolution
Bursitis		LAVENDER: Pain Relief and Realignment Technique QUARTZ: Life Force Infusion
Caffeine withdrawal	POPPY JASPER QUARTZ	
Cancer support	DARK GREEN AVENTURINE*+ EMERALD* LIGHT GREEN AVENTURINE* *As an adjunct to other treatments +Not during chemotherapy or radiation therapy	DARK GREEN AVENTURINE: Awakening the Body*+ EMERALD: Green Ray Infusion* *As an adjunct to other treatments +Not during chemotherapy or radiation therapy
Candida infection (yeast and fungal)	BLOODSTONE CARNELIAN	BLOODSTONE: Strengthening Localized Immune Response (on aggravated area) CARNELIAN: Revitalizing and Cleansing Infusion (on liver)
Canker sores/Fever blisters	BLOODSTONE CARNELIAN DARK GREEN AVENTURINE EMERALD LIGHT GREEN AVENTURINE	

Condition	Necklace to Wear	Therapy to Perform
Cartilage, any condition relating to	Indigo	Quartz: Life Force Infusion
Cause of illness, desire to understand	Aquamarine Opalight	Aquamarine: Discovering the Cause of Illness Opalight: Karmic Resolution Technique
Cellulite	Carnelian Poppy Jasper	Bloodstone: Strengthening Localized Immune Response Carnelian: Revitalizing and Cleansing Infusion Poppy Jasper: Enlivening Localized Areas
Chakra imbalance	Lapis Lazuli Lavender Quartz Sodalight	
Childbirth support (labor and transition phase)	Riverstone	
Childbirth support (pushing phase)	Poppy Jasper	
Childhood issues	Carnelian Mother of Pearl Rhodochrosite Rhodonite	
Childhood support	Mother of Pearl	
Chiropractic adjustment, enhancement of	Lavender Quartzite (following adjustment)	Citrine: Tension Release Lavender: Pain Relief and Realignment Technique Quartz: Life Force Infusion Quartzite: Stabilizing Positive Changes Riverstone: Enhancing Another Therapy
Chronic fatigue syndrome	Bloodstone Carnelian Emerald Lavender Quartz	

CONDITION	NECKLACE TO WEAR	THERAPY TO PERFORM
Chronic illness or disease	AMETHYST (for nerve cells or brain) BLUE SAPPHIRE (for vascular system, nerve sheaths, cerebrospinal fluid, sense organs, or brain) CARNELIAN (for lymphatic or immune system) CITRINE (for skin, kidneys, bladder, intestines, or eliminative aspects of liver) EMERALD (for organ or any other disease) INDIGO (for bones, joints, ligaments, or cartilage) RUBY (for muscles)	CARNELIAN: Revitalizing and Cleansing Infusion (on affected area) DARK GREEN AVENTURINE: Awakening the Body EMERALD: Green Ray Infusion MALACHITE: Dissolving Disharmony
Circulation, poor	AQUAMARINE BLUE SAPPHIRE	
Cold sore	BLOODSTONE CARNELIAN	
Color ray deficiency or imbalance	AMETHYST (purple) BLUE SAPPHIRE (blue) CARNELIAN (orange) CITRINE (yellow) EMERALD (green) INDIGO (indigo) PURPLE RAINBOW FLUORITE (indigo or purple) QUARTZ (all colors) RUBY (red)	AMETHYST: Chakra Therapies CARNELIAN: Revitalizing and Cleansing Infusion CITRINE: Tension Release EMERALD: Green Ray Infusion INDIGO: Removing Mental Blocks to Healing QUARTZ: Life Force Infusion
Common cold	BLOODSTONE CARNELIAN DARK GREEN AVENTURINE EMERALD	BLOODSTONE: Strengthening Localized Immune Response* CARNELIAN: Revitalizing and Cleansing Infusion* DARK GREEN AVENTURINE: Awakening the Body EMERALD: Green Ray Infusion* GREEN TOURMALINE: Hydrotherapy for Men *On chest, sinuses, or liver

CONDITION	NECKLACE TO WEAR	THERAPY TO PERFORM
Concentrating, difficulty	BLUE SAPPHIRE CARNELIAN ONYX SODALIGHT	ONYX: Grounding Technique
Conflict between heart and mind	LAPIS LAZULI	RHODOCHROSITE: Inner-Conflict Resolution
Confusing physical symptoms	LAVENDER	
Confusion, mental	BLUE SAPPHIRE CARNELIAN SODALIGHT	
Congestion, sinus (*See* Sinus congestion)		
Consciousness, desire to expand (*See* Awareness, desire to expand)		
Constipation	CITRINE POPPY JASPER	LAVENDER: Pain Relief and Realignment Technique POPPY JASPER: Enlivening Localized Areas QUARTZ: Life Force Infusion
Coordination, poor physical	BLUE SAPPHIRE MALACHITE	
Cough	BLOODSTONE CARNELIAN DARK GREEN AVENTURINE EMERALD MALACHITE	BLOODSTONE: Strengthening Localized Immune Response CARNELIAN: Revitalizing and Cleansing Infusion DARK GREEN AVENTURINE: Awakening the Body EMERALD: Green Ray Infusion
Cranio-sacral support	BLUE SAPPHIRE CITRINE LAVENDER	AMETHYST: Chakra Therapies (Crown Chakra) CITRINE: Tension Release
Creativity, desire for enhanced	AQUAMARINE	
Cysts (*See* Growths, cysts, and tumors)		

374

Condition	Necklace to Wear	Therapy to Perform
Depression	Aquamarine Carnelian Poppy Jasper Quartz Rhodonite Roselle Ruby Sodalight	Amethyst: Chakra Therapies (Crown Chakra) Rhodonite: Emotional Regulation Therapy Sodalight: Emotional Pain Resolution
Detoxification	Bloodstone Carnelian Citrine Dark Green Aventurine Emerald Lavender Light Green Aventurine	Bloodstone: Strengthening Localized Immune Response Carnelian: Revitalizing and Cleansing Infusion Dark Green Aventurine: Awakening the Body Emerald: Green Ray Infusion Green Tourmaline: Hydrotherapy for Men Light Green Aventurine: Organ Tonic
Diabetes support	Carnelian Citrine Dark Green Aventurine Emerald Light Green Aventurine	Carnelian: Revitalizing and Cleansing Infusion* Dark Green Aventurine: Awakening the Body Emerald: Green Ray Infusion* *On pancreas
Diarrhea	Bloodstone (when infectious) Citrine Dark Green Aventurine Emerald Light Green Aventurine	
Disconnection from natural environment	Agate Onyx	Onyx: Grounding Technique
Disconnection from others, feelings of	Mother of Pearl Ruby	Onyx: Grounding Technique
Disconnection from self	Amethyst Indigo Lapis Lazuli Lavender Mother of Pearl	Onyx: Grounding Technique

Condition	Necklace to Wear	Therapy to Perform
Disempowerment, feelings of	GREEN TOURMALINE (men) LAPIS LAZULI PINK TOURMALINE (women) RHODOCHROSITE	
Dizziness / Vertigo / Lightheadedness	BLOODSTONE (when post-infection) BLUE SAPPHIRE (when related to ear condition) CITRINE (when caused by fluid accumulation in the ear) ONYX	BLOODSTONE: Strengthening Localized Immune Response LAVENDER: Pain Relief and Realignment Technique (when caused by structural misalignment) ONYX: Grounding Technique
Dysmenorrhea (painful menstruation)	DARK GREEN AVENTURINE EMERALD PINK TOURMALINE	PINK TOURMALINE: Gynecological Health and Fertility Therapy
Ear infection / Otitis media	BLOODSTONE CARNELIAN DARK GREEN AVENTURINE	BLOODSTONE: Strengthening Localized Immune Response CARNELIAN: Revitalizing and Cleansing Infusion EMERALD: Green Ray Infusion QUARTZ: Life Force Infusion
Eczema	BLOODSTONE CARNELIAN CITRINE	BLOODSTONE: Strengthening Localized Immune Response* CARNELIAN: Revitalizing and Cleansing Infusion* *On liver and affected area
Edema	AGATE AQUAMARINE CITRINE LIGHT GREEN AVENTURINE MALACHITE	DARK GREEN AVENTURINE: Awakening the Body EMERALD: Green Ray Infusion LIGHT GREEN AVENTURINE: Organ Tonic (on affected area)
Effects of other gems, desire to enhance	AGATE CITRINE LAVENDER LEOPARDSKIN JASPER QUARTZ QUARTZITE RIVERSTONE	QUARTZITE: Stabilizing Positive Changes RIVERSTONE: Enhancing Another Therapy
Emotional exhaustion	MOTHER OF PEARL RHODONITE RUBY	RHODONITE: Emotional Regulation Therapy

CONDITION	NECKLACE TO WEAR	THERAPY TO PERFORM
Emotional expression, difficulty with	MOTHER OF PEARL ROSELLE	
Emotional imbalance or extremes	AMETHYST CARNELIAN MOTHER OF PEARL QUARTZ RHODONITE ROSELLE RUBY SODALIGHT	RHODONITE: Emotional Regulation Therapy
Emotional instability	MOTHER OF PEARL QUARTZ RHODONITE	ONYX: Grounding Technique RHODONITE: Emotional Regulation Therapy
Emotional pain	AQUAMARINE MOTHER OF PEARL RHODONITE ROSELLE RUBY	RHODONITE: Emotional Regulation Therapy SODALIGHT: Emotional Pain Resolution
Emotional patterns, unhealthy or destructive	PURPLE RAINBOW FLUORITE RHODOCHROSITE	
Emotional soothing, desire for	AQUAMARINE (when grieving) MOTHER OF PEARL RHODONITE	RHODONITE: Emotional Regulation Therapy SODALIGHT: Emotional Pain Resolution
Emotional withdrawal or flatness	ROSELLE RUBY	
Emotions, desire to understand	AQUAMARINE LAPIS LAZULI ROSELLE RUBY SODALIGHT	AMETHYST: Chakra Therapies (Heart and Brow Chakras) SODALIGHT: Emotional Pain Resolution
Emotions, suppressed	ROSELLE	
Emotionally burdened, sense of being	RHODOCHROSITE ROSELLE SODALIGHT	RHODONITE: Emotional Regulation Therapy ROSELLE: Releasing Stress in the Heart SODALIGHT: Emotional Pain Resolution

CONDITION	NECKLACE TO WEAR	THERAPY TO PERFORM
Endocrine imbalance	CARNELIAN GREEN TOURMALINE (men) LEOPARDSKIN JASPER PINK TOURMALINE (women)	CARNELIAN: Revitalizing and Cleansing Infusion LEOPARDSKIN JASPER: Regulation Therapy PINK TOURMALINE: Gynecological Health and Fertility Therapy RHODONITE: Emotional Regulation Therapy (when emotions are affected)
Endurance, desire to enhance	GREEN TOURMALINE	
Environmental allergies or sensitivities	BLOODSTONE CARNELIAN	BLOODSTONE: Strengthening Localized Immune Response (on affected area) CARNELIAN: Revitalizing and Cleansing Infusion (on liver)
Eye condition	BLUE SAPPHIRE	QUARTZ: Life Force Infusion
Eye fatigue or strain		BLUE SAPPHIRE: Eye Treatment QUARTZ: Life Force Infusion
Fascia, weakened or tight	RUBY	INDIGO: Removing Mental Blocks to Healing QUARTZ: Life Force Infusion
Fatigue	CARNELIAN EMERALD LAVENDER POPPY JASPER QUARTZ	
Fear	AQUAMARINE GREEN TOURMALINE (men) LAPIS LAZULI MOTHER OF PEARL PINK TOURMALINE (women) RHODOCHROSITE RHODONITE	RHODONITE: Emotional Regulation Therapy
Fever	BLOODSTONE CARNELIAN QUARTZ	BLOODSTONE: Strengthening Localized Immune Response (when caused by localized infection) DARK GREEN AVENTURINE: Awakening the Body

CONDITION	NECKLACE TO WEAR	THERAPY TO PERFORM
Fibromyalgia	BLOODSTONE CARNELIAN EMERALD LAVENDER QUARTZ	
Flu	BLOODSTONE CARNELIAN	BLOODSTONE: Strengthening Localized Immune Response (on affected area) CARNELIAN: Revitalizing and Cleansing Infusion (on liver or affected area) EMERALD: Green Ray Infusion GREEN TOURMALINE: Hydrotherapy for Men
Focusing, difficulty	AMETHYST BLUE SAPPHIRE ONYX POPPY JASPER SODALIGHT	ONYX: Grounding Technique
Gastrointestinal discomfort	CITRINE	AMETHYST: Chakra Therapies (Stomach Chakra)
Gem therapy, enhancement of	CITRINE LAVENDER LEOPARDSKIN JASPER QUARTZ RIVERSTONE	QUARTZITE: Stabilizing Positive Changes RIVERSTONE: Enhancing Another Therapy
Gender-related imbalance	GREEN TOURMALINE PINK TOURMALINE	
Gland, any complaint	CARNELIAN GREEN TOURMALINE (men) LEOPARDSKIN JASPER PINK TOURMALINE (women) POPPY JASPER (when sluggish)	CARNELIAN: Revitalizing and Cleansing Infusion LEOPARDSKIN JASPER: Regulation Therapy POPPY JASPER: Enlivening Localized Areas QUARTZ: Life Force Infusion
Goals, difficulty defining	CARNELIAN INDIGO LAPIS LAZULI LAVENDER SODALIGHT	LAPIS LAZULI: Inquiry Technique

CONDITION	NECKLACE TO WEAR	THERAPY TO PERFORM
Gout	AQUAMARINE BLOODSTONE CARNELIAN	AQUAMARINE WATER BLOODSTONE: Strengthening Localized Immune Response LAVENDER: Pain Relief and Realignment Technique QUARTZ: Life Force Infusion
Grief	AQUAMARINE MOTHER OF PEARL RHODONITE ROSELLE	RHODONITE: Emotional Regulation Therapy ROSELLE: Releasing Stress in the Heart SODALIGHT: Emotional Pain Resolution
Growths, cysts, and tumors	DARK GREEN AVENTURINE* EMERALD* *As an adjunct to other treatments	DARK GREEN AVENTURINE: Awakening the Body* EMERALD: Green Ray Infusion* *As an adjunct to other treatments
Habit, desire to break	ONYX RHODOCHROSITE	
Headache	LAVENDER	AMETHYST: Chakra Therapies (Brow and Crown Chakras) LAVENDER: Pain Relief and Realignment Technique QUARTZ: Life Force Infusion
Hearing problem	BLUE SAPPHIRE (when sensory organ problem underlies condition) CITRINE (when caused by fluid build-up)	
Heart, weakness in regulatory function	LEOPARDSKIN JASPER	LEOPARDSKIN JASPER: Regulation Therapy
Heart chakra, desire to heal or open	ROSELLE RUBY	ROSELLE: Releasing Stress in the Heart
Heart condition	EMERALD* LEOPARDSKIN JASPER (when condition involves regulatory function)* ROSELLE* RUBY* *As an adjunct to other treatments	LEOPARDSKIN JASPER: Regulation Therapy (when condition involves regulatory function)* QUARTZ: Life Force Infusion* ROSELLE: Releasing Stress in the Heart* *As an adjunct to other treatments

Condition	Necklace to Wear	Therapy to Perform
Hepatitis (*See* Organ disease or weakness)		
High blood pressure (hypertension)	Quartz Rhodonite* Roselle* *When stress underlies condition	Rhodonite: Emotional Regulation Therapy
High-rise, live or work in	Agate	
HIV/AIDS support	Bloodstone* Carnelian* Dark Green Aventurine* Emerald* Light Green Aventurine* Quartz* *As an adjunct to other treatments	Dark Green Aventurine: Awakening the Body* Green Tourmaline: Hydrotherapy for Men* Emerald: Green Ray Infusion* *As an adjunct to other treatments
Hormonal imbalance	Carnelian Green Tourmaline (men) Pink Tourmaline (women)	Green Tourmaline: Hydrotherapy for Men Pink Tourmaline: Gynecological Health and Fertility Therapy Rhodonite: Emotional Regulation Therapy (when emotions are affected)
Hyperactivity	Onyx Quartz Quartzite	
Hypersensitivity, emotional	Rhodonite Sodalight	Rhodonite: Emotional Regulation Therapy
Hypoglycemia	Carnelian Leopardskin Jasper Quartz	Carnelian: Revitalizing and Cleansing Infusion* Leopardskin Jasper: Regulation Therapy* Quartz: Life Force Infusion* *On affected glands
Hypothalamus, weakness or condition in	Carnelian Leopardskin Jasper	Carnelian: Revitalizing and Cleansing Infusion Leopardskin Jasper: Regulation Therapy Quartz: Life Force Infusion

CONDITION	NECKLACE TO WEAR	THERAPY TO PERFORM
Hysteria, pattern of	PURPLE RAINBOW FLUORITE QUARTZ RHODOCHROSITE RHODONITE	ONYX: Grounding Technique RHODONITE: Emotional Regulation Therapy
Illness, multiple conditions	BLOODSTONE CARNELIAN DARK GREEN AVENTURINE EMERALD LAVENDER	DARK GREEN AVENTURINE: Awakening the Body EMERALD: Green Ray Infusion
Immune function support	BLOODSTONE CARNELIAN	BLOODSTONE: Strengthening Localized Immune Response* CARNELIAN: Revitalizing and Cleansing Infusion* *On organs or glands involved in immune function
Indecision	LAPIS LAZULI RHODOCHROSITE SODALIGHT	LAPIS LAZULI: Inquiry Technique RHODOCHROSITE: Inner-Conflict Resolution
Indigestion, chronic	CITRINE RHODONITE (when emotions underlie condition)	AMETHYST: Chakra Therapies (Stomach Chakra) BLOODSTONE: Strengthening Localized Immune Response (when caused by infection) QUARTZ: Life Force Infusion
Ineffectiveness or difficulty putting ideas into action	CARNELIAN GREEN TOURMALINE (men) LAPIS LAZULI LAVENDER ONYX PINK TOURMALINE (women) SODALIGHT	ONYX: Grounding Technique
Infection	BLOODSTONE CARNELIAN EMERALD	BLOODSTONE: Strengthening Localized Immune Response EMERALD: Green Ray Infusion QUARTZ: Life Force Infusion
Infertility	GREEN TOURMALINE (men) PINK TOURMALINE (women)	GREEN TOURMALINE: Hydrotherapy for Men PINK TOURMALINE: Gynecological Health and Fertility Therapy

CONDITION	NECKLACE TO WEAR	THERAPY TO PERFORM
Inflammation	BLOODSTONE CARNELIAN EMERALD LIGHT GREEN AVENTURINE MALACHITE	AQUAMARINE WATER BLOODSTONE: Strengthening Localized Immune Response EMERALD: Green Ray Infusion LAVENDER: Pain Relief and Realignment Technique QUARTZ: Life Force Infusion
Inflexibility, mental or emotional	AQUAMARINE BLUE SAPPHIRE (mental) CARNELIAN CITRINE	
Inflexibility, physical	AQUAMARINE CITRINE	AQUAMARINE WATER CITRINE: Tension Release
Injury, acute or chronic	LAVENDER LEOPARDSKIN JASPER MALACHITE QUARTZ	AGATE: Improving Communication Within the Body LAVENDER: Pain Relief and Realignment Technique MALACHITE: Dissolving Disharmony QUARTZ: Life Force Infusion
Inner conflict	LAPIS LAZULI RHODOCHROSITE	RHODOCHROSITE: Inner-Conflict Resolution
Inner guidance, desire for	AMETHYST INDIGO LAVENDER	LAPIS LAZULI: Inquiry Technique
Insight, desire for	AMETHYST AQUAMARINE INDIGO	AMETHYST: Chakra Therapies (Heart Chakra) AQUAMARINE: Discovering the Cause of Illness LAPIS LAZULI: Inquiry Technique
Insomnia	AQUAMARINE OPALIGHT SODALIGHT	
Intestinal condition	BLOODSTONE (when caused by infection) CITRINE DARK GREEN AVENTURINE EMERALD	

CONDITION	NECKLACE TO WEAR	THERAPY TO PERFORM
Intuition, desire to develop	AQUAMARINE AMETHYST INDIGO LAVENDER	
Irritability	MOTHER OF PEARL RHODONITE	RHODONITE: Emotional Regulation Therapy
Irritable bowel syndrome	CITRINE DARK GREEN AVENTURINE EMERALD RHODONITE* MOTHER OF PEARL* *When stress aggravates condition	AMETHYST: Chakra Therapies (Stomach Chakra) CARNELIAN: Revitalizing and Cleansing Infusion RHODONITE: Emotional Regulation Therapy* *When stress aggravates condition
Jaw pain (*See* Joint pain or condition) (*See also* TMJ)		
Jet lag	AGATE PINK TOURMALINE	
Joint pain or condition	CITRINE INDIGO LAVENDER	AGATE: Improving Communication Within the Body AQUAMARINE WATER CITRINE: Tension Release INDIGO: Removing Mental Blocks to Healing LAVENDER: Pain Relief and Realignment Technique QUARTZ: Life Force Infusion
Karmic involvement in illness	OPALIGHT RHODOCHROSITE	AQUAMARINE: Discovering the Cause of Illness OPALIGHT: Karmic Resolution Technique
Kidney condition (*See* Organ disease or weakness)		
Knee pain (*See* Joint pain or condition)		
Letting go, difficulty in	AMETHYST CITRINE	
Libido / Impotence	GREEN TOURMALINE (men) PINK TOURMALINE (women)	

CONDITION	NECKLACE TO WEAR	THERAPY TO PERFORM
Life goals, desire to clarify	AMETHYST AQUAMARINE INDIGO LAPIS LAZULI LAVENDER	
Ligament condition	INDIGO	INDIGO: Removing Mental Blocks to Healing
Liver condition (*See* Organ disease or weakness)		
Low or sluggish energy	CARNELIAN EMERALD GREEN TOURMALINE (men) LAPIS LAZULI (when caused by sluggish meridian function) LAVENDER PINK TOURMALINE (women) POPPY JASPER QUARTZ SODALIGHT	DARK GREEN AVENTURINE: Awakening the Body EMERALD: Green Ray Infusion MALACHITE: Dissolving Disharmony RHODONITE: Emotional Regulation Therapy
Lupus (*See* Autoimmune condition support)		
Lymphatic condition	CARNELIAN	CARNELIAN: Revitalizing and Cleansing Infusion
Meditation, desire to enhance	AMETHYST LAVENDER PURPLE RAINBOW FLUORITE QUARTZITE RIVERSTONE	AMETHYST: Chakra Therapies (Brow Chakra)
Memories, persistent painful	SODALIGHT	SODALIGHT: Emotional Pain Resolution
Memory, desire to improve	BLUE SAPPHIRE CARNELIAN MOTHER OF PEARL SODALIGHT	
Memory loss	BLUE SAPPHIRE CARNELIAN SODALIGHT	
Menopause symptoms	CARNELIAN PINK TOURMALINE	PINK TOURMALINE: Gynecological Health and Fertility Therapy

CONDITION	NECKLACE TO WEAR	THERAPY TO PERFORM
Menstrual cramps	PINK TOURMALINE	LAVENDER: Pain Relief and Realignment Technique PINK TOURMALINE: Gynecological Health and Fertility Therapy QUARTZ: Life Force Infusion
Menstruation, irregular	CARNELIAN LEOPARDSKIN JASPER PINK TOURMALINE	PINK TOURMALINE: Gynecological Health and Fertility Therapy
Menstruation, painful (*See* Dysmenorrhea)		
Mental capacity, desire to expand	BLUE SAPPHIRE QUARTZ SODALIGHT	
Mental disorderliness or fog	BLUE SAPPHIRE CARNELIAN INDIGO SODALIGHT	
Mental instability	BLUE SAPPHIRE QUARTZ	ONYX: Grounding Technique
Meridian imbalance or sluggishness	LAPIS LAZULI LAVENDER SODALIGHT	
Metabolic condition or weakness	CARNELIAN LEOPARDSKIN JASPER	LEOPARDSKIN JASPER: Regulation Therapy
Migraine headache	BLUE SAPPHIRE* CARNELIAN (when hormonal imbalance underlies)* GREEN TOURMALINE (for men, when hormonal imbalance underlies)* LAVENDER*+ PINK TOURMALINE (for women, when hormonal imbalance underlies)* *For issues underlying chronic migraines +For relief of acute headache	CITRINE: Tension Release*+ DARK GREEN AVENTURINE: Awakening the Body* LAVENDER: Pain Relief and Realignment Technique*+ LEOPARDSKIN JASPER: Regulation Therapy* QUARTZ: Life Force Infusion*+ *For issues underlying chronic migraines +For relief of acute headache
Mood swings	RHODONITE SODALIGHT	RHODONITE: Emotional Regulation Therapy

CONDITION	NECKLACE TO WEAR	THERAPY TO PERFORM
Motion sickness, chronic	AGATE ONYX	ONYX: Grounding Technique
Motivation, desire for	CARNELIAN POPPY JASPER	
Multi-tasking	ONYX	
Multiple sclerosis, support (*See also* Autoimmune condition support)	BLOODSTONE BLUE SAPPHIRE CARNELIAN	
Muscle condition	RUBY	
Muscle strain		AGATE: Improving Communication Within the Body BLOODSTONE: Strengthening Localized Immune Response LAVENDER: Pain Relief and Realignment Technique QUARTZ: Life Force Infusion
Nausea, chronic	CITRINE (when chronic digestion issues underlie condition) LAVENDER	AMETHYST: Chakra Therapies (Stomach Chakra)
Neck pain (*See* Joint pain or condition)		
Negativity (negative attitude)	BLUE SAPPHIRE SODALIGHT	INDIGO: Removing Mental Blocks to Healing (when affects a physical condition)
Nervous system condition	AMETHYST PURPLE RAINBOW FLUORITE	
New environment, difficulty adapting to	AGATE	
Nutritional deficiency	BLOODSTONE CARNELIAN CITRINE LEOPARDSKIN JASPER	
Onset of acute illness	BLOODSTONE CARNELIAN EMERALD	DARK GREEN AVENTURINE: Awakening the Body EMERALD: Green Ray Infusion
Organ, sluggish	DARK GREEN AVENTURINE EMERALD LIGHT GREEN AVENTURINE	CARNELIAN: Revitalizing and Cleansing Infusion *(Continued on next page)*

CONDITION	NECKLACE TO WEAR	THERAPY TO PERFORM
Organ, sluggish (*Continued*)	POPPY JASPER	DARK GREEN AVENTURINE: Awakening the Body EMERALD: Green Ray Infusion LIGHT GREEN AVENTURINE: Organ Tonic POPPY JASPER: Enlivening Localized Areas
Organ disease or weakness	AMETHYST (for brain) BLOODSTONE (when infection underlies condition) BLUE SAPPHIRE (for brain or eyes) CARNELIAN (for liver) CITRINE (for stomach, kidneys, liver, or intestines) DARK GREEN AVENTURINE* EMERALD* LIGHT GREEN AVENTURINE* RUBY (for heart) *For any organ	BLOODSTONE: Strengthening Localized Immune Response (when infection underlies condition) CARNELIAN: Revitalizing and Cleansing Infusion DARK GREEN AVENTURINE: Awakening the Body EMERALD: Green Ray Infusion LIGHT GREEN AVENTURINE: Organ Tonic MALACHITE: Dissolving Disharmony
Osteoarthritis	AQUAMARINE INDIGO LAVENDER	AQUAMARINE WATER LAVENDER: Pain Relief and Realignment Technique
Osteoporosis	INDIGO SODALIGHT	
Ovarian cyst	CARNELIAN EMERALD PINK TOURMALINE	CARNELIAN: Revitalizing and Cleansing Infusion EMERALD: Green Ray Infusion PINK TOURMALINE: Gynecological Health and Fertility Therapy QUARTZ: Life Force Infusion
Overactive mind	AQUAMARINE BLUE SAPPHIRE LAPIS LAZULI OPALIGHT QUARTZITE	
Overwhelmed, sense of being	ONYX QUARTZITE RHODONITE SODALIGHT	ONYX: Grounding Technique RHODONITE: Emotional Regulation Therapy

CONDITION	NECKLACE TO WEAR	THERAPY TO PERFORM
Pain, emotional	AQUAMARINE MOTHER OF PEARL RHODONITE ROSELLE	RHODONITE: Emotional Regulation Therapy SODALIGHT: Emotional Pain Resolution
Pain, localized physical	AQUAMARINE LAVENDER MALACHITE QUARTZ	AGATE: Improving Communication Within the Body CITRINE: Tension Release EMERALD: Green Ray Infusion LAVENDER: Pain Relief and Realignment Technique MALACHITE: Dissolving Disharmony QUARTZ: Life Force Infusion RHODOCHROSITE: Inner-Conflict Resolution
Parkinson's disease and other palsy support	AMETHYST BLUE SAPPHIRE EMERALD	EMERALD: Green Ray Infusion
Persistent condition resistant to healing	AGATE LAVENDER LEOPARDSKIN JASPER PURPLE RAINBOW FLUORITE RHODOCHROSITE ROSELLE (when emotions underlie condition)	DARK GREEN AVENTURINE: Awakening the Body INDIGO: Removing Mental Blocks to Healing MALACHITE: Dissolving Disharmony RHODOCHROSITE: Inner-Conflict Resolution RIVERSTONE: Enhancing Another Therapy SODALIGHT: Emotional Pain Resolution
Personal boundary issues	LEOPARDSKIN JASPER PINK TOURMALINE (women) SODALIGHT	
Pessimism	CARNELIAN POPPY JASPER SODALIGHT	
Pineal gland, weakness or condition in	CARNELIAN LEOPARDSKIN JASPER	CARNELIAN: Revitalizing and Cleansing Infusion LEOPARDSKIN JASPER: Regulation Therapy QUARTZ: Life Force Infusion

CONDITION	NECKLACE TO WEAR	THERAPY TO PERFORM
Pituitary gland, weakness or condition in	CARNELIAN LEOPARDSKIN JASPER	CARNELIAN: Revitalizing and Cleansing Infusion LEOPARDSKIN JASPER: Regulation Therapy QUARTZ: Life Force Infusion
PMS (Premenstrual syndrome)	CARNELIAN PINK TOURMALINE QUARTZ	PINK TOURMALINE: Gynecological Health and Fertility Therapy
Postpartum care	CARNELIAN LIGHT GREEN AVENTURINE MOTHER OF PEARL PINK TOURMALINE	LIGHT GREEN AVENTURINE: Organ Tonic PINK TOURMALINE: Gynecological Health and Fertility Therapy
Post-traumatic stress disorder (PTSD)	RHODONITE SODALIGHT	
Pregnancy, desire to connect with child during	AQUAMARINE	AMETHYST: Chakra Therapies (Sacral Chakra)
Prevention of illness, desire for	BLOODSTONE CARNELIAN EMERALD LIGHT GREEN AVENTURINE	LIGHT GREEN AVENTURINE: Organ Tonic
Progress in life or health, stalled	RHODOCHROSITE RIVERSTONE	
Prostate, weakness or condition in	CARNELIAN GREEN TOURMALINE	CARNELIAN: Revitalizing and Cleansing Infusion GREEN TOURMALINE: Hydrotherapy for Men QUARTZ: Life Force Infusion
Protection from electromagnetic radiation	MOTHER OF PEARL PINK TOURMALINE	
Protection from negative mental or emotional energies, child's need for	MOTHER OF PEARL	
Protection from negative mental or emotional energies, desire for	MOTHER OF PEARL PINK TOURMALINE SODALIGHT	

CONDITION	NECKLACE TO WEAR	THERAPY TO PERFORM
Psoriasis, support	BLOODSTONE CITRINE DARK GREEN AVENTURINE LIGHT GREEN AVENTURINE	CARNELIAN: Revitalizing and Cleansing Infusion (on liver)
Public interaction, draining effects of	PINK TOURMALINE	
Public speaking, support for	AMETHYST (short necklace) RHODOCHROSITE	AMETHYST: Chakra Therapies (Throat Chakra)
Recent move, difficulty adapting to	AGATE	
Regulatory dysfunction	LEOPARDSKIN JASPER	
Relationship with mate, desire to enhance	GREEN TOURMALINE (men) PINK TOURMALINE (women)	
Relationship with pet, desire to enhance	SODALIGHT	
Relationships, pattern of unhealthy	GREEN TOURMALINE (men) PINK TOURMALINE (women) PURPLE RAINBOW FLUORITE RHODOCHROSITE	
Reproductive disorder or weakness	GREEN TOURMALINE (men) PINK TOURMALINE (women)	GREEN TOURMALINE: Hydrotherapy for Men PINK TOURMALINE: Gynecological Health and Fertility Therapy
Resistance to healing	AGATE BLOODSTONE LAVENDER LEOPARDSKIN JASPER PURPLE RAINBOW FLUORITE RHODOCHROSITE ROSELLE	DARK GREEN AVENTURINE: Awakening the Body INDIGO: Removing Mental Blocks to Healing MALACHITE: Dissolving Disharmony OPALIGHT: Karmic Resolution Technique RHODOCHROSITE: Inner-Conflict Resolution RIVERSTONE: Enhancing Another Therapy SODALIGHT: Emotional Pain Resolution
Rosacea	BLOODSTONE CITRINE	BLOODSTONE: Strengthening Localized Immune Response

CONDITION	NECKLACE TO WEAR	THERAPY TO PERFORM
Scattered, feeling	ONYX RHODONITE	ONYX: Grounding Technique
Sea, live or work at	AGATE	
Self-esteem, low	GREEN TOURMALINE (men) LAPIS LAZULI PINK TOURMALINE (women) RHODOCHROSITE	
Self-expression, difficulty with	AMETHYST ROSELLE	AMETHYST: Chakra Therapies (Throat Chakra)
Self-knowledge, desire for	AQUAMARINE LAPIS LAZULI OPALIGHT RHODONITE ROSELLE	AQUAMARINE: Discovering the Cause of Illness SODALIGHT: Emotional Pain Resolution
Sensory processing dysfunction	BLUE SAPPHIRE SODALIGHT	
Sexual dysfunction	GREEN TOURMALINE (men) PINK TOURMALINE (women)	
Sexual prowess, desire for	GREEN TOURMALINE (men) PINK TOURMALINE (women)	
Shoulder pain (*See* Joint pain or condition)		
Sinus congestion	BLOODSTONE BLUE SAPPHIRE CARNELIAN	BLOODSTONE: Strengthening Localized Immune Response CARNELIAN: Revitalizing and Cleansing Infusion EMERALD: Green Ray Infusion QUARTZ: Life Force Infusion
Sinusitis	BLOODSTONE (when infection involved) BLUE SAPPHIRE CARNELIAN CITRINE (when poor digestion underlies condition)	CARNELIAN: Revitalizing and Cleansing Infusion DARK GREEN AVENTURINE: Awakening the Body LAVENDER: Pain Relief and Realignment Technique QUARTZ: Life Force Infusion
Skin condition	BLOODSTONE (when infection involved) CITRINE	

CONDITION	NECKLACE TO WEAR	THERAPY TO PERFORM
Smoking, desire to quit	ONYX RHODOCHROSITE	
Soft tissue condition	CARNELIAN	CARNELIAN: Revitalizing and Cleansing Infusion
Sore throat	AMETHYST (short necklace, for strained voice) BLOODSTONE CARNELIAN DARK GREEN AVENTURINE EMERALD LIGHT GREEN AVENTURINE	BLOODSTONE: Strengthening Localized Immune Response CARNELIAN: Revitalizing and Cleansing Infusion LAVENDER: Pain Relief and Realignment Technique
Spaciness	AGATE ONYX QUARTZ	
Spinal misalignment	CITRINE LAVENDER	CITRINE: Tension Release LAVENDER: Pain Relief and Realignment Technique
Spiritual development, desire for	AMETHYST AQUAMARINE CITRINE INDIGO LAPIS LAZULI LAVENDER PURPLE RAINBOW FLUORITE	AMETHYST: Chakra Therapies (Brow Chakra)
Sprain (*See* Strains and sprains)		
Stabilize healthy changes or progress, desire to	QUARTZITE	QUARTZITE: Stabilizing Positive Changes
Stalled progress in life or health	LAVENDER RHODOCHROSITE RIVERSTONE	
Stiffness	AQUAMARINE CITRINE	AGATE: Improving Communication Within the Body AQUAMARINE WATER CITRINE: Tension Release QUARTZ: Life Force Infusion
Stimulants, craving for	ONYX POPPY JASPER QUARTZ	RHODONITE: Emotional Regulation Therapy

CONDITION	NECKLACE TO WEAR	THERAPY TO PERFORM
Stomach condition	CITRINE DARK GREEN AVENTURINE EMERALD LIGHT GREEN AVENTURINE	AMETHYST: Chakra Therapies (Stomach Chakra)
Stomachache	CITRINE (when chronic) RHODONITE (when emotions underlie condition)	AMETHYST: Chakra Therapies (Stomach Chakra) QUARTZ: Life Force Infusion
Strains and sprains		LAVENDER: Pain Relief and Realignment Technique QUARTZ: Life Force Infusion
Surgery, preparation for	LAVENDER	
Swollen glands	BLOODSTONE CARNELIAN	BLOODSTONE: Strengthening Localized Immune Response CARNELIAN: Revitalizing and Cleansing Infusion
Systemic illness	BLOODSTONE* CARNELIAN* EMERALD MALACHITE *When immune function involved	EMERALD: Green Ray Infusion GREEN TOURMALINE: Hydrotherapy for Men
Teething	MOTHER OF PEARL	LAVENDER: Pain Relief and Realignment Technique QUARTZ: Life Force Infusion
Tension, feelings of	AQUAMARINE CARNELIAN CITRINE ROSELLE	CITRINE: Tension Release
Therapy, preparation for any	LAVENDER	OPALIGHT: Karmic Resolution Technique QUARTZ: Life Force Infusion RIVERSTONE: Enhancing AnotherTherapy
Therapy, resistance to	AGATE PURPLE RAINBOW FLUORITE RIVERSTONE	CARNELIAN: Revitalizing and Cleansing Infusion DARK GREEN AVENTURINE: Awakening the Body INDIGO: Removing Mental Blocks to Healing

(Continued on next page)

CONDITION	NECKLACE TO WEAR	THERAPY TO PERFORM
Therapy, resistance to *(Continued)*		OPALIGHT: Karmic Resolution Technique RIVERSTONE: Enhancing Another Therapy
Thyroid, weakness or condition in	CARNELIAN LEOPARDSKIN JASPER	CARNELIAN: Revitalizing and Cleansing Infusion LEOPARDSKIN JASPER: Regulation Therapy QUARTZ: Life Force Infusion
Tight or tense muscles	AQUAMARINE CITRINE LAVENDER MALACHITE	CITRINE: Tension Release LAVENDER: Pain Relief and Realignment Technique MALACHITE: Dissolving Disharmony QUARTZ: Life Force Infusion RHODOCHROSITE: Inner-Conflict Resolution
TMJ (temporomandibular joint pain)	CITRINE LAVENDER	AQUAMARINE WATER CITRINE: Tension Release LAVENDER: Pain Relief and Realignment Technique QUARTZ: Life Force Infusion
Toothache	BLOODSTONE CARNELIAN EMERALD LAVENDER QUARTZ	BLOODSTONE: Strengthening Localized Immune Response CARNELIAN: Revitalizing and Cleansing Infusion EMERALD: Green Ray Infusion LAVENDER: Pain Relief and Realignment Technique QUARTZ: Life Force Infusion
Toxicity *(See Detoxification)*		
Trauma, emotional	CARNELIAN MOTHER OF PEARL RHODONITE	SODALIGHT: Emotional Pain Resolution
Trauma, physical (injury)	QUARTZ	QUARTZ: Life Force Infusion
Travel, desire to minimize the negative effects of	AGATE PINK TOURMALINE	
Tumor *(See Growths, cysts, and tumors)*		

Condition	Necklace to Wear	Therapy to Perform
Ulcers	Bloodstone Citrine	Quartz: Life Force Infusion Rhodonite: Emotional Regulation Therapy
Urban setting, live or work in	Agate	
Urinary tract infection	Bloodstone Carnelian Citrine	Bloodstone: Strengthening Localized Immune Response Carnelian: Revitalizing and Cleansing Infusion
Uterine fibroids	Pink Tourmaline	Carnelian: Revitalizing and Cleansing Infusion (on liver and fibroids) Pink Tourmaline: Gynecological Health and Fertility Therapy
Vaginitis	Bloodstone Emerald Pink Tourmaline	Dark Green Aventurine: Awakening the Body Malachite: Dissolving Disharmony Pink Tourmaline: Gynecological Health and Fertility Therapy
Vascular condition	Bloodstone (when infectious) Blue Sapphire	
Viral infection	Bloodstone Carnelian Emerald	Bloodstone: Strengthening Localized Immune Response
Vision problem	Blue Sapphire	Blue Sapphire: Eye Treatment
Voice, desire to strengthen	Amethyst (short necklace)	Amethyst: Chakra Therapies (Throat Chakra)
Water retention (*See* Edema)		
Weakness, physical	Citrine Green Tourmaline (men) Ruby (when muscular)	Agate: Improving Communication Within the Body Dark Green Aventurine: Awakening the Body Malachite: Dissolving Disharmony
Weight loss /Obesity	Carnelian Poppy Jasper	Emerald: Green Ray Infusion Poppy Jasper: Enlivening Localized Areas
Yeast infection (*See also* Candida infection)	Bloodstone (when chronic or acute) Carnelian (when chronic)	Bloodstone: Strengthening Localized Immune Response

Care and Cleansing of Therapeutic Gems

Like all expressions of life, gemstones need and deserve care to retain their vitality. As therapeutic gemstones help us release energetic impurities and blockages, some of these released energies cling to the surface of the gemstones. These disharmonious energies quickly build up on the surface of the gems, inhibiting their ability to work at peak capacity. Regular cleansing clears these energies and restores the gemstones to their naturally vibrant state. Several minutes of care given regularly will keep therapeutic gemstones vital and ready to help us take our next step in growth and healing.

Basic Care Guidelines

- When using a therapeutic gemstone necklace regularly, cleanse it at least two to three times a week using one of the following methods: Water Rinse, Salt Bed, Plant Rejuvenation, or Sunbath (see descriptions below).
- When not in use, store cleansed gemstones in a drawer, covered container, or jewelry roll.
- Handle all therapeutic gemstones with care. Some are particularly fragile, such as Purple Rainbow Fluorite, Malachite, Mother of Pearl, and Rhodochrosite. They naturally break, scratch, and chip more easily than other gemstones.

To Be Avoided

- Avoid storing gemstones near strong electromagnetic fields, such as those emitted by televisions and computers, which can disrupt the gemstones' energies.
- Avoid exposing gemstones to x-rays, such as at the dentist, in a hospital, or at an airport security station. X-rays will be absorbed by the gemstones and released later into the user's aura.

- Avoid wearing gemstones in chlorinated swimming pools or hot tubs. Chlorine weakens natural-fiber thread and adversely affects the surface of certain gems.
- Avoid smoking and wearing synthetic perfume when wearing therapeutic gemstones, especially porous stones. The fumes can interfere with the free flow of a gemstone's energy.

To Protect the Thread's Longevity

- Do not wear necklaces longer than 20 inches to bed. Instead, lay them within three feet of your body.
- During intense physical activity, such as jogging, remove your necklace and place it in a secure pocket.
- In general, be sure that the thread is completely dry before wearing or storing a necklace. For example, you can rinse a necklace before you go to bed and leave it flat to dry within three feet of your body while you sleep.

Four Cleansing Methods

Any of the four methods described below can cleanse therapeutic gems of the disharmonious energies they tend to collect during use. For certain gemstones, some methods are more appropriate than others; these special considerations are noted where required.

Water Rinse

Two to three times a week, or more often as needed

Rinsing gemstones in alternating hot and cold running water gently shocks the gems into releasing their accumulated energies and then washes these energies away. Hold the entire necklace under hot running tap water for about 5-10 seconds and then immediately switch to cold running water for 5-10 seconds. Repeat this process three to five times. To ensure that the hot water doesn't become too hot, which can cause some gems to crack, test the temperature with your fingers; if the water is too hot for your fingers, it may be too hot for the gems. If you are going to wear the necklace immediately after cleansing it, end the rinse with hot water; otherwise, end with cold water.

After rinsing, pat the gems dry with a soft cloth or towel. Unless there's an immediate need to place the necklace around your neck, lay it flat for at least several hours to allow the thread to dry completely. Putting a necklace with wet thread around one's neck can stretch and weaken the thread.

Special considerations:
Rinsing will dull the polish of Rhodochrosite, Lapis Lazuli, Malachite, Sodalight, Indigo, and Mother of Pearl. Therefore, use other cleansing methods for these gems.

Every three to four weeks:
For gemstones that tolerate rinsing, occasionally use a small amount of mild, non-synthetic soap to remove body oils from the surface of the gems.

Salt Bed
Two to three times a week, or more often as needed
Sea salt absorbs the disharmonious energies that accumulate on the surface of therapeutic gems. Before going to sleep for the night, lay the gemstones in a dish or bowl of sea salt, directly on the salt. If possible, place the dish within three feet of your bed to maintain the gems' energetic connection with your aura. Replace the salt about every two weeks.

Plant Rejuvenation
Two to three times a week, or more often as needed
Plants generate a living energy field that can absorb and transform the disharmonious energies we release. At the end of the day, wrap the gemstone necklace around the base of a healthy houseplant, or lay the necklace in its branches. If possible, place the plant within three feet of your bed to maintain the gems' energetic connection with your aura. During the night, the gemstones will be gently

cleared of any accumulated energies. For a deeper cleansing and rejuvenation, place the gemstones outside underneath or in the branches of a shrub or tree for several days.

Sunbath

Every one to two weeks, or more often as needed

Sunlight provides the deepest cleansing of any in-home method. Sunshine clears, energizes, and revitalizes therapeutic gems. Unless the gems are water-sensitive, first rinse them in hot and cold running water as described above. Then lay the gems in direct sunlight for up to one hour. Ideally, expose the gems to the sun directly, rather than through a glass windowpane. If possible, lay the gems directly on the earth, grass (preferably untreated), or branches of a plant. On a cloudy day, gems can be left in the sun for two to three hours. Avoid excessive exposure to the sun, since this has a negative effect similar to that of sunburn on human beings.

Special Treats

For an especially deep and refreshing cleansing, you can use either of the following methods with any gemstone for which a water rinse is appropriate:

Streaming water

You can provide a gemstone necklace with a powerful cleansing and rejuvenation by holding or placing it in a natural stream or creek or in gentle ocean waves lapping onto the shore. Keep the gems in the water for up to 20 minutes. Be sure to secure the gems adequately, so as not to lose them in the moving water.

Rain bath

Placing gems in the grass during a rainfall for several hours or overnight will also thoroughly cleanse and refresh them.

Cleansing Guidelines for Individual Gemstones

The chart below provides gem-specific details for the Water Rinse and Sunbath methods described above. Special Care notes indicate additional needs of certain gems.

GEMSTONE	WATER RINSE *Details*	SUNBATH *Maximum Time*	SPECIAL CARE
AGATE	2–3 times a week	1 hour	
AMETHYST	Every day for the first two weeks of constant use. Thereafter, 2–3 times a week.	15 minutes	
AQUAMARINE	2–3 times a week	5 minutes	
BLOODSTONE	2–3 times a week	1 hour	
BLUE SAPPHIRE	2–3 times a week	1 hour	
CARNELIAN	Every day for the first two weeks of constant use. Thereafter, at least 2–3 times a week.	1 hour	Store in closed container to · counteract its tendency to pick up unwanted energies from the atmosphere.
CITRINE	2–3 times a week. Begin with a long cold rinse, and always end with cold water.	5 minutes	Alternative: Place in snow.
DARK GREEN AVENTURINE	Every day for the first two weeks of constant use. Thereafter, 2–3 times a week.	15 minutes	Alternative: Place on grass in rain for minimum of 30 minutes.
EMERALD	2–3 times a week	1 hour	
GREEN TOURMALINE	2–3 times a week	1 hour	
INDIGO	Avoid rinsing. Rinsing dulls polish.	5 minutes	Wipe with a soft cloth 2–3 times a week. Alternative: Place in moonlight.
LAPIS LAZULI	Avoid rinsing. Rinsing dulls polish.	15 minutes	Wipe with a soft cloth 2–3 times a week.
LAVENDER	2–3 times a week	1 hour	
LEOPARDSKIN JASPER	2–3 times a week	15 minutes	

GEMSTONE	WATER RINSE *Details*	SUNBATH *Maximum Time*	SPECIAL CARE
LIGHT GREEN AVENTURINE	Every day for the first two weeks of constant use. Thereafter, 2–3 times a week.	15 minutes	Alternative: Place on grass in rain for minimum of 30 minutes.
MALACHITE	Avoid rinsing. Rinsing dulls polish.	30 minutes	Wipe with a soft cloth 2–3 times a week.
MOTHER OF PEARL	Avoid rinsing. Rinsing dulls polish.	15 minutes	Wipe with a soft cloth 2–3 times a week.
ONYX	2–3 times a week	1 hour	
OPALIGHT	2–3 times a week	1 hour	
PINK TOURMALINE	2–3 times a week	1 hour	
POPPY JASPER	2–3 times a week	1 hour	
PURPLE RAINBOW FLUORITE	Avoid rinsing. Rinsing dulls polish.	15 minutes	Wipe with a soft cloth 2–3 times a week. Store separately to prevent scratching and breakage.
QUARTZ	Every day for the first two weeks of constant use. Thereafter, 2–3 times a week.	1 hour	Occasionally wash with mild natural soap to remove body oils and restore frosted appearance.
QUARTZITE	Avoid rinsing.	1 hour	Wipe with a soft cloth 2–3 times a week.
RHODOCHROSITE	Avoid rinsing. Rinsing dulls polish.	1 hour	Wipe with a soft cloth 2–3 times a week. Store separately to prevent scratching and breakage.
RHODONITE	2–3 times a week	1 hour	
RIVERSTONE	2–3 times a week	1 hour	
ROSELLE	Every day for the first two weeks of constant use. Thereafter, 2–3 times a week.	5 minutes	
RUBY	2–3 times a week	1 hour	
SODALIGHT	Avoid rinsing. Rinsing dulls polish.	5 minutes	Wipe with a soft cloth 2–3 times a week. Avoid contact with plastic; Sodalight absorbs gases released by it (see page 202 for more information).

Sphere Size and Necklace Length

Gemstone Mass and Therapeutic Power

In addition to shape and therapeutic quality, another factor in determining a gemstone necklace's therapeutic power is mass. When it comes to gemstone spheres, more mass generally means greater power. Thus, *quality being equal*, larger spheres and longer necklaces are more potent than smaller spheres and shorter necklaces of the same gemstone. For example, a necklace of 10-millimeter Quartz spheres will work more quickly and forcefully than a necklace of 8-millimeter Quartz spheres. Similarly, a 25-inch-long Carnelian necklace will work more forcefully than an 18-inch-long Carnelian necklace of the same sphere size.

It is helpful to keep in mind, however, that not all situations call for greater force and speed. Sometimes a gentler, more gradual approach to healing is more effective.

Of course, the larger the size of the gemstone spheres in a necklace, the heavier the necklace will be. This is an especially important factor if your neck is sensitive to weight. If a 10-millimeter or 12-millimeter necklace causes any discomfort, it's best to choose a necklace with smaller spheres.

Children

In general, it is best for young children to use spheres no larger than 8 millimeters in diameter.

Maximum Sphere Size

Gemstone spheres larger than 16 millimeters in diameter should not be used for therapeutic purposes. Such large spheres do not resonate as effectively with human beings as smaller spheres do, primarily because larger spheres affect the aura somewhat differently. In general, it's best not to use spheres larger than 12 millimeters in a therapeutic necklace.

Index